Stories, Stats and Stuff About OU Football

By Jim Weeks

Printed in the United States of America by
Mennonite Press, Inc.

ISBN 1-880652-78-1

PHOTO CREDITS Photographs courtesy of the
University of Oklahoma and the Jim Weeks
Collection.

ACKNOWLEDGMENTS

Certainly acknowledgment should be extended first and foremost to the men who coached and played football at the University of Oklahoma in the previous 100 years.

This book would not exist without their dedication and sacrifices.

Also acknowledgment should be extended to the many loyal fans of OU football who have shared cheers of joy and tears of disappointment with the Sooners.

Much of the information comes from notes and stories written during my own career as a sportswriter. The people who supplied that information know who they are and that they are appreciated.

Information also was obtained from books written by Harold Keith, Volney Meece, Dr. George L. Cross, Ken Farris, Jay Wilkinson, and Barry Switzer. Thanks for the help.

Mike Prusinski, Debbie Copp, and Betty Klima of the OU Athletic Department provided many of the photographs and allowed me to rifle their files. Gena Cadman of the University of Minnesota Sports Information Office was particularly helpful by providing the early photographs of Bud Wilkinson.

I know the photographs throughout the book will have special meaning. Lack of space and lack of identification keeps me from acknowledging each photographer by name. But their work is essential to telling the story of OU football.

A special thank you is extended to the staff members of Midwest Sports Publications, and particularly Bruce Janssen, my assigned editor, for providing the opportunity for me to rekindle so many pleasant memories.

While you are reading this book, I will acknowledge another group by getting reacquainted with my family and friends.

Jim Weeks

INTRODUCTION

So many dedicated, skilled athletes.
So many knowledgeable coaches.
So many game-deciding plays.
So many thrilling encounters.
So many championship campaigns.
So many near-championship seasons.
So many all-everything football players.
So many significant stories.
So many humorous quotations.
So many descriptive statements.
So many records and statistics and scores.
So little space.

Getting everything about everyone who is important in the history of OU football into one limited volume is an impossible task. So I chose to write about the most important events and people and let them set the tone of one of the great college football programs in the nation.

I have attempted to make up in some small measure for not mentioning everyone and everything in the narrative chapters by listing lettermen and a wealth of statistics in the chapter named *By the Numbers*.

OU football was elevated to a program that competed on the national level consistently starting in the late-1940s. The intention was to restore pride to the residents of Oklahoma after the devastating Dust Bowl in the late 1930s. The major portion of this book is dedicated to the two men who were most instrumental in achieving that purpose: Bud Wilkinson and Barry Switzer.

As OU enters a new era with a new head coach, perhaps now is the proper time to look at the history-making, exciting past and see how the Sooners got to where they are today.

Jim Weeks

TABLE OF CONTENTS

John Blake

John Blake became the 20th head coach in OU history on Dec. 31, 1995.

The sturdily built, nearly square-shaped man stood at the end of the ramp leading to the humpback, lush green surface called Owen Field.

FEED THE MONSTER John Blake was one of the young men who realized his dreams as an OU football player at Owen Field. Now as the Sooners' coach, he hopes to step into football history. Many already view him as the next coach who will feed the Monster.

"Bud created the Monster, and I just fed it," said Barry Switzer, referring to the roles played by Bud Wilkinson and himself. Wilkinson brought the Sooners to national prominence in the 1950s. Two decades later, Switzer concocted Sooner Magic, rejuvenating the Monster. It was he who pointed out that the insatiable Monster was requiring more and bigger football triumphs.

Another two decades have passed, and one of Switzer's protégés, John Blake, has tackled that task. Blake, a member of the Sooner Family, is expected by his siblings to breathe life back into a program that has struggled since Switzer left seven unfulfilled seasons ago.

DIFFERENT SITUATION But Blake finds himself in an entirely different situation than either Wilkinson or Switzer faced in his first campaign. Both of those men

The 1956 backfield of quarterback Jimmy Harris (15), fullback Billy Pricer (43) and halfbacks Clendon Thomas and Tommy McDonald is considered the Sooners' best by some observers.

inherited teams that were on the upswing and blessed with players considered among the best in OU's illustrious history.

Going into the 1996 campaign, OU has not posted a winning record the past two seasons, hasn't won a championship since Switzer left, and doesn't have a player considered among the Sooner greats.

Also OU is entering a new era. The Big Eight Conference schools have joined Texas, Texas A&M,

OWEN FIELD:

■ Where Wilkinson created the Monster and Switzer created Sooner Magic.

■ Where Tyree, Owens, Manley, Paine, Burris, McNabb, Rapacz, Greathouse, Andros, West, Walker, Giese, Dinkins, Goad, Mitchell, Royal, Wallace, Golding, Davis, and Sarratt returned from the battlefield to the playing field.

■ Where the family names of Johnson, Burris, Owens, and Selmon are legend.

■ Where Mule Train was more than a popular song.

■ Where Weatherall booted ball carriers and extra points.

■ Where Vessels raced to the Heisman and became perhaps the greatest of the great Sooners.

■ Where Heady Eddie hid the ball.

■ Where Liggins, McAdams, Aycock, Shoate, Cumby, and Casillas found the ball and its carriers.

■ Where the guys up front – Mayes, Roberts (J.D. and Greg), Bolinger, Gray, Krisher, Harrison, Neely, Brahaney, Foster, Roush, Vaughan, Webb, Oubre, Crouch, Hutson, and Phillips – are not forgotten.

■ Where Tubbs was ready to play

wherever he was needed.

■ Where Harris, McDonald, Thomas, and Pricer formed a backfield for all time.

■ Where the Irish shattered dreams (and the Jayhawks and Hurricanes nearly did the same).

■ Where Owens ran and ran and ran to the Heisman.

■ Where Mildren, Davis, Lott, Bradley, Watts, and Holieway worked their Wishbone wizardry.

■ Where Bosworth made good on his boasts.

■ Where von Schamann became Von Foot.

■ Where Gautt, Kalsu, and Key left their marks in special ways.

■ Where Jones, Royal, Lisak, Barrett, Hughes, Henderson, Ray, and Dixon formed the last line of defense.

■ Where Boydston, Zabel, and Jackson made All-America the old-fashioned way.

■ Where Washington darted like a bug on water.

■ Where Sims slashed and dashed to the Heisman.

■ Where every youngster knows the significance of 47 straight and 123 in a row.

OU's three Heisman Trophy winners are Billy Vessels in 1952, Billy Sims in 1978 and Steve Owens in 1969.

Halfback Joe Washington's running style was compared to "smoke through a keyhole."

Baylor, and Texas Tech, formerly of the storied Southwest Conference, to form the Big 12 Conference. That league will open play for the first time in the fall of 1996.

However, the mood is upbeat and more comfortable where the wind comes sweeping down the plains. That is so mainly because John Blake is upbeat and makes others feel comfortable.

SOMETHING SPECIAL "Everyone has something special, everyone has gifts from God, but sometimes they need it to be pointed out to them," said the former Sooner player and assistant coach. "I want to instill in these kids that we can truly love people for who they are regardless of anything else.

"I was at Oklahoma when we were on top. I was there. I know what the people expect at Oklahoma. There is absolutely no other place I want to be. There is no other job that interests me. I'm right where I want to be for the rest of my life."

Blake may not possess the impressive credentials of the OU head coaches who have preceded him in the past 50 years. But Blake apparently was hired (after having been snubbed once) for something other than credentials. His ability to communicate with other people (notable traits of Wilkinson and Switzer), the strong support of Switzer, and the approval of several influential former OU players were major factors in his selection.

ONE OF OUR OWN "We have selected one of our own, an Oklahoman who truly cares about our state, as our next head coach," said OU President David Lyle Boren at a news conference that bordered on being a party. After all, the announcement came on New Year's Eve 1995. More than 300 people, only a small percentage of whom represented the media, were there along with a five-piece band, red and white (or perhaps crimson and cream) balloons, and former OU coaches and players. "Above all, he will be a players' coach who cares about student-athletes and wants to make a positive difference in their lives."

"John Blake's pedigree. passion, and patience made him the right hire at the University of Oklahoma," wrote John Klein, associate sports editor of the *Tulsa World*, following the celebrated announcement.

"BOO BOO" John Fitzgerald Blake was born March 6, 1961, in Rockford, Ill., one of six children of James L. and Dorothy Jean Haley Blake. His father is a diesel mechanic and operator of heavy equipment, and his mother, who is a cousin of the late author Alex Haley, is a social worker. In 1972, they moved to Buford Colony in the south part of Sand Springs, which borders Tulsa on the northwest.

Blake already was playing flag football and recalled: "I was real fast for my size. In fact, they used to call me

SOONER QUIZ

1. What were OU's original school colors?

John Blake charges into his senior campaign in 1982.

SOONER QUIZ

2. Name the years OU played in more than one bowl game in the same calendar year.

'Lightning.' "

The nickname didn't stick. But he got a nickname at OU that he still answers to today: "Boo," shortened from the original "Boo Boo."

"In practice, I was always smiling and trying to keep guys going," said Blake. "One day someone said, 'There's "Boo Boo," he's always smiling like Yogi Bear (referring to the popular television cartoon character of that era).' It just caught on."

Blake believes his natural interest in others and ability to relate to all types of people came from his family background.

BIG JIM "My Dad is a funny person, but he is a serious person," said Blake, who speaks in a soothing tone. "He said he would do anything for anyone, if they just asked him.

"People always said: 'Big Jim can do this and Big Jim can do that.' My Dad always took pride in anything he did. He was a very competent person. When he did something, he exaggerated about how well he had done it. And he did it well. But if he did it all the time the way he exaggerated it, he might have built a spaceship," he said, laughing.

But success has not come to John Blake readily. While playing regularly, Blake earned a starting role at OU his senior season. His early attempts to become a full-fledged member of a college coaching staff were unsuccessful. And his first bid to be hired as OU head coach apparently was not taken seriously.

John Blake zeroes in on a Kansas State player.

By the time he got into Charles Page High School in Sand Springs, Blake was considered one of the outstanding football players in town. As a tailback on offense and a nose guard on defense, he was selected to the prestigious Tulsa all-metro team as a sophomore. By the next year, Blake had decided he wanted to play at OU, although Earl Campbell, the great fullback and 1977 Heisman Trophy winner at Texas, was one of his heroes.

EARLY RECRUITER While he was being recruited by OU, Blake demonstrated his potential as a recruiter. He talked Buggar Paul Parker, a star tackle at Tulsa Washington High School, into going to OU after the Sooner coaches thought they might be out of the running with Parker, the most prized line prospect in the state that year. Parker started at offensive guard in his senior year at OU.

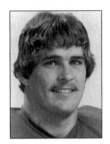

Tackle Rick Bryan played beside Blake for two seasons and was a consensus All-American in 1982 and 1983.

Blake played a reserve role as a freshman. But he was so impressive in the spring drills his freshman year that he was named the outstanding lineman in the Varsity-Alumni game, and OU coaches abandoned plans to redshirt him as a sophomore. At 5-11, 250 pounds, Blake was one of the strongest players at OU and could bench press 420 pounds.

FIRST START As a sophomore, Blake gained his first starting assignment in the last regular season game in 1980 against Oklahoma State. The Sooners claimed the Big Eight Conference title, defeated Florida State, 18-17, in the Orange Bowl, and finished with a 10-2 record. OU was ranked third in the nation behind No. 1 Georgia and Pittsburgh. Blake and the Sooners struggled in 1981. OU finished second to Nebraska in the Big Eight race, posted a 7-4-1 record, and wound up ranked 20th. Blake was a reserve at nose guard again and missed games against Nebraska and OSU after suffering a knee injury in a stunning loss to Missouri, which finished fifth in the conference race.

Blake faced another setback coming into spring training in 1982. He suffered a fractured arm during spring practice but came back to gain the starting nose guard position in his senior campaign. Still the Sooners struggled, again placing second to Nebraska in the Big Eight race. They finished with an 8-4 record after losing to Arizona State in the Fiesta Bowl. OU was ranked 16th.

SOONER QUIZ

3. Name the four Sooners who won the Outland Trophy.

STOP THE LONGHORNS Blake made the most memorable play of his college career in the 1982 Texas game during his senior year.

OU was unranked with a 2-2 record. Texas, which had beaten the Sooners in their previous three meetings, had a 3-0 record and was ranked 13th in the nation.

Safety Keith Stanberry teamed with Blake to halt Texas' last threat in OU's victory in 1982.

The Longhorns scored twice in the fourth quarter to narrow OU's lead to 28-22. But Blake made the key defensive play of the game. He broke into the Texas backfield on second down at the OU 46-yard line to tackle Robert Brewer. The Longhorn quarterback suffered a 9-yard loss and his fumble was recovered by OU safety Keith Stanberry, halting Texas' last threat with 6:16 left.

SOONER QUIZ

4. What two seasons did OU not have an official captain?

WANTED TO COACH "In my junior year here at Oklahoma, I decided I wanted to be a coach, and I was a teacher on the field," said Blake. "I observed how Coach Switzer did things, how the (offensive and defensive) coordinators did things. I was a student of the game. I watched how the assistant coaches got things across to players. I knew those players' personalities and characters. I would think: How are you going to teach this guy to do this? He's not paying attention. I know what his agenda is. I would think to myself: Coach needs to tell him this way because this is how he would comprehend it.

"Now I've learned a lot more about coaching," said Blake.

"When you have players' attention as a football coach, you can share other things with them. Football is important, but it's also a way I can get their confidence and share things about life, about God, and things that their parents tried to instill in them."

But Blake had to wait to become a coach.

He earned a bachelor's degree in recreation from OU in 1984 and got a non-paying job as a volunteer coach at OU in 1985. In order to afford to live in Norman, Blake worked on the 11 p.m. to 7 a.m. shift at a wholesale food distributor in Oklahoma City.

5. When was the last year OU had only one captain?

VALUABLE LESSONS Blake had learned some valuable lessons from his father, and he applied those experiences during this demanding period.

"My dad didn't let things bother him," he said. "When something happened, he just always dealt with it. And you never knew if it was affecting him much. When his business was slow, he always found a way to get us through. I'd just listen to him and watch how he did things. I just saw my dad provide. I learned it didn't take much to be happy. I didn't have to go to McDonald's and get something that looked real pretty. We had chickens, and hogs, and a garden, and hunted rabbits, and we'd just harvest and survive.

"I felt I could make it in life; I could survive."

Switzer was impressed by Blake's willingness to work all night and then work as a volunteer coach, sometimes on only a few hours of sleep. He also recognized his recruiting skills when Blake hosted prospective athletes on weekends.

Blake reached the next level as a graduate assistant coach at OU in 1986 and 1987. He still was not a regular staff member, but at least he was receiving some financial compensation.

A REGULAR JOB In fact, Blake's first job as a regular coaching staff member did not come at OU. Dave Rader hired him to coach tight ends and receivers at Tulsa in 1988.

The next year Switzer hired Blake as the defensive line coach, a job he held when Gary Gibbs was named OU head coach. Blake held the job through the 1992 season.

"Coach Gibbs is a guy that some people maybe took the wrong way," said Blake. "He was a guy that meant well for the kids and wanted them to do their best. He worked diligent and hard."

Blake's career and life changed dramatically in 1993.

Jimmy Johnson hired Blake as the defensive line coach of the Dallas Cowboys of the National Football League that year. The move not only provided Blake with invaluable experience in the professional game but distanced him from the disappointments of the Gibbs era.

6. Name the colleges where Bud Wilkinson's son, Jay, and Barry Switzer's son, Greg, played football.

Merv Johnson has been an assistant coach at OU since 1979. He has the unique distinction of being on the staffs of the last four OU coaches, Barry Switzer, Gary Gibbs, Howard Schnellenberger, and John Blake.

SOONER QUIZ

7. What season did all three Selmons start at OU?

WEDDING BELLS In 1993, Blake also married Freda LaShone Harris, a graduate of Tulsa Washington High School and the University of Central Oklahoma in Edmond. They had met when Blake was at OU and dated while he was coaching in Tulsa. They were married June 11 in Tulsa. Their first child — a son, Jourdan Fitzgerald — arrived April 23, 1996.

When Gibbs resigned after the 1994 season, Blake, who still was with the Dallas Cowboys, sought the job. Switzer, who had become the Cowboys' head coach, publicly campaigned for Blake. Because Switzer had resigned as OU head coach six years earlier, his support may not have been a plus for Blake. There was a belief in some quarters that Blake was too young — 33 — and had not established his reputation in coaching.

Nevertheless, Blake received an interview, although the procedure was a courtesy.

IT'S HOWARD OU selected Howard Schnellenberger, who had been the head coach at Louisville the previous 10 seasons and had coached Miami to its first national championship during the 1983 season.

Immediately, Blake evaluated what had happened and began preparing in case he got another chance, not knowing that such an opportunity would come much sooner than anyone could anticipate.

"I always study and look, and then I go do it," said Blake.

His opportunity came one year later, when Schnellenberger was forced to resign following the 1995 campaign.

Once again Switzer campaigned for Blake, who had trimmed his weight to 225 pounds. Even so, other changes became more significant.

Boren had taken a more active role in the football situation, and Switzer had gained Boren's confidence. Boren, who had had a highly successful political career as governor and then as a U.S. senator from Oklahoma, was astute enough to realize that Switzer remained extremely popular with many OU fans and supporters.

Because he had not been at OU when Switzer had been pressured to resign, Boren could accept Switzer's counsel without appearing to reverse fields. Also several former OU players had been turned off by the Schnellenberger regime and favored replacing him with one of their own.

VALUABLE ENDORSEMENTS This time around, Blake had friends in high places.

"John is more prepared to be a head coach than I was," said Switzer.

OU President David L. Boren and Howard Schnellenberger chat during happier times.

Steve Owens, who remained as dedicated an alumnus as he was as an overworked tailback in the 1960s, publicly endorsed Blake. Owens was named to the selection committee two days later, enhancing Blake's chances. A list of some 50 candidates was trimmed to 10, but Blake reportedly was the only candidate who was interviewed, at least on the OU campus.

Blake's selection apparently was sealed when Boren sought and received the clinching advice. He contacted retired OU President George Lynn Cross, who had been most influential in his dealings with the athletic department during his 25 years on campus.

"I asked Dr. Cross if he had any advice for me in selecting a new football coach," Boren said. "He said he was glad that I called and that he had been studying the situation. He asked if I wanted the long version or the short version. I told him to let me have it and then he said: 'Hire John Blake.' "

NOW IT'S JOHN At that point, Boren had heard enough.

Speaking of Blake, Boren said: "In the past year, I think he sat down, did a lot of self-evaluation and said, 'I've got to get myself ready if the opportunity ever comes again.' I think he showed a lot of discipline, a lot of personal soul-searching, a lot of attempts to improve himself. I think he made himself more ready."

Why had OU officials changed their minds in such a short period of time?

"You're never too old to learn," commented Boren.

John Blake is OU's 20th head football coach and the fourth former Sooner player to hold the job.

At 34 years old, Blake became the youngest active

SOONER QUIZ

8. Who scored OU's first touchdown in the Wishbone era?

Former OU Athletic Director Donnie Duncan.

head football coach in Division I-A of the NCAA in 1996. He is OU's youngest head coach since 33-year-old Chuck Fairbanks was selected in 1967.

Switzer also put the situation in perspective.

"John has an opportunity to do something that's never been done in the history of college football: He's the first minority coach at a perennial national power," he said. "That says something to the university and to President Boren to do what they believe to be right and is best for the program."

DIFFERENT DEMEANOR While his capabilities as a head coach still have not been tested, it is clear that Blake brings a different demeanor to the OU job.

In his one year at OU, Schnellenberger was seen as dictatorial, and many of his players viewed their 61-year-old coach as an old man. Gibbs, who was only 42 when his six-year tenure ended, was considered aloof by some players.

On the other hand, Blake is viewed as affable and as a peacemaker with a youthful and strong physical appearance.

He looks like a football player and can bench press 480 pounds, something that even today's big linemen can appreciate.

SWITZER ADMIRED Naturally Blake admires his mentor.

"Coach Switzer's consistent as far as his emotions, because they are true," he said. "He loves human beings. I felt he was a friend when I was a player and I felt that same way when I worked for him. He has a way of bringing out the best in you. If you had a shortcoming, he would let you recognize it but, at the same time, encourage you to do better. The way he would talk to you about things would lift you up.

"He's been through a lot in life, so he understands where you're coming from and where you're going: don't let success override your family and friends. If he won the Super Bowl and his best friend wasn't happy, why his friend wasn't happy would be the most important thing to him."

BEAT TEXAS Gibbs, who attended the announcement of Blake's selection after keeping an extremely low profile since his resignation, also helped put Blake's situation in perspective. "My only advice to John right now would be, 'Beat Texas,'" said Gibbs, whose teams had a 1-5 record in OU's barometer contest.

Some people questioned Blake's lack of credentials, even though he had developed four Pro Bowl players and had helped win two Super Bowls. The players he had

SOONER QUIZ

9. Name the former OU split end and punter who played major league baseball.

coached while with the Cowboys consistently ranked among the NFL leaders in individual and team performance. He had never been a coordinator, a job that would have placed him in charge of the offense or the defense. And he certainty was not as widely recognized as a head coaching prospect as were his two most successful predecessors: Wilkinson and Switzer.

"First of all, you've got to understand one year in professional football is like two college seasons," said Switzer, disputing the critics. "His three years with the Cowboys are like six years at the collegiate level.

"And John has been around some strong coaches and their coaching philosophies. The one qualification he does have that is critical, and he's always had, is he has compassion, caring, love, a gift to relate to people, especially young men.

"That's more important than anything any coach will ever know. That will win more football games and recruit more players and mothers and fathers for you more than anything."

WHAT'S IN A TITLE? "A title is something someone gives you," said Blake.

"The coordinator is the guy who makes the call on game day. I know exactly what our coordinator did at the Cowboys, and I know why he did it. Titles may identify your position, but they do not identify your capabilities."

But he is not totally unaware of the possible benefits of titles.

"Fishing is the only thing that can truly relax me. I'm a bass fisherman. I used to have a special place near Purcell (south of Norman). But I figure now that I'm the head coach, I'll get a lot of places to fish. That's one thing about a title, if it's the right one," he said with a big smile.

SOONER QUIZ

10. What are the names of the facilities where OU plays home football games?

SOONER QUIZ

11. Name the head coaches who had the most victories and the most losses in the OU-Texas series.

Bud & Barry

They grew up on the proverbial opposite sides of the tracks.

One came from a prominent family in the big city. The other from a dysfunctional family in a rural community.

Their childhood experiences were about as distant as their homes in Minnesota and Arkansas.

One prepared for college in a private school. The other attended a small public school.

One gained success in athletics almost immediately when he got to college. The other struggled to establish himself on the football team.

One spoke with the skill of an orator and rarely used a foul expression. The other liked to say "ain't" for emphasis, and it seemed natural for him to occasionally use earthy expressions.

Bud Wilkinson and defensive back Ed Lisak (45) react to the Sooners' victory over Texas in 1948, marking the first win for Wilkinson over the Longhorns.

Each was considered a handsome man: One in a classic fashion, the other in a more rugged manner.

One was honored early in his coaching career by his peers. The other struggled for the acceptance that never came from some of his peers.

One was Bud Wilkinson, the other Barry Switzer.

RIGHT PLACE, RIGHT TIME The story of OU football is the story of these two men.

Wilkinson brought the Sooners to national prominence during the 1950s, and Switzer rejuvenated the program, taking it to equal heights during the 1970s.

It is doubtful that any other college football program has had two such successful coaches over an equivalent period. The influence of Wilkinson and Switzer dominated OU football for half a century.

Their situation is interesting because the personalities and backgrounds of Wilkinson and Switzer were so different. Yet their lives and their careers in football have some remarkable similarities.

Barry Switzer addresses a huge gathering in the Myriad in Oklahoma City to celebrate the Sooners' national championship in 1974. Bud Wilkinson, who was the guest speaker, is seated at the right.

Significant changes involving the game itself, the backgrounds of the players, and trappings of the game occurred in college football in the 10 years that separated their head coaching careers at OU. It is doubtful that the approach of one would have worked in the era of the other. But it certainly worked in the era in which each coached.

But to understand what their teams did and how they did it, it's important to understand some of the men's similarities and some of their differences.

SIMILARITIES Here are some of the similarities shared by Wilkinson and Switzer:

• Each lost his mother while he was relatively young.

• Each gained confidence and respect when he was young through his success in athletics.

• Each came to OU as an assistant coach.

• Each was head coach at OU for nearly the same

TWO ERAS

In only one year during the past half-century (1995) has the influence of Bud Wilkinson and Barry Switzer not been both profound and obvious.

■ In 1946, Wilkinson becomes an assistant to Coach Jim Tatum.

■ From 1947 to 1963, Wilkinson is the head coach.

■ From 1964 to 1965: Gomer Jones, a former assistant to Wilkinson, is head coach.

■ In 1966: Switzer becomes an assistant to Jim Mackenzie.

■ From 1967 to 1972, Switzer is an assistant to Chuck Fairbanks.

■ From 1973 to 1988, Switzer is head coach.

■ From 1989 to 1994: Gary Gibbs, a former player and assistant to Switzer, is head coach.

■ In 1996, John Blake, a former player of Switzer's, becomes head coach.

During that time, OU won six national championships, won or shared 29 conference championships and won 18 times and tied once in 28 bowl games. All of the national championships and all of the conference championships, save three, were won when either Wilkinson or Switzer was head coach.

number of years: Wilkinson, 17, and Switzer, 16.

• Each became OU head coach in his 30s: Wilkinson at 31 and Switzer at 35.

• Their records as OU head coach were remarkably similar: Wilkinson's teams had 145 wins, 29 losses and 4 ties for a percentage of .826 and Switzer's teams had 157 wins, 29 losses and 4 ties for a percentage of .837.

• Each had the best won-lost career record in the nation during his coaching era.

• Each coached three Sooner teams to national championships: Wilkinson in 1950, 1955, and 1956 and Switzer in 1974, 1975, and 1985 (Switzer's 1973 and 1978 teams also were selected national champions by ranking systems acknowledged by the NCAA but not otherwise widely accepted.).

• Each had impressive winning streaks: Wilkinson's teams won 31 straight games from 1948 to 1950 and 47 straight games from 1953 to 1957. Switzer's teams won 28 straight games from 1973 to 1975.

• Each coached OU during NCAA record scoring streaks: Wilkinson with 123 straight in 1946-58 (Jim Tatum coached in 1946) and Switzer with 181 straight games in 1965-82 (Gomer Jones, Jim Mackenzie and Chuck Fairbanks also coached during part of the streak.).

• Each did what is needed for survival at OU — win against selected opponents: Wilkinson had a 9-8 record against Texas, had only nine losses and one tie in 17 years of conference play and had a 17-0 mark against intrastate rival Oklahoma State. Switzer had a 9-5-2 record against Texas, a 12-4 mark against his major conference rival, Nebraska, and had a 15-1 record against OSU.

• Each dominated the conference in which OU played: Wilkinson's teams tied for one Big Six championship, won 10 straight Big Seven championships and three Big Eight titles. Switzer's teams won eight outright championships and tied for four more titles in the Big Eight Conference.

• Each had one Heisman Trophy winner: Halfback Billy Vessels played for Wilkinson in 1952. Halfback Billy Sims played for Switzer in 1978.

• Each had two Outland Trophy winners: Tackle Jim Weatherall in 1951 and guard J.D. Roberts in 1953 for Wilkinson, and tackle Lee Roy Selmon in 1975 and guard Greg Roberts in 1978 for Switzer.

• Each was better known for his team's offensive achievements, but his best teams also were outstanding defensively.

• Each gained his greatest success with an option-oriented, run-dominated offense: Wilkinson with the Split-T and Switzer with the Wishbone.

• Each dismissed for disciplinary reasons a back who

Barry Switzer and assistant coach Gene Hochevar get a victory ride from Eddie Foster, Gary Baccus and Kyle Davis after OU defeated Texas, 52-13, in 1973 for Switzer's first triumph over the Longhorns.

12. What was the last year in which OU and Texas football teams met in a game that was not a sellout?

might have been one of his greatest players: Joe Don Looney by Wilkinson in 1963 and Marcus Dupree by Switzer in 1983. And, too, each was dismissed after the Texas game.

• Each changed offensive styles briefly during his career at OU.

• Late in each man's career, he had difficulty defeating teams coached by men whom he had helped: OU lost to Texas, coached by former Sooner Darrell Royal, in each of Wilkinson's last six years as OU coach. Switzer's teams suffered three of their last six losses during his OU career to Miami. The Hurricanes were coached by Jimmy Johnson, whom Switzer had coached at Arkansas and had helped obtain his first job in college coaching.

• Each underwent a painful divorce.

• Each was head coach during two periods in which penalties were inflicted by the NCAA. (It should be pointed out that Switzer was head coach when penalties were in effect but was not head coach when the infractions occurred in one of these situations.)

• Each became a head coach in the National Football League after leaving OU and after being out of coaching for a few years.

Bud Wilkinson was captain of the 1932 football team at Shattuck School.

MINNESOTA NATIVE Charles Burham Wilkinson was born in Minneapolis, Minn., on Easter Sunday, April 23, 1916. He was the second of two sons of Charles Patton and Edith Wilkinson. C.P., as his father was known, was a successful mortgage broker and, as was common at that time, expected his sons to follow in his business. That assumption created a situation that took years for Wilkinson and his father to resolve.

Wilkinson was introduced to music early in this life by his father, who liked to sing, and by his mother, who was a soloist in the church choir and played the piano. While not known for his musical talent, Wilkinson would later use his enjoyment of singing and playing the organ to help relieve the stress of coaching.

Wilkinson experienced personal tragedy when he was very young. In 1922, his family was involved in a railroad accident that left his mother a semi-invalid. A year later when he was seven years old, she died.

When Wilkinson was 13 years old, his father decided both of his sons needed the military style discipline and academic emphasis offered by a private school. So, in 1929, Wilkinson was sent to the highly regarded Shattuck School in Faribault, Minn.

Wilkinson adjusted to the situation by becoming involved in the school's wide range of athletic activities. In fact, he eventually won the Williams Cup as the school's best all-around athlete. He lettered four years in

Wilkinson was the "running guard" for Minnesota's national champions in 1934.

baseball, three years in football, three years in hockey, and one year in basketball.

Wilkinson continued his outstanding achievements as a student and an athlete at Minnesota. During his three seasons of varsity competition, the Golden Gophers had a 23-1 record and were recognized as national champions during each of those seasons.

He started at guard in 1934 and 1935 and at quarterback in 1936. Minnesota ran the single wing offense, and the quarterback was primarily a blocking back.

Grantland Rice, perhaps the most famous sportswriter in American history, cited Wilkinson as the "outstanding running guard in college football" after the 1935 campaign when he was selected All-America.

CHAMPIONSHIP SEASONS Minnesota had 8-0 records in 1934 and 1935 and won the Big Ten Conference championship with a 5-0 mark each season. The Gophers had a 7-1 record, losing only to Northwestern, 6-0, in 1936. Northwestern claimed the Big Ten title but lost to Notre Dame late in the season. Minnesota was voted No. 1

SOONER QUIZ

13. Why was the OU-Texas series interrupted in 1919?

and Northwestern No. 7 when The Associated Press conducted its first nationwide poll in 1936.

Wilkinson played goalie in hockey and was the captain of the golf team. As a senior, he received the Big Ten Medal for his achievements as an athlete and scholar and received a bachelor's degree in English.

Wilkinson closed his playing career as the quarterback of the College All-Star team. He played three quarters in the first victory in the storied series for the collegiate team, defeating the National Football League champion Green Bay Packers in 1937 in that now-defunct summer classic in Chicago.

He was an assistant coach at Syracuse and Minnesota and obtained a master's degree in English Education while at Syracuse. These additional studies were important, enabling him to refine his speaking skills and style. They also furthered his interest in prose and poetry, which he enjoyed as one release from the stresses of coaching.

MARY In the meantime, he married Mary Shifflett of Grinnell, Iowa, whom he had met when he was in college at Minnesota and she was attending nearby Carlton College.

With the onset of World War II, Wilkinson joined the Navy in 1942. He saw duty aboard the U.S.S. Enterprise aircraft carrier as a hangar deck officer in the battles off Iwo Jima, Kiushiu, and Okinawa in the Pacific Theater.

But before seeing sea duty, Wilkinson trained at Iowa Pre-Flight Naval Air Station at Iowa City in 1943. There he met Don Faurot and Jim Tatum, who would play significant roles in his life. Faurot was the head coach

Wilkinson started for three seasons for the Golden Gophers.

The National Football Coaches Association honored Wilkinson as Coach of the Year in 1949. The award was presented by Joe Williams (center), sports columnist of the New York World-Telegram and the Sun, and L. R. "Dutch" Meyer, head coach at Texas Christian and president of the NFCA.

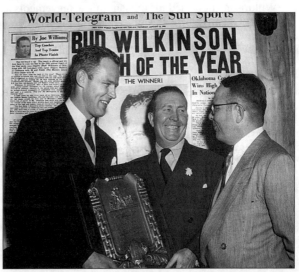

and Tatum was the line coach at Iowa Pre-Flight. The military used its athletic programs as a morale booster.

ENTER SPLIT-T Faurot had been the head football coach from 1935 through 1942 at Missouri. He devised a unique, new offense which was a variation of the popular T formation. Wilkinson, who coached the centers and quarterbacks at Iowa Pre-Flight, was intrigued by the system.

Faurot had called the formation various names, including the Missouri T and the Sliding T. But the name that stuck was the Split-T, because of the unusually wide distances between the linemen. Missouri had led the nation in rushing in 1941 with the new formation, which helped make Faurot famous and would help make Wilkinson incredibly successful after the war.

Tatum had been the head coach for one year at North Carolina before the war. After the war, Tatum would be instrumental in Wilkinson's coming to OU. Eventually, both Faurot and Tatum would suffer devastating setbacks against teams coached by Wilkinson.

Wilkinson is shown with the other members of his coaching staff in 1963, his last season at OU. The other coaches are (from left) Gomer Jones, Jay O'Neal, Bobby Drake Keith, Jerry Thompson and George Dickson.

AT HOME IN ARKANSAS Barry Layne Switzer was born on October 5, 1937, in the small, southeast Arkansas town of Crossett, the first of two sons of Frank Mays Switzer and Mary Louise Wood. The family lived on a houseboat in the Ouachita River west of town, where swamp bottom and pine forests decorate the landscape. The major industry in the area remains the paper mills.

Barry Switzer graduates from Crossett High School.

Switzer's father was a bootlegger, selling whiskey illegally. In fact, it was illegal for anyone to sell whiskey in those days. But plenty of people bought it, and local authorities often looked the other way. After all, some of the most prominent citizens in town were customers of "Mr. Frank." Most of them sent their black laborers to pick up the whiskey, not wanting to be seen participating in such an exchange themselves. Switzer's father also had his own loan business, but he did not operate it out of a bank and the interest might be as high as 20 percent.

HOME LIFE From his early days, Switzer remembered that his father drank heavily, had a violent temper, and often shot holes in the walls of their house.

Switzer's mother had been the valedictorian of her senior class at Crossett High School. But she was bothered by her husband's lifestyle, was withdrawn, and eventually began to rely on alcohol and barbiturates to deal with her unhappiness.

Switzer became the starting center at Arkansas in 1959 on the Razorbacks' Southwest Conference co-champion.

BLACK FRIENDS Switzer learned to read by the light of a coal-oil lamp and listened to a battery-powered radio in the "shotgun house" (so named because theoretically one could fire a shotgun through the front door and the pellets would exit the back door without hitting anything). Many of his friends were the children of neighboring blacks. Those early and meaningful experiences with African-Americans proved vital to him later as a recruiter and coach.

In the seventh grade, Switzer quit playing football, not because he didn't like the game, but because he had to walk the five miles from school to home in the dark after practice. The bus that took him to school did not operate that late in the day.

However, Lynn Yarborough, who was a physical education teacher, recognized Switzer's potential in athletics and thought he might have a future in football. Yarborough convinced the football coach, Harry Denson, that the bootlegger's son would be worth some special attention. Yarborough and Denson talked Switzer into trying football again with the understanding that one of them would provide a ride home after each practice.

Switzer also had help in overcoming another obstacle. Although the good people of Crossett didn't mind buying goods sold by Mr. Frank, more than a few didn't want their daughters' dating the bootlegger's son. With a hint of the creativity that he would demonstrate later in life — and with some help from his friends — he devised a solution. He would double-date with a friend, who would go to the door at each girl's home. But Switzer may have missed a few good-night kisses since he couldn't take his date home either.

PRISON TIME When Switzer was a senior at Crossett High School, his father was convicted of bootlegging and sent to the Cummins Unit of the Arkansas State Prison outside Varner, a small town 60 miles north of Crossett.

One of Switzer's duties was to drive his mother and brother to visit his father every other Sunday. Here is the description of one such visit from Switzer's book, *Bootlegger's Boy*:

"Of course, my brother and I were embarrassed to go see Daddy in the pen. Occasionally, we'd see some other kids we knew who had relatives behind bars and we'd all kind of act like we hadn't seen each other.

"But I loved Daddy and I know he loved us, even though I can't remember that he ever told Donnie or me that he did. Daddy never kissed me or Donnie or hugged either one of us. I guess it just didn't occur to him. And Mother loved him dearly despite all the crap he had put her through.

"Every time we visited him in prison, he was laughing and in good humor."

Switzer's father never saw him play football. But

Switzer and Arkansas Head Coach Frank Broyles attended Barry Switzer Day in Crossett after the 1959 season.

Barry Switzer came to OU in 1966 as an assistant coach. The Sooner coaches that year were (front row from left) Chuck Fairbanks, Pat James, Head Coach Jim Mackenzie, Homer Rice, Switzer, (back row) trainer Ken Rawlinson, Galen Hall, Billy Gray, Robert E. "Swede" Lee, Larry Lacewell and Port Robertson. Notice how the football staffs had increased since 1963.

plenty of other people recognized his athletic achievements. Although he was only 16 years old when his senior season started, Switzer was considered one of the top high-school lineman in Arkansas. He also set the school record and placed first in the shot put in the state track and field meet as a senior. Switzer was a solid student. In fact, he was offered a provisional appointment to the United States Naval Academy at Annapolis, Md., but decided not to accept it.

Coaches from Arkansas and Louisiana State were trying to persuade Switzer to play football at their schools. He had become a fan of football at Arkansas and wanted to play for the Razorbacks. Arkansas assistant coach George Cole visited Crossett to convince Switzer that the Razorbacks wanted him.

RECRUITING CHANGED Switzer later wrote in *Bootlegger's Boy*:

> "George, a great player and assistant coach who later became athletic director at Arkansas, took me out to the Wagon Wheel Cafe. After we ate our chicken-fried steak, he gave me his recruiting speech: 'I'll tell you what, son. I'm going to give you a bed to sleep in and a plate to eat off of, and as long as you make your bed and behave yourself, I won't break your plate.'

> "I thought that sounded really good. Recruiting is a hell of a lot different today."

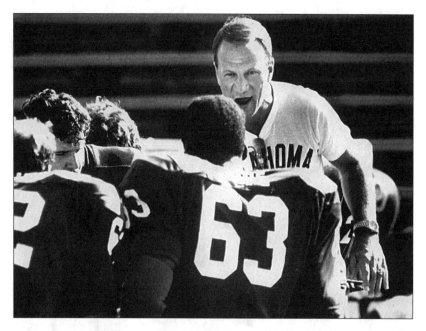

Two significant events in Switzer's life occurred in the fall of 1955: He packed his belongings in an Early Times whisky box and headed for college, and his father was released from prison.

Switzer had a difficult time at first at Arkansas. He neglected his studies, was redshirted, and lost confidence in his athletic skills.

"I didn't know how to go about my business … to improve and become a better product," he said of the situation. "It took me two years to make a decision to learn how to go about it and learn to give effort. I wasn't as sophisticated as young men are today. I had a lot of hang-ups and complexes that I look back on and laugh at today."

RAZORBACKS RALLY The Razorbacks had mediocre seasons the first two years Switzer was eligible for varsity play. He was redshirted in 1956. Arkansas had a 6-4 record in 1957 and a 4-6 record in 1958 and tied for fifth place in the Southwest Conference each season. But the Razorbacks rallied late in the 1958 season. Frank Broyles had come to Arkansas as head coach in 1958 and changed the offense to the Delaware Wing T. The attack was a disaster and the season nearly was, too. Arkansas was shut out twice and scored six, seven, 12 and 14 points in its first six games. Broyles switched to the Wing T and Split-T, and Arkansas won its last four games.

Switzer was hampered the last half of the season by a

Although he let his assistants do most of the coaching, sometimes Barry Switzer couldn't help but get involved.

Barry Switzer and the Sooners celebrate their 25-10 victory over No. 1-ranked Penn State in the 1986 Orange Bowl game. The triumph propelled OU to No. 1 in the final poll for the 1985 season. That was the Sooners' most recent national championship.

shoulder injury he sustained in the fifth game, but he and his teammates looked forward to the 1959 campaign.

However, 1959 was to be a year of conflicting emotions for Barry Switzer. He would experience one of the tormenting calamities of his life, enjoy his most successful season as a football player, and meet his future wife.

He lived at home and worked in the paper mill during the summer of 1959.

On August 26, Switzer's mother came to his room to kiss him good night. He turned his head away because she smelled of whisky. A few minutes later, she shot herself.

"I was in total shock," Switzer wrote in his book. "I felt like I was the one who had caused her to pull the trigger. All she wanted was my love, and I had turned my face away. I have carried this guilt with me the rest of my life."

SIMILAR EXPERIENCES Twenty years later, Switzer would learn that his brother had had a similar experience with their mother that night. (Their mother also left a suicide note, leading professionals to conclude that she would have killed herself no matter what her sons had done.)

Some have speculated that this experience was influential in Switzer's giving troubled players at OU second and third chances, something that would contribute to his own problems late in his career.

But Switzer's football fortunes were on an upswing,

despite the fact that Arkansas was picked fifth in a preseason SWC poll in 1959. He was elected tri-captain, playing primarily on offense.

HOG HEAVEN Arkansas posted a 9-2 record, its best mark since 1927, tied Texas and Texas Christian for the Southwest Conference championship, and capped the campaign with a 14-9 victory over Coach Frank Broyles' alma mater, Georgia Tech, in the Gator Bowl. The Razorbacks were ranked ninth in the nation, their highest ranking in history to that point, and had lost only to No. 2-ranked Mississippi and No. 4-ranked Texas. Arkansas had won only three outright titles and tied for another championship in the Southwest Conference in the previous 44 years

That year at Arkansas, Switzer met Kay McCollum, a freshman from Stuttgart, Ark., who was attractive, a skilled athlete as a majorette, and one of the most effective duck callers in the state. Switzer was an avid outdoorsman, and he later used hunting and fishing to combat the stresses of coaching. Barry and Kay were married in 1963. Switzer became an assistant coach on Broyles' staff after serving an abbreviated stint on active duty in the Army. During this time, Switzer also became a protégé of Jim Mackenzie, who was the assistant head coach and defensive coordinator at Arkansas. That close relationship would lead Switzer to Oklahoma.

SOONER QUIZ

14. Who was the most recent Sooner named all-conference as a running back?

Bud Wilkinson

When he came to Oklahoma in 1946, Bud Wilkinson made a commitment to stay one year as an assistant coach. When he resigned 18 years later, OU football and the expectations of Sooner fans had been changed forever. Wilkinson had established OU as a national football power and had become one of the most successful and most respected coaches in the history of the American college game.

Under his leadership, the Sooners set some standards that still are national records and others that took years to eclipse. He propelled OU from a contender for conference championships to a regular contender for the national championship.

NATIONAL CHAMPIONS Wilkinson-coached teams claimed national championships in 1950, 1955, and 1956, and his teams were ranked in the nation's Top 20 in each of

Bud Wilkinson (right) and Gomer Jones paced many sidelines together.

his first 13 seasons and 15 of the 17 years he was head coach.

During the same period, the Sooners dominated their conference as no team had before or after. The Sooners shared the Big Six Conference title in his first season in 1947, won outright titles during each of the 10 years the conference was the Big Seven and won outright titles the first two years in the Big Eight. The Sooners won the Big Eight title again in 1962, his next-to-last year as OU coach.

Meticulous Ken Farris organized and personally held together the financial aspects of a rapidly growing athletic department through prosperous and lean times from 1950 through 1981.

47 STRAIGHT Wilkinson's record of 145 victories, 29 losses and 4 ties places him eighth in overall winning percentage among NCAA major-college coaches. The Sooners' record of 47 straight victories during the '50s remains the longest win streak in college history. OU also went 48 straight games without a loss during that period. Oklahoma set the NCAA record by scoring in 123 straight games from 1946 to 1957, a remarkable achievement considering defensive play dominated much of that era. Beginning in the 1948 season and extending into the 1950 season, the Sooners also had a streak of 31 straight victories, seventh-longest streak in college history.

Starting in 1946 and ending in 1959, Oklahoma went an inconceivable 74 straight games without a loss in conference play. That streak included 72 wins (all except two with Wilkinson as head coach) and two ties. OU also won a record 44 straight conference games during the 1950s.

Wilkinson's modifications improved the Split-T offense. He and his long-time assistant, Gomer Jones, developed the most popular defensive alignment of their era – the 7-2 defense which became known as the Oklahoma defense. (Actually, they called it the Oklahoma 72 defense.)

Wilkinson made two other highly significant contributions to OU's athletic history: He recruited the school's first black football player (despite open opposition from some of the program's most influential supporters,) and he stressed the importance of academics — 87 percent of his players received degrees.

Port Robertson was hated but later loved for his physical and figurative headlock used to guide many otherwise misguided young men through college from the late 1940s through the late 1970s.

HIRING TATUM In 1945, OU's Board of Regents linked the head football coach's job to state morale. John Steinbeck's classic 1939 saga *The Grapes of Wrath* was regarded as anything but a classic by many Oklahomans. Influential residents thought the author's depiction of the flat-broke Joad family fleeing the Dust Bowl for work as fruit pickers in California had left too many Americans with a one-dimensional view of the Sooner

Jim Tatum brought a wealth of players to OU in his one season as head coach in 1946.

State. Lloyd Noble, a member of the board and an oilman from Ardmore, touted the idea of building a football team that would boost state pride, pointing out that many outstanding athletes would be returning after World War II.

But how was OU going to get its share (or maybe more than its share) of these players?

Athletic Director Lawrence E. "Jap" Haskell had a suggestion. He recommended hiring Jim Tatum as head coach. Haskell had met Tatum at the Jacksonville Naval Air Station. The regents also considered W. H. "Red" Drew, who later coached at Alabama, and Henry Frnka, who had successful coaching stints at Tulsa and Tulane.

GETTING BUD, TOO The regents told Dr. George L. Cross, who had a meteoric rise from assistant professor of botany to OU president in 1944, to arrange an interview with Tatum. The 32-year-old former North Carolina head coach made a special request concerning the interview: Tatum wanted to be accompanied by someone he considered a prospective assistant coach. Cross wisely agreed.

On January 9, 1946, Tatum and Bud Wilkinson met with the regents. Tatum did most of the talking, but some of the regents also were impressed by Wilkinson's poise and what was described as his "winsome smile." Noble, in fact, was so impressed that he suggested Wilkinson be offered the job. Cross thought "institutional ethics might be compromised" if that were to occur. So the regents compromised: Tatum would be offered the job if he agreed to bring Wilkinson with him. Wilkinson was working in his family owned Wilkinson Home Finance Company in Minneapolis and had attended the interview only as a favor to Tatum. But when confronted with the unusual circumstances, Wilkinson agreed to be an assistant coach for one year.

SUPER FORECASTER James Moore Tatum proved to be the man to carry out the regents' wishes. He conducted a nationwide recruiting spree.

"Jim Tatum was a super, super forecaster of what a youngster would do some two or three years later in his growth and his ability to perform," said Wade Walker, a native of North Carolina who had played for Tatum at Jacksonville. "I think he was one of the best organizers that I have ever been around. He was flamboyant. Maybe a little bit over boisterous."

Walker, who was an OU cocaptain in 1947 and 1948 and OU athletic director in 1971-86, was one of many military veterans on the 1946 Sooners. In fact, all 11 starters and 31 of the top 33 players were military

SOONER QUIZ

15. Name the three Sooners who were selected all-conference in four seasons.

John Rapacz was the starting center on the Sooners' first team after World War II.

veterans, the overwhelming majority being Oklahomans.

Taking advantage of liberal NCAA rules governing try-outs and transfers, Tatum gathered the material for a powerful team and the cornerstone for OU's emergence as a national contender. In all, about 275 athletes reportedly tried out. The roster was reduced to 140 during the summer and then cut to the 40 top players.

VETERANS RETURN The starters in the first game in 1946 were ends Jim Tyree and Warren Geise, tackles Wade Walker and Homer Paine, guards Plato Andros and Buddy Burris, center John Rapacz, quarterback Dave Wallace, halfbacks Darrell Royal and Joe Golding, and fullback Eddie Davis. Most of them had been highly decorated in the battles of the Rhineland, the Bulge, Central Germany, and the Marshall and Gilbert Islands in the South Pacific. They were well-prepared to survive what was one of the most extensive try-out systems in college history. Most of the reserves had comparable records as football players and servicemen.

Even with all that potential, OU faced several

SOONER QUIZ

16. Name the Sooner selected all-conference in two different leagues. (Do not consider the Big Six, Big Seven, and Big Eight to be different conferences.)

Plato Andros returned from the war to start at guard.

SOONER QUIZ

17. Name two OU quarterbacks named Watts.

obstacles. It had been several years since most of the Sooners had played football. Few of them had ever played on the same team. They were learning a new attack, the Split-T. And OU faced an incredible challenge immediately, opening the 1946 season against Army.

The Cadets had won back-to-back national championships in 1944 and 1945 and entered the contest with an 19-game winning streak. Plus the team was returning two of its all-time great players: halfback Glenn "Junior" Davis and fullback Felix "Doc" Blanchard. However Blanchard, who was a cousin of Tatum, would not play against the Sooners because of a leg injury.

The untested Sooners made an impressive showing against heavily favored Army at Michie Field, where President Harry S. Truman became the first U.S. president to attend a game in West Point, N.Y. With the Sooners threatening to score in the fourth quarter, Army's Arnold Tucker picked up an OU pitchout and raced 86 yards for the clinching score in a 21-7 victory. (At the end of the season, Army would be ranked second in the nation, after a 0-0 deadlock with Notre Dame vaulted the Fighting Irish to the No. 1 spot.)

TOO MANY COACHES A few years later, Plato Andros jokingly remarked: "We had too many coaches and not enough players in the lineup."

Seven players on the Sooner roster became major college head coaches: Royal at Mississippi State, Washington, and Texas; Jim Owens at Washington; Jack Mitchell at Wichita State, Arkansas, and Kansas; Demosthenes (known to his teammates as Dee) Andros at Oregon State; Walker at Mississippi State; Giese at South Carolina, and Alonzo (known to his teammates as Pete) Tillman at Wichita State.

Jim Owens was an All-American end and later head coach at Washington.

MORE CHALLENGES After the loss to Army, OU's offense continued to sputter. The Sooners claimed a 10-7 win over Texas A&M, which won only four games in 1946. But Texas gained its seventh straight win over OU, 20-13. However, when Jack Mitchell was promoted to starting quarterback, OU began to win.

A setback came against Kansas, 16-13. But OU and Kansas shared the Big Six Conference championship when OU won its remaining league games, and the Jayhawks fell to Nebraska, 16-14.

But one score remained to be settled in 1946. Led by the great Bob Fenimore, Oklahoma A&M (which changed its name to Oklahoma State in 1957), had humiliated the Sooners, 47-0, in the final game of the 1945 season. (That game remains the most decisive loss in Sooner history.)

Tatum wanted his players in a bad mood for the 1946 contest, so he made them practice on Thanksgiving Day.

"He didn't think he was doing a good job unless he had everybody mad at him," said team captain Jim Tyree. "And he was gifted at that."

It appeared the tactic had backfired when the out-manned Aggies, who entered the game with a 3-6-1 record, gained a 12-0 lead. However, the Sooners rallied for a resounding 73-12 win.

OU finished the season with an 8-3 record and was ranked 14th in the nation. Joe Golding had set a school record with 923 yards rushing.

Tatum, apparently overestimating the influence that came with his team's success, continually overplayed his hand with OU officials. Before his team's 34-13 victory in the Gator Bowl, rumors spread that Tatum might be hired by Maryland. It was then that Noble renewed his campaign to hire Bud Wilkinson. He sent his company plane to fly Cross to Gainesville, Fla., and offer Wilkinson the job. Actually, OU was fortunate Wilkinson was available. Two weeks earlier, Drake had selected Al Kawal over Wilkinson as its coach.

When Tatum went to Maryland, OU hired the 31-year-old Wilkinson as its 13th head coach.

SOONER QUIZ

18. In 1952, Billy Vessels ranked second and Buck McPhail ranked third in the nation in rushing. The player who was first played for an Oklahoma college. Who was he?

"Bud, what position do you play?" Wade Walker asked Wilkinson when they met during the summer of 1946, thinking he was one of the players.

NO HINT OF FUTURE Wilkinson's first season as OU head coach did not provide a hint of what was to come. But even before his first season began, Wilkinson made the type of decision that would become the hallmark of his career: He hired Gomer Jones, an All-America center at Ohio State in 1935 and line coach at Nebraska in 1946, as his line coach. Jones remained during Wilkinson's entire career at OU, and many people viewed them as a team.

The Sooners struggled early in the 1947 campaign, posting a 2-2-1 record after five games. The team appeared to be on a downward spiral even though many of the servicemen and highly recruited players had returned from the previous season.

Wilkinson had been aware from the start that some observers thought he might be too young and too soft-spoken to guide the vets. At 31, he was only four or five years older than some of the players.

LACK OF CHIN STRAP OU won its first two games but squeaked by in the opener, a 24-20 triumph at unheralded Detroit in a Friday night contest that was televised in the Detroit area. (It was estimated that Detroit had 5,000 television sets at the time.) Wilkinson recalled a situation in the opening game that might have strengthened the views of his doubters. Detroit scored one of its touchdowns when linebacker Myrle Greathouse, who had lost his helmet chin strap, left the game. OU did not get a substitute on the field before the scoring play started.

"Well, if we lose the game for having 10 guys on the field in my first game as head coach ... ," Wilkinson said, not finishing the sentence but knowing what people would think.

SOONER QUIZ

19. Name the 1950s OU halfback who became a movie and television actor.

SISCO CALLS OU suffered one of its losses to Texas, 34-14, marking the eighth straight win for the Longhorns in the series. The game has become infamous in OU annals because of two calls by official Jack Sisco. One of the calls gave Texas another offensive play after the field clock showed no time remaining in the first half. The Longhorns scored on the extra play.

The second call kept another Texas scoring drive alive when OU was called for roughing the passer after Darrell Royal intercepted a Longhorn pass. Sooner fans were outraged and threw bottles on the field. Some order finally was restored, and Sisco was escorted from the field by the police after the game. But to this day, Sooner fans use the word "Sisco" to denote something derogatory.

Royal played significant roles in two other OU games that shaped Wilkinson's first season: a tie with Kansas and a victory at Missouri. The 163-pound Royal was a versatile player, had started as a freshman the previous season, and became OU's quarterback in 1948. He also was an outstanding defensive back and an accurate and crafty punter. In fact, he still holds the OU record with 17 interceptions in his career.

"Royal probably is the best punter I've ever seen," Wilkinson said.

CROSSROADS The Sooners battled a star-studded Kansas eleven to a 13-13 tie before 34,700 fans, a record crowd, at Owen Field. Royal's punting played a key role, and the tie meant OU and Kansas would eventually tie for the title in the final season of Big Six play. (Colorado joined the league in 1948 to make it the Big Seven.)

But the following week, OU bowed, 20-7, to mediocre Texas Christian, which claimed only three other wins.

At that point, Wilkinson took three steps that influenced the rest of the season. He conducted a two-hour scrimmage on Monday, usually a day of light practice; elevated some reserves to starting roles, and told the Sooners to elect captains, intending to promote player leadership. Tyree and Walker were selected as the captains.

SOONER QUIZ

20. Bud Wilkinson considered leaving OU to coach at another college. What school did he consider?

Darrell Royal dealt opponents misery as an OU halfback and quarterback and later dealt OU misery as the coach at Texas.

CRUCIAL ENCOUNTER

CRUCIAL ENCOUNTER Wilkinson considered the clash at Missouri a crucial encounter, not only for the season but in his coaching career. OU was unranked, but Missouri, with Head Coach Don Faurot having returned from military duty, had been rejuvenated and was ranked 17th in the nation.

Royal's punting backed Missouri into its own territory, a brilliant defensive effort held the Tigers there, and Mitchell, known as General Jack for his demeanor in the huddle, led the attack in OU's 21-12 triumph.

President George L. Cross and his wife, Cleo, were among OU's most loyal fans.

Missouri, which averaged 258.1 yards a game rushing, was held to only 81 yards.

"Missouri was really a pivotal game — not just for that season, but it was the springboard to our becoming a fine football team," Wilkinson said. "It gave the team and coaching staff confidence and gave the public confidence in our program. And the environment of the players is one of the essential elements in a successful program."

OU finished with a 7-2-1 record, ranked 16th in the nation.

Some OU supporters still had doubts about Wilkinson. But he had a strong supporter in President Cross, who not only rode out the tide of dissatisfaction but recommended that Wilkinson be appointed athletic director. In the meantime, Wilkinson had turned down an offer to coach at the U.S. Naval Academy. (Navy later hired George Sauer, whose Kansas teams had tied OU for the conference title the previous two seasons.)

DOUBTS QUIETED During the next 11 seasons, the Sooners quieted any remaining Wilkinson detractors.

Starting in 1948 and continuing through the 1958 season, the Sooners won 107 games, lost only 8 and tied 2. It is unlikely that any college team has matched or even approached such consistency in the post-World War II era.

During that period:

• OU won three national championships (1950, 1955 and 1956).

• OU had four all-victorious seasons (1949, 1954, 1955 and 1956).

• OU had 11 wins in two seasons and 10 wins in five other seasons.

• OU's worst record was 8-2 (in 1951).

• OU was ranked lower than fifth in the nation at the end of only one season.

MORE CHANGES But the 1948 campaign did not start without its problems.

OU jumped to a 17-7 lead at Santa Clara in the opening game. But the Broncos rallied to win, 20-17. Concerned by the collapse, Wilkinson met with cocaptains Wade Walker and Homer Paine, who suggested line reserves spell the starters as a unit since the Sooners had so many outstanding players. Wilkinson bought the idea.

Wilkinson also made other successful changes. He moved Jack Mitchell from halfback to quarterback and brought back the Split-T after trying the traditional T. In the coming weeks, he also replaced three starters with

21. What are the real names of Steve Owens and Tinker Owens?

22. Name the seven different bowls in which OU has played. (Consider the Sun Bowl and John Hancock the same bowl.)

The Sooners celebrate with the bronze Cowboy Hat after defeating Texas for the first time in nine years in 1948. It was Bud Wilkinson's first triumph over the Longhorns.

In 1948, guard Buddy Burris became the Sooners' first consensus All-American in 10 years.

sophomores: guard Clair Mayes, halfback Lindell Pearson, and fullback Leon Heath.

OU finally won the annual bloodletting in Dallas, defeating Texas, 20-14, and giving the Sooners a reason to celebrate after eight barren seasons in the Red River rivalry.

The Sooners were unchallenged in the Big Seven Conference, defeating runner-up Missouri, 41-7, before a record crowd of 39,297 at Owen Field.

HOUSE AFIRE OU did face a challenge against third-ranked North Carolina in the Sugar Bowl. Before the largest crowd that had ever seen the Sooners play — 80,383 — OU won, 14-6, scoring on a 7-yard run by Pearson and a 1-yard run by Mitchell, set up by a 70-yard pass interception return by linebacker Myrle Greathouse.

"When OU walked out on the field, they looked like a bunch of noncommittal, couldn't care less, slouch-around guys," said Mitchell, who was selected as the Most Valuable Player in the Sugar Bowl contest. "They looked like they were going to a funeral. But it was the damnedest revelation you've ever seen. When they blew that whistle, it was like a house afire."

OU finished with a 10-1 record and vaulted to fifth in the national rankings. Guard Paul "Buddy" Burris became OU's first consensus All-America since end Roland "Waddy" Young in 1938. (Some say Buddy was the best of the Burris brothers, but it would not be safe

Quarterback Jack Mitchell was known as General Jack, but he is with the real general here.

to say that if you were surrounded by Buddy, Kurt, and Robert.)

Wilkinson gained some added job security, getting a separate contact as athletic director and professor of physical education. His salary also was raised — to $15,000, more than the OU president was paid at the time.

WIN 'EM ALL OU enjoyed its first all-victorious season in 31 years in 1949. Some observers still consider the '49 Sooners the best team in school history. OU had a cohesive mixture of former servicemen and fresh Wilkinson recruits and was ranked second in the nation only to all-victorious Notre Dame.

But the Monster was being created.

Darrell Royal, who had been in Wilkinson's meetings with quarterbacks for four seasons and probably qualified for a doctorate in the subject, took over the leadership role at quarterback, aided by end Jim Owens, tackle Wade Walker, guard Stan West, and halfback George Thomas, who led the nation in scoring with 117 points.

The Sooners posted their second straight 20-14 win

Stan West was an all-conference guard in 1949.

TABOO TURNS INTO TOUCHDOWN

A play during 1948's 42-0 rout of Kansas State gave Coach Bud Wilkinson an opportunity to show his sense of humor, something he did not often do in public. On a K-State punt, Jack Mitchell fielded the ball and handed off to Darrell Royal, who went 96 yards for a touchdown.

At that time, Wilkinson met with the Oklahoma City Quarterback Club and reporters weekly during the season. Here is how he described the play to that group:

"I had told the boys never to catch a punt inside the 10-yard line. When Mitchell caught the ball around the four, I ran down the sideline yelling, 'Don't catch it! Don't catch it!' Then Darrell took the ball from Mitchell on the crisscross, and suddenly he was open for the touchdown. I ran up the sideline with him, yelling, 'Way to go! Way to go!' I guess that's what you call being an adaptable coach."

Mitchell, incidentally, was a game-breaking punt returner, averaging 23.6 yards a return. He still holds the OU career record of 922 yards in punt returns.

---

over Texas before a record crowd of 75,347 fans in the Cotton Bowl and claimed another Big Seven title with a 27-7 clinching victory over Missouri before a record crowd of 37,152 fans at Columbia.

But it was the game against Santa Clara, the last foe to have beaten the Sooners, that exposed how mammoth the Monster was becoming. An overflow crowd of 60,145 fans gathered for the clash. (The Sooners were able to sell that many tickets because of the foresight of Cross, who had approved a stadium expansion from 30,000 to 55,000 seats during the off-season. Critics derided the OU president's decision, referring to it as Cross's Folly.) OU rallied to defeat the Broncos, 28-21, on touchdown runs of 81 yards by Heath and 24 yards by Thomas.

19 STRAIGHT The victory boosted OU's winning streak to a school-record 19 games.

The Sugar Bowl attempted to set up a national playoff game between OU and Notre Dame, but the Irish did not compete in bowl games at that time. So Louisiana State, a local favorite ranked ninth in the nation, was selected. The contest received an unexpected spark when a former LSU player was accused of spying on OU practices. LSU denied the charges, saying Wilkinson simply was trying to motivate the Sooners. "That was the only time I ever saw Bud real angry," said assistant coach Frank "Pop" Ivy. "His face was white."

Halfback George Thomas led the nation in scoring with 117 points in 1949.

Whatever the situation, OU won, 35-0, the most decisive contest in Sugar Bowl history. Heath, who ripped LSU for 170 yards rushing and 11.3 yards a carry, received the Outstanding Player Award.

'49 STRONGEST Years later, Wilkinson analyzed the 11-0 season.

"I would say that 1949 probably was the strongest team I coached with this reservation: All the athletes from 1941 through 1945 went into the service and were back together. So you had the unusual situation of four or five classes of seniors coming together at one time. It's unlikely that it will ever happen again. So it is really unfair to compare this team with what I call a normal college team.

"Many of the 1949 players had combat experience and had been athletes in the service. It was the last big group of veterans, and they were mature, highly competent, and unflappable. We did not have any weakness."

Wilkinson was presented the American Football Coaches Association Coach of the Year Award following the 1949 season. He remains the only OU coach ever to receive that prestigious award.

SOONER QUIZ

23. What was the identical score of the first bowl games of Bud Wilkinson and Barry Switzer?

President George L. Cross gets a victory ride after the Sooners defeated Louisiana State, 35-0, in the 1950 Sugar Bowl.

24. OU's first football field, which was unnamed, was located where? a) Where Owen Field is today, b) north of Owen Field, c) under the law library, d) north of Holmberg Hall.

Wilkinson confers with quarterback Claude Arnold during OU's 14-13 triumph over Texas in 1950.

BITTERSWEET MEMORIES The 1950 season was marked by two of OU's most memorable victories, contests against Texas A&M and Nebraska, and by two history-making events. The Sooners won their first national championship and saw their 31-game winning streak ended.

OU faced a major rebuilding job, with fullback Leon Heath on offense and halfback Ed Lisak and safety Wilbur "Buddy" Jones on defense the only returning starters. But the Sooners were aided by several returning reserves who had played regularly and a smashing sophomore class. Four other players, including starting halfback Tom Carroll, had been called to active military duty with the 45th Infantry Division because of the Korean War.

OU also had its least experienced quarterback in some time, Claude Arnold, who had been recruited from the intramural touch football scene two years earlier. Arnold remains overshadowed by OU's more sensational quarterbacks, but none of them came close to his mark of allowing only one interception in 114 passes in 1950. Also Arnold's 13 touchdown passes remained an OU one-season record for 43 years.

THE FINEST FINISH In what many call the most exciting game ever played at Owen Field, OU trailed Texas A&M, 28-27, with only 3:36 remaining when tackle Jim Weatherall's point-after attempt went wide of the goal posts. Weatherall left the field crying, thinking his miss had lost the game.

46   *Sooners Handbook*

"Bud said he thought it was the thing that won the ball game for us," Weatherall recalled. "Otherwise we might have settled for a tie."

But the Sooners weren't settling for a loss either. OU held A&M on downs, and Heath raced four yards for a touchdown with only 44 seconds remaining.

"That was the finest football finish I have ever seen," Wilkinson said of the 34-28 victory. "I still don't see how we did it. You just don't move 69 yards in one minute and nine seconds against a team as good as the Texas Aggies."

Heath had a rare combination of power and speed and his running overshadowed his excellent blocking. He was nicknamed "Mule Train," a song made popular in the 1950s by singer Frankie Laine. Heath got the name because of his stubbornness in continuing to run after defenders hit him.

BILLY THE KID The Sooners also came from behind in the fourth quarter the next week to topple Texas, 14-13. Sophomore Billy Vessels, who had been moved from starting defensive halfback to replace Carroll on offense, scored both OU touchdowns, the final one coming on an

SOONER QUIZ

25. A 1950s OU halfback had a brother who became OU track and field coach and the coach had a son who played football for the Sooners in the 1970s. Name the men.

Fullback Leon Heath was known as "Mule Train" because he was so difficult to bring down.

*26. Name three sets
of brothers who
played at OU in the
1950s.*

11-yard tackle-breaking run with only 3:46 remaining.

But Vessels would have his most outstanding game as a sophomore against 6-1-1 Nebraska. The game also pitted Vessels against the most celebrated sophomore in the conference, Cornhusker halfback Bobby Reynolds, who had rushed for 1,260 yards and scored 19 touchdowns.

Reynolds lived up to his reputation, rushing for 81 yards and leading Nebraska to a 21-14 advantage in the first half. However, Reynolds gained only one yard in the second half. Vessels rushed for an OU one-game record of 208 yards and scored three touchdowns as the Sooners won, 49-35, before 53,066 fans, the largest crowd to watch a Big Seven game at that time.

After the game, Reynolds sought out Wilkinson and asked: "Where's Buddy Jones? I want to shake hands with him. He was wonderful."

The 155-pound Jones had dogged Reynolds most of the second half, but he had suffered a knee injury — a loss that would cost OU dearly in the postseason.

OU was ranked No. 1 in the final poll by The Associated Press to claim the school's first national championship.

The Sooners struggled in the Sugar Bowl against seventh-ranked Kentucky, coached by the legendary

*Wilkinson and
Gomer Jones visited
with Notre Dame
Coach Frank Leahy
as the schools
planned a home-
and-home series in
1952 and 1953.*

Paul "Bear" Bryant. Quarterback Vito "Babe" Parilli passed for two touchdowns — highlighting how sorely the Sooners missed the injured Jones — in a 13-7 setback that ended OU's 31-game victory streak. The Sooners lost five of seven fumbles. Vessels, who had a 51-yard run to the Kentucky 14-yard line nullified, passed to another sophomore, Merrill Green, for 17 yards and OU's only touchdown. At least, OU had extended its scoring streak.

OU finished the season with a 10-1 record. (The team's No. 1 ranking didn't change, because polls were not taken after bowl games at that time.)

UNCERTAINTIES The Sooners faced serious uncertainties going into the 1951 season. They returned only four offensive starters, including Weatherall and Vessels. OU had its most inexperienced quarterback since 1945, because starter Eddie Crowder had played only sparingly in 1950 after suffering a bruised kidney. And OU had lost one of the strengths of its defense: its entire secondary, including stalwarts Buddy Jones and Ed Lisak.

OU's inexperience was demonstrated when the Sooners bowed to Texas A&M in their second game and to Texas in their third contest. Vessels and Crowder were injured on the same play in the loss to the Longhorns. Vessels was sidelined for the rest of the season by a knee injury. Crowder would return in two weeks.

A week later, determined fullback Coleman "Buck" McPhail, rushed for 215 yards against Kansas, eclipsing Vessels' school mark.

WHERE'S THE BALL Against once-beaten Colorado, Crowder returned with a remarkable feat. Heavy rain

27. Name three sets of brothers who played at OU in the 1970s.

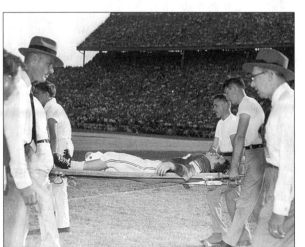

Billy Vessels was sidelined the rest of the season after suffering a knee injury against Texas in 1951. Bud Wilkinson is at the left.

Fullback Buck McPhail set a school record of 215 yards against Kansas in 1951 and gained 1,018 rushing in 1952.

SOONER QUIZ

28. Who held most of the OU major career passing records before Cale Gundy bettered them in 1993?

had been forecast for late in the day, so Wilkinson tried to get an early lead. Crowder was uncanny at faking a hand-off to fullback McPhail, while hiding the ball on one hip and fading to pass. McPhail played a major role in the act, charging full tilt into the line.

The Golden Buffaloes, and a vast majority of the crowd of 46,686, were fooled four times. Crowder took advantage of CU's befuddlement by passing for four touchdowns in the first 17 minutes, 16 seconds of the 55-14 triumph.

(Interestingly, Crowder later became the head coach — from 1963 to 1973 — and athletic director — from 1965 to 1984 — at Colorado.)

OU posted an 8-2 record, going virtually unchallenged in the conference race and ranking 10th in the nation.

"BEST EVER"

"BEST EVER" The Sooners had another banner year in 1952, although OU was surprised in a 21-21 tie with Colorado in Boulder — the first time the Sooners had not beaten a conference team since they were tied by Kansas 29 league games earlier in 1947.

Led by one of its all-time great backfields and center/linebacker Tom Catlin, OU rallied the rest of the season, smashing 10th-ranked Texas, 49-20, and breezing through the rest of the Big Seven Conference schedule.

Sportswriter Dick Cullum of The Minneapolis Tribune obviously was impressed, writing:

"When Buddy Leake, the right halfback, was well, the Oklahoma backfield of Eddie Crowder, Billy Vessels, Leake and Buck McPhail was the best-balanced, most versatile backfield I have ever seen. Every one of them was at the All-American level. Oklahoma had the best offensive platoon of the season and as far as I know, the best ever."

SETBACK AT SOUTH BEND OU suffered its only loss in 1952 in perhaps Vessels' greatest game of his career. The fourth-ranked Sooners faced once-beaten, once-tied 10th-ranked Notre Dame in South Bend, Ind. In a rugged, emotional seesaw battle, Notre Dame scored on a controversial drive in the fourth quarter to win, 27-21. The drive was controversial because Notre Dame used what became known as "the sucker shift," which was considered a deliberate attempt to draw the opponent offside. It worked on OU, and Notre Dame

Quarterback Eddie Crowder fakes a handoff to fullback Buck McPhail (41) and fades to pass against Texas. Crowder fooled many opposing players, fans and cameramen with his play.

All-American center Tom Catlin was one of OU's captains in 1952.

got a first down on its 3-yard line on the winning series. The NCAA outlawed the shift the next year.

Halfback Larry Grigg, who lost a fumble on a kickoff return before Notre Dame's winning drive, gave OU a chance at victory when he blocked the conversion attempt. If it could score again, OU could win with a conversion. The Sooners reached the Notre Dame 25-yard line in the closing seconds. Crowder called a screen pass to speedy sophomore left end Max Boydston. But when he looked down field, Crowder could not find Boydston, and the Sooners threat ended. (Boydston had gotten back to line late and was told the wrong play call by a teammate.)

Tackle Jim Weatherall was a two-time consensus All-American and won the Outland Trophy in 1951.

Vessels ran for 195 yards, the most ever by an individual against Notre Dame and a mark that stood until 1973. He scored on touchdown runs of 62 and 44 yards and on a pass from Crowder on a play covering 28 yards.

After the game, Vessels told Wilkinson: "Remember, coach, when I was a freshman, and you told me it was the team that counted and not the individual? I know what you mean now."

The Sooners ended the season ranked fourth with an 8-1-1 record.

FIRST OUTLAND WINNER

In 1951, Jim Weatherall broke new ground. Finally, a player from OU and the Big Seven Conference won one of college football's major individual awards when he was presented the Outland Trophy as the nation's best lineman.

"One of the things that I think helped me most was that when I came onto the team, we had a lot of older-type fellows from the standpoint that they had been in the service," said Weatherall, who was an overpowering defensive tackle. "Their thinking was more mature, and this seemed to be passed on to the younger guys. I think that this prevailed over the years.

"I think I learned a lot more football quicker. With that old bunch, you nearly had to or you'd get killed."

"He was everything you're looking for in a football player," Wilkinson said of the 6-foot-4, 230 pounder. "Highly intelligent. Very strong physically. And he had that desire to excel. He became just a superb lineman."

OU's outstanding backfield in 1952 includes Buddy Leake, Billy Vessels, Eddie Crowder, and Buck McPhail.

In his memoirs, published in Look magazine, Notre Dame Coach Frank Leahy wrote: "The best team our lads ever faced — I did not see the powerful Army aggregations of '44 and '45 because I was in the service — was Oklahoma of '52. Upsetting them was my greatest coaching thrill."

Many observers consider Vessels the greatest OU player of all time. He had everything: size, speed, strength, and an insatiable desire to win. Had he not been the best offensive player on the team, Vessels would have been the best defensive player. In fact, he did play defense in special situations.

Billy Vessels sets sail on one of his three touchdown plays against Notre Dame in 1952.

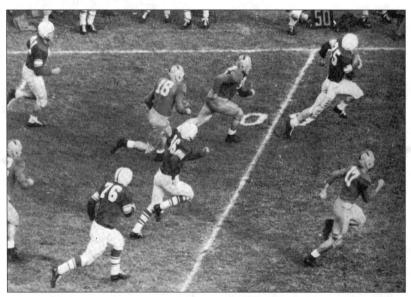

In 1952, Billy Vessels became the first OU player and first Big Seven player to win the Heisman Trophy.

His performance against Notre Dame in OU's first nationally televised game was credited with gaining Vessels the Heisman Trophy, symbolic of the nation's outstanding college football player. He received 525 points to 367 for the runner-up Maryland quarterback Jack Scarbath. Catlin was 10th and Crowder 12th in the voting.

FASTEST & TOUGHEST "Billy is one of the classic examples of what athletics will do for you. Without athletics, there wasn't any way," Wilkinson said of Vessels, who had a disruptive family life in the small northeastern Oklahoma town of Cleveland.

"Billy was a remarkable athlete. He was the first player that I had ever been around who was the fastest man on the field and also the toughest. Those two things don't normally go together. But Vessels was just unbelievably strong and tough and also the fastest man we had. And totally dedicated. A truly great player. He really was. His senior year, he was just unreal. He could do everything."

The 6-1, 185-pound Vessels finished the season with a school-record 1,072 yards. McPhail rushed for 1,018 yards, making them the first teammates to rush for 1,000 yards or more in the same season in NCAA history.

SOONER QUIZ

29. Steve Owens holds nine of the top 10 marks for most rushes in a game at OU. Who is the only other Sooner in the top 10?

Bud Wilkinson and quarterback Eddie Crowder celebrate a 41-6 win over Oklahoma A&M in 1951.

FRONT SEAT IN HELL OU faced a number of changes in 1953. For one thing, the rules had been changed to eliminate offensive and defensive platoons, meaning players could not be substituted freely.

The Sooners faced Notre Dame in the opening game. The Irish returned many of the players who had helped upset OU in 1952, were ranked No. 1 in the nation, and handed OU a 28-21 setback. The inexperienced Sooners helped the Irish by yielding five fumbles, two interceptions, and a blocked punt.

"I'd give up my seat on the front row in hell to play them again," said guard Virgilee "Bo" Bolinger, who never got another shot at Notre Dame but was named a consensus All-American in 1955.

The next week, OU struggled to a 7-7 tie at Pittsburgh.

The situation demanded bold action. Going into the annual grudge match against Texas, Wilkinson moved Gene Dan Calame to quarterback. Calame, who at 5-10, 165 pounds was wiry and tough, had started at defensive end in his freshman and sophomore seasons in 1951 and 1952. Calame learned the quarterback duties quickly, and the new rules that forced players to also play defense were right down his alley.

SOONER QUIZ

30. Cale Gundy and Garrick McGee hold nine of the top 10 yards passing marks in one game at OU. Who is the only other Sooner in the top 10?

Halfback Merrill Green raced 51 yards for a touchdown with 36 seconds left in OU's 27-20 win over Colorado in 1953.

The Sooners beat Texas, 19-14, to start what was to become the longest winning streak in the history of the college game. But during the remainder of OU's season, more close encounters remained. Merrill Green ran 51 yards for a touchdown with 36 seconds left to beat Colorado, 27-20, and Larry Grigg scored on a 1-yard run to beat Missouri, 14-7.

BUD VS. TATUM The season reversal and 8-1-1 record sent the fourth-ranked Sooners into the Orange Bowl against Maryland for the first of three clashes with Wilkinson's former boss, Jim Tatum. The all-victorious Terrapins had claimed 10 straight wins and allowed only five touchdowns the entire season. In the Orange Bowl, Maryland allowed only one more touchdown. But Grigg's 25-yard touchdown run was enough for OU to win, 7-0, blanking the Terrapins for the first time in 52 games.

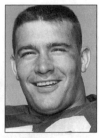

Bo Bolinger was a consensus All-American guard in 1955.

OU had lost its first- and second-team quarterbacks by the second half, and the awesome duties fell to Jack Van Pool, a senior who had played sparingly in his career. Van Pool defused a touchy situation when he went into the huddle, telling his teammates, "I know I'm not very good, but I promise you guys if you'll stick with me through this, I won't fumble." His hands were trembling at the time, and the humor of the situation relieved the tension. He didn't fumble, his teammates stuck with him, and the team ended the season with a 9-1-1 record. The Sooners ranking did not change because votes still were not taken after bowl games.

SUPER COMPETITOR The Sooners gained another major individual award in 1953, when guard J.D. Roberts of Dallas was presented the Outland Trophy as the nation's

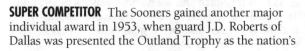

Guard J.D. Roberts (left) won the Outland Trophy in 1953 and tackle Roger Nelson was one of the Sooners' cocaptains the same season.

outstanding interior lineman.

"J.D. was a boy who really was not physically as impressive as Weatherall, for example," said Wilkinson. "He was not tall (5-10). Yet he had extremely fast reflexes. Again, that burning desire to excel. A super competitor.

"He played his first couple of years at about 230 and 220. He was an excellent player, but he was just a little bit slow in relative terms. He was still an excellent player. But his senior year, he got down to 200 pounds, and that gave him that extra couple of steps in speed that he had not had up to that time. With that little bit of added speed, he became just remarkable.

"He was the first dominant type nose guard that I recall. We didn't play him the way Nebraska played Rich Glover (in 1971 and 1972), but he was that important to us, and he was that effective."

Roberts, who became the head coach of the New Orleans Saints (1972-74), also was named Lineman of the Year by The Associated Press and United Press International.

ENTER THE SOPHS The 1954 Sooners were not sensational. But OU posted its second all-victorious season in

SOONER QUIZ

31. When was the OU team season scoring record set?

Wilkinson's career. And a group of fast-advancing sophomores gave a hint of what was to come.

OU faced a crucial situation when quarterback Gene Dan Calame was sidelined indefinitely after being injured in the second game of the season. Enter Jimmy Harris, a raw-boned, 168-pound sophomore. No one could have known at the time, but Harris was to be OU's quarterback for most of three seasons, and the Sooners never would lose with him at the helm. (Harris shared playing time with Calame late in 1954.)

With Texas coming up, Wilkinson also realized OU needed more running punch. He made a masterful but daring position change, moving third-team sophomore center Jerry Tubbs to first-team fullback. Tubbs had never played in the backfield, but he was extremely strong for a 205 pounder and was an exceptional linebacker.

Quarterback Gene Dan Calame picks up 20 yards against Kansas.

Wilkinson also started spelling his starters with a complete second team that he called the alternate unit.

Wilkinson's emphasis on defense was playing off. OU shut out four foes, allowed three others only one touchdown and gave up its most points in a 21-16 win over Texas Christian.

But the all-victorious Sooners were only ranked third in the national polls. Two other all-victorious teams, Ohio State and UCLA, were ranked first in the wire service polls.

Still, the Monster was growing.

NCAA MARK The 1954 team also pushed OU past the NCAA record for scoring in consecutive games, reaching 90 in a row with its defeat of Kansas State in the fifth game of the season. The mark had been set by Catawba College of Salisbury, N.C., over ten seasons, 1944-53.

"If anybody had told us before the season began that we would go through all-victorious, I'd have thought they were crazy," said Wilkinson. "But our 1954 team had a world of fight and was always able to show a little more of it than the other team when the going became tough and the chips were down. That's the mark of a champion."

In a highly unusual situation, two players, center Kurt Burris and end Max Boydston, both from the relatively small town of Muskogee, were consensus All-America choices and, in another unique situation, were named linemen of the year.

Burris was named Player of the Year by the Helms and Citizens Savings Athletic Foundation, Lineman of the Year by the Philadelphia Sports Writers Association, and finished second to fullback Alan Ameche of Wisconsin in the Heisman Trophy voting – the highest finish for an interior lineman to that time.

Boydston caught only 11 passes as a senior, but he was an excellent all-around player and punter and was named Lineman of the Year by the Washington (D.C.) Touchdown Club.

Although many of the previous year's starters had departed, the alternate-team sophomores of 1954 had been promoted in 1955 and were nearly as experienced as they were unheralded. The Sooners picked up where they left off the previous season after surviving a 13-6 scare against North Carolina. The 1955 Sooners wouldn't have another close contest until they faced Maryland in a battle of No. 1 and 2 teams in the Orange Bowl.

'BOOMER SOONER' Halfback Clendon Thomas recalled Wilkinson's method of guiding players, telling him he was good enough to start, but the team needed him on

SOONER QUIZ

32. Name the three Sooners who led in rushing three consecutive seasons.

Max Boydston was a consensus All-American selection at end and Lineman of the Year in 1954.

Kurt Burris was a consensus All-American choice at center and Lineman of the Year in 1954.

Halfback Bob Burris was a starting halfback on OU's 1955 national championship team.

the alternate unit in 1955.

"He would do a snow job on you," Thomas said. "He just had a way of making you wave the flag and come out singing, 'Boomer Sooner.' "

The Sooners scored 40 points or more in six of their regular-season games. But what was often overlooked was that the Sooners shut out five foes and held three others to only one touchdown each.

The reputation of the offense was enhanced because of what was called the "Hurry-up Offense" and "Go-Go Offense." The Sooners ran back to the huddle after each play or sometimes returned to the line of scrimmage without a huddle and called the next play there. The tactic demoralized many opponents, who already felt out-manned. Also OU's use of two teams helped the Sooners.

GO-GO OFFENSE Wilkinson got the idea to crank up his offense after watching halfback Tommy McDonald, a consensus All-American in 1955 and 1956. The 169-pound McDonald was quick, could pass accurately on the run, and was an excellent secondary player. But most of all, McDonald was spirited.

"McDonald is a funny kid," Wilkinson said. "He figures any play that doesn't go for a touchdown is a failure. When he doesn't score, Tommy jumps up and tears back to the huddle, running almost as hard as if he had the ball. It became contagious. The other boys, more or less, picked it up from him and then we started working on it, seeing how fast we could go. Tommy was convinced that he was going to win, and that rubbed off on the people around him."

The 1955 Orange Bowl once again pitted Wilkinson against Maryland and Tatum, but this time with the Sooners being the No. 1 team. Maryland, which was considered the best defensive team in the country, gained a 6-0 halftime lead.

"Sit down," Wilkinson ordered in the dressing room. "If you guys don't get busy and start playing football, you're going to get the hell beat out of you."

It was the first time many of the Sooners had ever heard Wilkinson cuss, and that got their attention.

SOONER QUIZ

33. Name the two Sooners who led in passing four consecutive seasons.

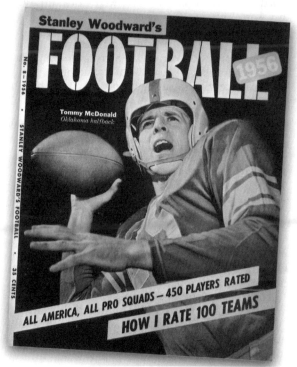

Tommy McDonald graced the cover of Stanley Woodward's Football preview magazine in 1956.

OU's 1956 preseason starters are (front row from left) John Bell, Tom Emerson, Bill Krisher, Jerry Tubbs, Ken Northcutt, Edmon Gray, Don Stiller, (back row) Clendon Thomas, Jimmy Harris, Billy Pricer and Tommy McDonald. However, Northcutt was injured before the season started and did not play in 1956.

OU also got Maryland's attention by using the "Go-Go Offense" in the second half.

"It was all you could do to last through it," Thomas recalled. "After four or five quick plays, if they hadn't called time-out, we'd have to. We were just as tired as they were. They just didn't know it."

McDonald scored on a 4-yard run, reserve quarterback Jay O'Neal scored on a 1-yard run, and halfback Carl Dodd returned an interception 82 yards for the closing touchdown in OU's 20-6 triumph.

"That's the most satisfying victory we've ever had," Wilkinson said.

Tatum was gracious in defeat, commenting: "Oklahoma is definitely the best team in the country. I've never seen a team with all the equipment this one has."

"I don't know if we're the best," said Wilkinson, "but we haven't been beaten yet."

The Sooners were 11-0 for their second straight all-victorious campaign, had extended their winning streak to 30 games, and were national champions for the second time.

Could the Monster grow any more?

ANOTHER CHAMPIONSHIP The 1956 season was truly a campaign of history-making events.

The Sooners were all-victorious for the third year in a row and set a national record in consecutive victories. OU also handed Notre Dame its most decisive loss to that time. OU had only one close contest and claimed its second-straight national title.

Although it went virtually unnoticed in 1956, Wilkinson quietly recruited a player named Prentice Gautt and changed the face of OU football forever.

Wilkinson had his last face-to-face encounters with his Iowa Pre-Flight associates, Jim Tatum and Don Faurot. The Sooners beat Tatum's North Carolina team, 36-0, in their opening game, giving Wilkinson a 3-0 mark against his former boss. And the Sooners routed Missouri, 67-14, giving Wilkinson a 10-0 record over Faurot, who retired after the 1956 campaign.

The confident and experienced Sooners posted a 10-0 record and averaged 47 points to only six points a game for their opponents, six of whom did not score. A Big Seven rule at that time barred teams from going to a bowl two years in a row.

BEST NORMAL TEAM Many consider the 1956 Sooners the best OU team ever. After he left OU, Wilkinson called them "the best normal college team I coached," distinguishing the '56 team from the serviceman-packed 1949 unit. The returning Sooners reported to fall practice six pounds per player lighter than they had been the previous season. Wilkinson liked trim, fast players. Wilkinson rewarded the Sooners by telling them that their 10:30 curfew on school nights still was in effect but coaches would not make room checks.

The Sooners were ready when they faced a sub-par Notre Dame at South Bend, Ind., on October 27, before a record crowd of 60,128 and a national television audience.

"He didn't have to say much," Thomas said of Wilkinson. "He had us ready. He knew when to say things and when not to. There was no rah-rah stuff. They were in for it. We had an outstanding ball team. We had unbelievable depth.

"I guess (center and cocaptain) Jerry Tubbs was as good a collegiate player as I've ever seen. First play out of the hat, he stuck Hornung (Notre Dame quarterback Paul Hornung, 1956 Heisman Trophy winner) in the face and chest. That was the keynote address for that ball game."

BEAT THE IRISH OU dominated the game, 40-0. The Sooners intercepted four passes, two by Tommy McDonald (who had been told he was too small to play at Notre Dame), who returned one for 55 yards and a touchdown, and another by Thomas, who returned it 36 yards for a touchdown.

The win was Wilkinson's only victory over the Irish in six encounters.

The next week, the Sooners went to once-beaten and

Only one thing could dampen the Sooners' national championship giddiness, and the NCAA provided it, placing OU on two-years' probation in 1955 for extending scholarships past eligibility, paying medical expenses of athletes' families, and providing clothes, cash, and gifts to athletes.

SOONER QUIZ

34. Name the two Sooners who led in pass receiving three consecutive seasons.

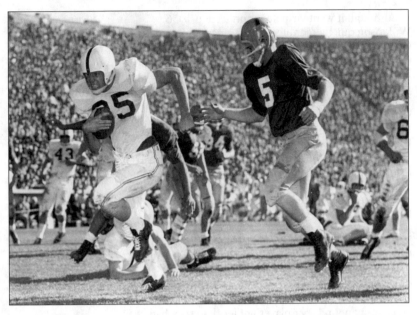

Clendon Thomas speeds past Heisman Trophy winner Paul Hornung (5) for a touchdown in OU's 40-0 win over Notre Dame in 1956.

upset-minded Colorado, which had not beaten OU since 1912. Folsom Field had been expanded earlier in the year and a record crowd of 46,563 gathered despite 27-degree temperature.

It appeared the Sooners might have met their match when the Golden Buffaloes took a 19-6 lead at halftime.

Stories differ as what was said at halftime, but Thomas remembered:

"That's one of the few times in my career with Mr. Wilkinson that he ever really got mad. That day, he made a comment to the effect that we didn't deserve to wear the red jerseys that we had on our backs. He was talking about the tradition, the winning streak, and us as ball players."

Some reports add that Wilkinson also made some defensive adjustments.

On its first offensive series of the second half, OU gambled when it was two yards short of a first down with a fourth down on its own 28-yard line. Thomas made three yards on a quick-hitter, setting the tone for the rest of the game. McDonald threw a 6-yard pass to Thomas for a touchdown and then ran 11 yards after taking a pitchout from quarterback Jimmy Harris to score on the ensuing series. The Sooners won, 27-19.

LET GRAY SCORE When they ended the season with a 53-0 win over Oklahoma A&M, the Sooners had stretched their winning streak to 40 straight games, topping the previous national mark of 39 set by Washington from

1908 to 1914. OU also established national single-season records by averaging 391 yards rushing and gaining an average of 22.2 first downs a game.

Left tackle and cocaptain Edmon Gray held two distinctions: He was the only player who had started every game during the three consecutive all-victorious seasons and the roughshod, fun-loving fellow was the only player from the era who ever dared to call Wilkinson "Bud" to his face. But Gray had never scored a touchdown in his entire career. So he traded positions with Thomas late in his final game and smashed over for a touchdown.

"Wilkinson went crazy," Thomas remembered. "He loved it. We loved it, too."

McDonald won the Robert W. Maxwell Award and The Sporting News Award as the nation's outstanding player, and Tubbs, who had been moved back to center as a junior in 1955, won the Walter Camp Trophy as the nation's outstanding player and was selected Lineman of the Year by UPI. Thomas led the nation in scoring with 108 points, six more than McDonald scored.

HARRIS UNDERRATED Years later, Wilkinson made the type of comment he rarely made while coaching:

"Jimmy Harris was probably the most underrated

Jerry Tubbs accepted the Washington Touchdown Club trophy for the national championship and the Rockne Trophy as Lineman of the Year in 1956. Presenting the awards are Vice President Richard M. Nixon (left) and House Speaker Sam Rayburn.

Quarterback Jimmy Harris stiff-arms Texas' Don Marony on an 8-yard touchdown run in 1956.

athlete who ever played."

Twelve seniors completed their careers as all-victorious, three-year lettermen. They were ends John Bell, Bob Timberlake, and Delbert Long; tackles Gray, Tom Emerson, and Wayne Greenlee; center Tubbs; quarterbacks Harris and Jay O'Neal; halfbacks McDonald and Robert Derrick, and fullback Billy Pricer.

Many believe the 1956 starting backfield of Harris, McDonald, Thomas, and Pricer was the best in OU history, considering its play on both offense and defense.

And many believed the Monster would never be beaten.

The 1957 Sooners, led by guard Bill Krisher and half-back Clendon Thomas, escaped another close call against Colorado, handed Wilkinson his last victory over Texas, claimed the Big Seven championship and won in the Orange Bowl. But 1957 will be remembered as the year the longest winning streak in college football history ended.

OU UNBEATABLE? November 16, 1957, when No. 2-ranked OU faced unranked Notre Dame at Owen Field, remains the darkest day in OU football history. But hardly anyone could foresee the outcome. OU was an 18-point favorite, and Sooners Illustrated had just published a cover story entitled, "Why Oklahoma is Unbeatable."

The teams waged a classic defensive struggle. The Irish stopped OU on downs at the Notre Dame 13-yard line on OU's opening drive. That was as close as the Sooners came to scoring on that gray, chilly Saturday. OU turned back one Notre Dame threat at the 1-yard line and another by intercepting a pass in the end zone.

Finally, Notre Dame put together a 20-play drive, featuring the pounding of 205-pound fullback Nick Pietrosante. On fourth down from the 3-yard line, the Irish faked a hand-off to Pietrosante, and halfback Dick Lynch etched his place in history with a touchdown run around right end with 3:50 left. Monte Stickles kicked the conversion, and Notre Dame had all the points it needed for a 7-0 triumph.

Notre Dame not only ended OU's national record victory streak at 47 games but also ended OU's national record consecutive scoring streak at 123 games.

Many in the record partisan crowd of 63,170 sat stunned for several minutes after the game, almost as though they expected OU to return to the field and win.

"Father, I want to congratulate you," Coach Bud Wilkinson told the Reverend Edmund P. Joyce, executive vice president of Notre Dame, who visited the OU dressing room afterward. "You have a great ball team. We played as well as we could every minute of the game."

On their way to the president's home, a short walk from the stadium, Joyce told OU President George L. Cross:

"In all my years — and there are many — I've never heard a losing coach say his team played as well as it could. They always explain how the team didn't play so well. What a fine spirit it was for a coach to have. How gentlemanly and sportsmanly his boys were."

OU halfback Clendon Thomas looked back on the situation years later, saying:

"At that time, we had a tradition to uphold. There were three seasons of teams that had set that thing in motion. You were letting those guys down, if you didn't continue. You felt obligated, and you're under a lot of strain. The whole team for some reason was just dead that day.

"But the guys never really felt all that guilty about losing to Notre Dame. They felt bad because that streak was over. But we also felt a sigh of relief, too. That was a big strain, and it was over. I think the strain finally caught up with a bunch of guys."

Thomas scored 36 touchdowns in three seasons to better by one the OU record held by George "Junior" Thomas (1947-49) and Billy Vessels (1950-52).

NO SIMPLE ISSUE Before the 1956 season, Wilkinson

made a far-reaching decision.

"Prentice Gautt was probably the best player in Oklahoma that year," said Wilkinson. "We're now faced with a problem of do we or don't we give him a scholarship. This was no simple issue."

It was no simple issue because Gautt was black, and OU had never had a black football player. Black students had begun attending OU in the early 1950s. Buddy Hudson, a black basketball player from Purcell, had lettered in the early 1950s with no public fanfare.

Gautt had been the best player at Oklahoma City Douglass, a segregated high school that had won 76 games in a row. Even so, some of OU's influential supporters opposed recruiting Gautt. But Wilkinson struck a deal: Gautt would come to OU without a scholarship and would have to demonstrate he could be successful in the classroom and on the football field. "I knew he would make it," said Wilkinson. Gautt was supported by a group of professionals in the black community and received a scholarship after one semester.

"There was lots of positive reinforcement coming from guys like Bob Burris (then a freshman coach) and Eddie Crowder (a varsity assistant coach)," Gautt recalled. "And, of course, Bud. I still say that Bud had a lot to do with my emotional stability. It was almost like he was protecting me. I think he tried to see to it that I never had any real pressures placed on me. At least, none that I couldn't handle.

"I know he got some awfully nasty letters. Of course, I got some, too, but I didn't realize the pressures that he went through in terms of getting me to play there. I guess I got the feeling that he really wanted me to make it. And I guess I kinda looked at him as a father image to some extent."

WE ALL GREW Another of Gautt's strong supporters was Jakie Sandefer, a popular halfback from Breckenridge, Texas.

"I think Jakie was asked if he wanted to be my roommate (on road trips)," Gautt said. "I believe that he accepted that as sort of a modeling thing for my acceptance."

"I've never felt that this was like the stories I've read about Jackie Robinson and Branch Rickey (integrating professional baseball) at all," Wilkinson said. "The professional situation is different than the amateur. You're talking about a relatively young person who wanted to do it, but I don't think he really knew at the start what he was getting into either. But he grew with it. We all did."

Gautt led OU in rushing and in tackles for two

SOONER QUIZ

35. Name the OU lineman who finished highest in the balloting for the Heisman Trophy.

SOONER QUIZ

36. Name four sets of brothers who played at OU in the 1960s.

Bill Krisher was a consensus All-American guard in 1957.

seasons and was selected to the 1959 Academic All-American team. The 5-11, 196-pound fullback rushed for 627 yards in 1958 and 674 yards in 1959.

The Sooners' only setback in 1958 came in a 15-14 loss to Texas. OU was ranked fifth in the nation, claimed another conference title, defeated Syracuse in the Orange Bowl, and once again relied on defense, shutting out five foes and allowing four others only one touchdown each.

The Monster still was riding high.

Center Bob Harrison was named Lineman of the Year by UPI.

NORTHWESTERN NAUSEA The Sooners were brought down to earth in 1959.

OU opened the season against Northwestern in perhaps the most mysterious and suspicious chapter in OU football history. Thirteen players, including 10 on the first and second teams, became ill during dinner at the famous Chez Paree nightclub in Chicago two days before the game. Most of the players missed practice Friday and many made what trainer Ken Rawlinson described as "only token appearances" when Northwestern won, 45-13, handing Wilkinson the most decisive loss of his career. The Wildcats scored the most points ever against a Wilkinson-coached OU team. Gamblers were suspected of being involved, but nothing ever was proven.

Halfback Clendon Thomas led the nation in scoring with 108 points in 1956 and was a consensus All-American choice in 1957.

Jakie Sandefer was an OU halfback in 1955-57.

"SUCH A SORRY COACH" One of the other losses in 1959 also was a history-making setback.

Nebraska upset the Sooners, 25-21, in Lincoln, for OU's first loss in conference play in 75 games. OU had not lost a conference game since Jim Tatum's Sooners had bowed to Kansas, 16-13, in 1946. (OU and Kansas had tied, 13-13, in 1947, and OU and Colorado had tied, 21-21, in 1952.) The 74 games without a loss and OU's 44-game winning streak — starting in 1952 and ending in 1959 — remain conference records.

After the loss, Wilkinson reportedly apologized to his players for being "such a sorry coach." He reportedly told them he was not upset that they lost but because he had not prepared them well enough.

OU posted a 7-3 record and was ranked 15th in the nation, marking the first time in 12 years that the Sooners had not been in the top 10.

Ken Rawlinson was OU's football trainer in 1953-78.

BOLD PREDICTION In 1960, the NCAA put OU on probation indefinitely for operating a "slush fund" for recruiting. The Sooners were barred from bowls and TV appearances in 1960.

OU struggled the next two seasons. The Sooners suffered through Wilkinson's only losing season, 3-6-1 in 1960, and posted a 5-5 record in 1961 in what some believe may have been Wilkinson's best job of coaching, considering the Sooners lost their first five games.

"The pressures of losing were getting heavy," Wilkinson remembered years after the 1961 campaign. "I said we were going to win the next five games (on his statewide Sunday night television show) in an effort to give everybody the feeling we could.

"Our teams in the early 1960s just did not have enough quality athletes," said Wilkinson, later evaluating the situation. He took the responsibility for what he called his own "poor recruiting."

"In retrospect, I believe the ease of traveling by air had extended recruiting boundaries, and we just hadn't realized it at the time," he said.

OU returned only two starters in 1962, but an exceptional class of sophomores not only was challenging for playing time but for starting assignments. OU also got a surprising boost from halfback Joe Don Looney, the only junior-college transfer during the Wilkinson era. On his first play at OU, Looney ran 60 yards for a touchdown in OU's 7-3 win over Syracuse in the season opener. One of the sophomores, end Rick McCurdy, recovered three Syracuse fumbles.

The Sooners bowed to Notre Dame and Texas in their next two games.

The offense got boosts from Looney, although he had

David Baker was the Sooners' quarterback in 1958 and one of the stars of OU's win in the 1958 Orange Bowl.

All-American center Bob Harrison (left) and Joe Rector were OU captains in 1958.

become a problem because of his open adversity to practice and team rules, and sophomore fullback Jim Grisham. Looney led the nation in punting with an average of 43.4 yards

But once again, defensive play was instrumental: OU shut out four foes and allowed four other opponents one touchdown or less.

OU won the conference championship for the first time in four seasons, had an 8-3 record and was ranked eighth in the nation. But the comeback was sidetracked by Alabama, led by quarterback Joe Namath and linebacker Lee Roy Jordan, in a 17-0 loss in the Orange Bowl.

BUD'S FAREWELL The Sooners grabbed a mixed bag in 1963, not knowing it would be Wilkinson's last season

OU's 1959 backfield included quarterback Bobby Boyd, halfback Jimmy Carpenter, halfback Brewster Hobby and fullback Prentice Gautt.

President John F. Kennedy visited the OU dressing room before the Sooners' ill-fated clash with Alabama in the 1963 Orange Bowl.

In his second year as Texas coach, former Sooner Darrell Royal made timely use of a new rule to claim his first victory over his alma mater. For the first time, college teams could try for two points by running or passing on the conversion play after a touchdown. The Longhorns scored on a conversion pass after their first touchdown to claim their first win over OU in eight seasons, 15-14.

at OU.

OU upset defending national champion Southern California, 17-12, in a contest played in 110-degree temperature in Los Angeles. The victory vaulted OU to the top of the national polls going into the Sooners' annual clash with No. 2-ranked Texas, marking the only time the bitter rivals have met when ranked 1-2. Stories vary concerning what happened, but apparently dissension had mounted because of halfback Joe Don Looney's aversion to practice and team rules. Texas, which went on to win Darrell Royal's first national championship, dominated the Sooners, 28-7.

The next week Wilkinson dismissed Looney.

But OU faced one more disappointment in 1963. The Sooners appeared on their way to another conference title going into their clash with Nebraska, which was rebuilding in its second year with Bob Devaney as coach. The conference title contest was scheduled in Lincoln on November 23. But on the afternoon before the game, President John F. Kennedy was assassinated in Dallas. Wilkinson had worked with Kennedy as a recreation consultant, and the President had visited the Sooners' dressing room before the 1963 Orange Bowl clash. Many of the OU players wanted to postpone the game. But after conferring with OU and state officials and representatives of the Kennedy family, OU agreed to Nebraska's request to play the game as scheduled. The Cornhuskers won, 29-20, gaining their first of four straight Big Eight Conference championships (OSU had joined the conference in 1960.).

Someone commented to Wilkinson that the events in Dallas had made the OU-Nebraska game seem less important. He replied: "It never was as important as some people thought it was."

OU posted an 8-2 record and was ranked 10th in the nation.

Less than two months after the 1963 season, Wilkinson revealed his plans to resign as head football coach. At the time, he had the best record of any major college coach in the nation. Only six coaches in the history of the game had ever had better records. Bud Wilkinson was 47 years old at the time.

"Wilkinson worried that what he was doing would not be a source of satisfaction to him later in life," President George L. Cross said. "We often talked about this. I think he really lost his zest for coaching near the end of his career. Recruiting fell off. The probation was a handicap."

After leaving OU, Wilkinson conducted an unsuccessful campaign for a U.S. Senate seat from Oklahoma in 1964.

Wilkinson preached that the will to prepare was more important than the will to win. He theorized that every player had the will to win on game day, but only the most successful players had the will to prepare before the contest. He told his players that the will to prepare would serve them long after their football careers.

He was known for conducting short, well-organized practices.

He had a policy of working his teams the hardest when they were going to face the least threatening foes. Against the most challenging teams, he reduced the number of offensive plays and defensive formations in hopes of eliminating mistakes.

SPECIAL SKILLS He repeatedly visualized the best player on the next opposing team making a winning play against the Sooners. Once he convinced himself that could happen, Wilkinson believed he could persuade his players.

Halfback Joe Don Looney came and left in a whirlwind in 1962 and 1963.

Tackle Billy White was OU captain in 1961 and the Sooners' only all-conference selection in 1960 and 1961.

Center Wayne Lee and guard Leon "Old Rugged" Cross were OU captains in 1962.

Wilkinson acknowledges his reception at the halftime of the OU-North Texas game during "A Tribute for Bud Wilkinson" in 1991.

His assistants also were amazed how often he prepared his teams for trick plays and new formations used by opponents.

Wilkinson often told his teams mythical stories to illustrate a point. Perhaps the favorite of these stories was what became known as the "bird story." The gist of the story was that a young man confronted an older wise man with the following situation: The young man had a bird in his hands and asked the old man, "Is the bird dead or alive?" The young man could kill the bird or let it go, making whatever the old man answered wrong. But the old man's answer was "You hold destiny in your hands." Obviously, Wilkinson's point was that his players held their destiny in their hands.

In 1956, when he thought one of his greatest teams was not well-prepared for its clash against Texas, Wilkinson told his team it was going to lose to the Longhorns and did not appear for a pregame talk. But cocaptain Edmon Gray put things in perspective by telling his teammates: "I guess the old man isn't going to tell us that damned bird story today, so we better go out and win this one on our own."

End John Flynn fields a 40-yard pass from Monte Deere against Nebraska in 1962.

All-American tackle Edmon Gray, embracing Gomer Jones, was the only Sooner to start every game during 1954-56.

The Sooners won, 45-0.

Wilkinson's record as an athletic director often is overlooked. He was a frugal manager. In his tenure, his athletic department provided some $400,000 to OU projects that had nothing to do with athletics.

Wilkinson later was involved in several ventures, including being a commentator on televised college football games, sponsoring coaching clinics, working on President Richard Nixon's administrative staff, and being head coach of the St. Louis Cardinals in the National Football League in 1978 and 1979. During that time, St. Louis tackle Dan Dierdorf coined perhaps the most descriptive phase of Wilkinson when he called him "the Velvet Hammer."

Wilkinson was inducted into the National Football Coaches Hall of Fame and the Helms and Citizens Savings Athletic Coaches Hall of Fame in 1969. He was honored at "A Tribute for Bud Wilkinson" attended by more than 200 of his former players in Oklahoma in 1991.

Wilkinson died of congestive heart failure at his home in St. Louis on February 9, 1994. He was 77 years old.

SOONER QUIZ

37. Name the 1960s OU halfback who was related to the principal chief of the Choctaw Nation.

Barry Switzer

It's doubtful any head coach ever started his career with such a mixed combination of situations as did Barry Switzer in his first three campaigns in 1973, 1974, and 1975.

Switzer had been warned by his mentor, and former OU head coach, Jim Mackenzie to get out of coaching if he had not been named a head coach by the time he was 35 years old. Fortunately for OU, Switzer waited a little longer than advised. Five months after his 35th birthday, Switzer was named OU head coach on Jan. 29, 1973, after Chuck Fairbanks resigned to take the head coaching of the New England Patriots of the NFL.

A popular bumper sticker read: Oklahoma is Switzerland.

SOONER MAGIC The phrase Sooner Magic was coined during the Switzer era. OU's thrilling comeback victories, particularly against powerful Nebraska, often were credited to Sooner Magic.

The Sooners got a whirlwind start, posting a 10-0-1 record in 1973, an 11-0 mark in 1974 and an 11-1 standard in 1975, winning national championships in 1974 and 1975.

Here's the gospel according to Switzer.

"If you look at who played then, that's really why we

Split end Tinker Owens and tight end Wayne Hoffman celebrate a Sooner victory.

won," said Switzer, who always was lavish in praising his players. "We just had unbelievable talent, starting with Little Joe Washington. We found a quarterback in (Steve) Davis. That's back when you could recruit a bunch of numbers. Great players. All of them could play today," he said in 1982.

Eight players on offense and seven on defense were selected on at least one All-America team during their careers.

Guard John Roush (left) was a consensus All-American choice in 1974.

Terry Webb (middle) was an All-American guard in 1975.

Joe Washington (right), established the OU career rushing record with 3,995 in 1972-75.

The offensive players were split ends Tinker Owens and Billy Brooks; tackles Mike Vaughan and Eddie Foster; guards John Roush and Terry Webb; center Kyle Davis, and halfback Joe Washington. The defensive players were end Jimbo Elrod; tackle Lee Roy Selmon; nose guard/tackle Dewey Selmon; nose guard Lucious Selmon; linebacker Rod Shoate, and safeties Randy Hughes and Zac Henderson. In addition, four other starters also were All-Big Eight choices: tight end Wayne Hoffman and tackle Jerry Arnold on offense, end Gary Baccus on defense and place-kicker Tony DiRienzo.

SOONER QUIZ

38. Name four players from OU's 1958 team who were OU assistant coaches in 1966.

NCAA PROBATION But the Sooners had some obstacles to overcome before claiming the conference crown and being voted third in the nation in 1973.

Before spring practice that year, OU had been placed on probation by the NCAA. The primary charge centered on the fact that school records of Kerry Jackson, a quarterback from Galveston (Texas) Ball High School, had been altered to make him eligible to enter college. The NCAA never determined who altered the records but concluded OU knew of the change.

What the NCAA called a two-year probation actually affected four seasons: OU forfeited three Big Eight games in which Jackson had played in 1972; was barred from bowl games in 1973 and 1974 and barred from television appearances in 1974 and 1975. The TV ban did not start in 1973 because OU already had signed contracts for some televised games.

Switzer, who was not mentioned in the NCAA report, took a positive approach, declaring:

"Bowl games and playing on TV, to me, are fine incentives for a football team. But I'm going to tell you what: There isn't but one reward, one great reward for playing the game of football, and that's winning.

"And winning is a matter of pride. We've been put on probation by the NCAA. The cards have been dealt now. And we have to live by it. But they didn't say that we couldn't beat the teams that are going to play on TV and go to bowl games, and they didn't say we couldn't win the Big Eight championship."

For nearly 50 years, a Keith served as OU sports information director. John Keith (foreground) was director in 1969-78 after succeeding his father, Harold, who had been director since 1929.

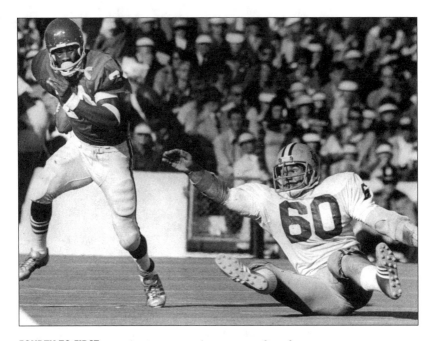

FOURTH TO FIRST But the Sooners, who were predicted to finish fourth in the conference, faced even more challenges. Sophomore tackle Lee Roy Selmon suffered from pericarditis (an inflammation around the heart) and was withheld from the first two games. Lee Roy was expected to start in the defensive line with his brothers, nose guard Lucious and tackle Dewey. Starting split end John Carroll was sidelined for the season with a knee injury in preseason drills. And starting right halfback Grant Burget was sidelined for the season after suffering a knee injury in the opening game.

Joe Washington left many opponents, including Iowa State's Brad Storm, grabbing nothing but air.

In the second game of the 1973 season, OU gave a hint of the future when it tied No. 1-ranked and defending national champion Southern California, which had a 14-game winning streak. Washington made one of his most memorable punt returns. It appeared the retreating, dodging, twisting silver-shoed darter bounced off or was spun around by every Trojan in the Los Angeles Coliseum in a play that covered 20 yards. The net result was a minus-4 yards and several near heart attacks. The play had to be seen to be appreciated.

SEMIS & PICKUPS "It sounded like trucks running together," said Switzer, describing the 7-7 contest. "They had semis, and we had pickups."

After coming from behind to beat Miami, 24-20, OU went unchallenged the rest of the season, which included two landmark triumphs.

The Eyes of Texas were upon split end Tinker Owens on his way to a touchdown against the Longhorns.

Kyle Davis was an All-American center in 1974.

The Sooners handed Darrell Royal the most decisive loss in his 21-year career at Texas with a 52-13 victory.

"I looked across the field at Darrell and his bunch and thought about all the bad mail and calls they were going to get," Switzer said with empathy after the game.

OU stunned Nebraska, which finished at 9-2-1, with a 27-0 win. Nebraska had only one offensive play in OU territory the entire game, and the Cornhuskers, who averaged 418 yards rushing, were held to only 174 yards.

"The nation had a chance today to see the finest defensive team in the country," said Switzer of the Sooners, who would not be seen on television the next two years.

In OU's closest conference contest, the margin was 17 points. Switzer's team dominated the Big Eight as no team had since the 1956 Sooners. Eight of OU's 11 opponents were ranked in the nation's Top 20 at some time during the season.

OU, which finished with a 10-0-1 record, paid dearly for not being able to go to a bowl game. All-victorious Notre Dame beat previously unbeaten Alabama in the Sugar Bowl to be ranked No. 1. And unbeaten, but once-tied Ohio State defeated Southern California in the Rose Bowl to be ranked No. 2.

Washington had 1,173 yards and fullback Waymon Clark had 1,014 yards to become only the third teammates to top 1,000 yards rushing in the same season.

Sports Illustrated got it correct in its 1974 preseason issue, calling the Sooners "The Best Team You'll Never See." OU was barred from television and bowl games.

In addition, the American Football Coaches

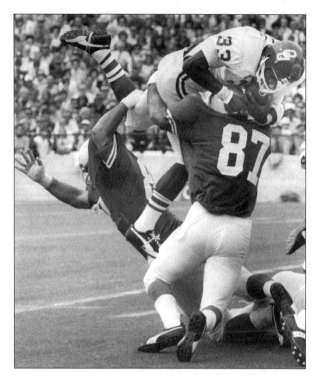

Fullback Waymon Clark charges into Texas' Kevin Henry.

Association voted to bar any team on probation from national rankings. The coaches voted in the UPI poll. The move created a rift between some coaches and Switzer, who interpreted the policy as a direct slap at OU. However, OU still could be ranked in The AP ranking in which sportswriters and sportscasters participate.

The Sooners had only one close game all season.

TEXAS SLUGFEST "Texas is always a slugfest," said quarterback Steve Davis of his team's 16-13 win, OU's fourth-straight triumph over the Longhorns. "Any time you can win the ball game, that's what you've got to be happy about."

"Roderick Shoate's play was outstanding," said Switzer of the OU linebacker who made 21 tackles against the Longhorns. "And I bet nobody in the stands knew he played with just one arm in the second half. His shoulder got knocked down, and we had to ice it down at half time, and he still played that way in the second half."

The 213-pound Shoate was known for his speed, great range, and vicious tackling.

"Rod Shoate has been places on the football field that no other linebacker has ever seen," said defensive coordinator Larry Lacewell.

Linebacker Rod Shoate was a consensus All-American in 1973 and 1974.

A LOT CLOSER Another comeback on offense and stingy defensive play carried OU to its third straight win over rugged Nebraska.

"It was a lot closer than 28-14," said Davis. The Cornhuskers took a 14-7 lead into the second half before 76,636 of the NU faithful at Lincoln, but OU came back with three long scoring drives. Aided by three interceptions by safety Randy Hughes, OU blanked Nebraska in the final 26 1/2 minutes and allowed only three first downs rushing in the second half.

"Randy probably was the most intense player that I've ever been around," Davis recalled. "I remember one time Randy really got upset in 1974 when we were not playing well against Oklahoma State. He came to the sideline, yelling at the offense, literally screaming at us

GENTLE GIANTS

The most popular bumper sticker in Oklahoma in 1973 read: Thank you, Mrs. Selmon. Jesse Selmon said it should have mentioned Mr. Selmon, too.

Of course, the sticker referred to the mother of the Selmon brothers. Their story truly is a once-in-a-lifetime tale that may never be repeated in college football. The three brothers, who had grown up in a four-room farmhouse outside the eastern Oklahoma town of Eufaula, played side-by-side in the defensive line. Lucious was a senior and Lee Roy and Dewey were sophomores.

They became known as the Gentle Giants.

"All three were bona-fide All-Americans," said Coach Barry Switzer. "No one brother carried the other. They were unspoiled, uncorrupted, and unselfish. They were the same kind of polite, unassuming young men they were the day I first met them."

"The older boys didn't have the chances they did," said Jesse, who also had three other sons and three daughters. "They were very interested in sports, but they didn't have the chance to play. The schools in Eufaula didn't integrate until the younger boys were in high school."

In fact, Lucious almost missed the opportunity to play at OU.

"The fact is I wasn't impressed at first," said OU defensive coordinator Larry Lacewell. "Lucious was a 5-10, 220-pound fullback when I first saw him, and his brothers were already bigger than he was. The day I arrived to talk to him, he was sweeping out the halls of the high school. No one up til then had offered him a scholarship, and we didn't need a janitor. But when I got to know more about him, I began to warm to the idea that he had to be a prospect for something."

Jesse told Lacewell what type of prospect she wanted Lucious to be.

"You're recruiting my boy as a football player, but I'm sending him to Oklahoma to get an education," she said. "He won't be a football player forever."

(Dewey, incidentally, was 11

for our poor performance. And he was justified. We said, 'Let's go out and put this game away, so Hughes doesn't have a heart attack.' "

COACH OF THE YEAR In 1974, OU claimed its first national championship and first all-victorious season (11-0) since 1956. The Sooners averaged 43 points and held their foes to an average of eight points a game.

Switzer was named the Walter Camp National Coach of the Year.

The Monster lived.

OU returned a veteran team in 1975 and was favored to repeat as national champion. The Sooners appeared to have lost their claim to the title but got a second chance under unexpected circumstances.

Randy Hughes was an All-American safety in 1974.

months older than Lee Roy. But Lee Roy was so lonely the first day Dewey went to school that their mother told Lee Roy to go to school with Dewey from then on. That's how they wound up in the same class.)

Lucious was a consensus All-America choice and finished second to Ohio State tackle John Hicks in the voting for the Outland Trophy in 1973.

The Selmon brothers, Lee Roy, Lucious and Dewey, provided OU with a formidable wall on defense in 1973.

Quarterback Steve Davis guided the Sooners to a 32-1-1 record and two national titles in 1973-75.

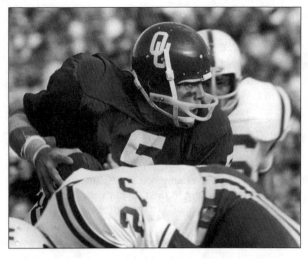

"We struggled for a lot of different reasons," said quarterback Steve Davis. "We were kinda holding our breath every week. Football is a game of momentum. I think we began to see other teams gain confidence because of the way we were playing."

THE HILL HIT The most memorable play of OU's 46-10 win over a Pittsburgh team that won the national championship in 1976 came when the Sooners were on defense. Trailing, 20-0, and with fourth down and 1-yard to go on the OU 34-yard line, the Panthers sent their great tailback, Tony Dorsett, around left end. Just short of the line of scrimmage, Dorsett was met by OU safety Scott Hill, who had hurdled a blocker and hit Dorsett almost like a projectile. The drive was halted.

"It was one of those plays you never forget," said Switzer. "It happened right in front of me."

Dorsett, who gained only 17 yards on 12 carries, probably will not forget it either.

OU survived the next three contests, beating Miami, 20-17; Colorado, 21-20; and Texas, 24-17.

KANSAS SPOILER But disaster struck on November 8, 1975.

OU was a solid favorite over Kansas, which had a 5-3 record and had not beaten the Sooners since 1964.

"I felt the pressure building in the winning streak," said Switzer. "The first couple of years I really didn't think anything about it. Then I got into it. I think we all felt it. I'm sure there was more pressure then than I will actually admit today. It's over with before you can say what really occurred, and what really went into it."

OU had not lost in 30 games since Switzer became head coach in 1973. He had a record of 29-0-1. The

SOONER QUIZ

39. Name the OU football player who is believed to have the longest last name.

Sooners had not lost in 37 straight games, going back to Chuck Fairbanks' tenure when they lost to Colorado in 1972. And OU had won 28 straight games since tying USC in the second game of the 1973 season.

Joe Washington shows Kansas State players a bit of Sooner Magic.

"Had we jumped on Kansas and put them down 10 to nothing, I would suspect Kansas probably would have quit," said Davis. However, OU held only a 3-0 lead after missing two other scoring chances. "But what happened is that we just kept feeding their confidence."

The Jayhawks blocked an OU punt and gained a 7-3 lead in the first half. And on their next eight possessions, the defending national champions lost the ball on four interceptions and four fumbles.

The Jayhawks had pulled one of the all-time upsets in college football history, 23-3.

"It ain't much fun," Switzer admitted. "When we did lose, I knew we'd have to help whoever beat us. And we sure won the mistake race today."

"God, what a win!" said Kansas center John Morgan. "None of the others even come close."

SOONER QUIZ

UNEXPECTED SCENARIO OU needed come-from-behind wins against Missouri and Nebraska to avoid other losses. Washington raced 71 yards for a touchdown and ran for a two-point conversion with 4:20 left in the 28-27 win over Missouri. After trailing, 10-7, in the third quarter, OU scored on four of its next six possessions for a 35-10 win over previously all-victorious Nebraska.

40. In what bowl game did OU not punt?

Sooner Magic.

The Sooners' first bowl appearance in three years came against Michigan in the Orange Bowl. The event also marked the first time a Big Ten team had played in any bowl game other than the Rose Bowl.

SOONER QUIZ

41. Who did his teammates call Tommy Trophy?

"We didn't imagine that scenario would develop," said Davis. "We went down to Miami to enjoy the rewards of three good years of playing football at the university. We did not talk about national championships."

But the scenario referred to by Davis was: Ohio State had finished No. 1 and Texas A&M No. 2 in the final regular-season poll. A&M lost in its final regular-season contest played after the poll was taken. And UCLA knocked off Ohio State, 23-10, in the Rose Bowl before the Orange Bowl game on January 1.

MORE IMPORTANT "I'll never forget; Galen Hall came up to me," said Davis, referring to the OU offensive coordinator. "He's biting his nails. His forehead wrinkled up and he smiled and said: 'Steve, this game just got a little bit more important.' It did. We felt revived. We had a second chance."

Once again, Hill played a key role, intercepting passes by Michigan quarterback Rich Leach on the fourth play of the game and also on the last play of the contest.

Hall, who was known for his conservative play calling, came up with a brilliant one-two punch in the first half. Davis passed to split end Tinker Owens for 40 yards to the Michigan 39-yard line. On the next play, OU ran a reverse with split end Billy Brooks racing around left end for the touchdown.

"We ran the reverse play – Left 17, reverse on one – a reserve end-around with Brooks carrying the ball," Davis recalled. "I pitched the ball and there was a defensive man between me and Billy. Number 77. I can't remember his name, but I remember his jersey because I was looking right into his back. I don't know how he got there. Great athlete that he was, Billy just made one sidestep and kissed him good-bye."

No. 77 was Michigan tackle Greg Morton, who played a brilliant game, making 14 tackles.

End Jimbo Elrod was a consensus All-American in 1975.

NO. 1 AGAIN Davis scored on a 10-yard keeper on a fourth down in the final quarter, and Michigan's only score in OU's 14-6 triumph came after recovering a fumble on the OU 2-yard line. Davis and Lee Roy Selmon were named the Most Valuable Players.

Sooner Magic.

Arizona State challenged for the No. 1 spot after finishing with a 12-0 record. But OU received 54 1/2 first-place votes and 1,257 points and Arizona State received five first-place votes and 1,038 points in the final AP poll. For the first time in the history of the polls, a school had won back-to-back national championships twice. OU's previous achievement came in 1955 and 1956.

In an unprecedented situation, not only were Lee Roy and Dewey Selmon consensus All-Americans but end Jimbo Elrod also was so honored. That meant OU had three of the five top selections in the defensive line.

"Jimbo was one of the truly free spirits of our football team," said Davis of the 6-0, 210-pounder. "He had an unbelievable canny about him, knowing where the football was. His reckless style of living in his personal life was also displayed on the field because he did play and tackle with reckless abandon."

GIANTS GONE The last of the Gentle Giants also finished their brilliant careers at OU in 1975.

"The most amazing thing about the Selmons to me is they are the only great defensive players I've ever seen who were not vicious," said defensive coordinator Larry Lacewell. "They just wouldn't get vicious. Dewey was the most aggressive, but his mean streak was pretty small. I've only seen Lucious get mad a few times, and then it wasn't safe. Fortunately, I don't think Lee Roy has ever been mad at anybody. If he ever gets mad, I am afraid we may be going to a funeral."

"Lee Roy was in a category by himself," said Switzer

Daryl Hunt tries to block a punt by Colorado's Stan Koleski.

SOONER QUIZ

42. Name the Sooner who was conference offensive player of the year in 1984.

of the 1975 winner of Outland Trophy and Lombardi Award as the nation's outstanding interior line.

"Hey, somebody made a misprint," Dewey told Lee Roy after seeing the trophy. "That's supposed to be D. Selmon, not L. Selmon."

"That group of players through '74 and '75 was the greatest group," said Switzer. "The one characteristic about them all was that they played with character. They weren't concerned about personal gain — how many yards they made, petty things. Especially our offensive line. We had so much character — great workers, leaders."

GIFTED MOTIVATOR "Coach is probably the most gifted motivator of college athletes I've ever been around," said Davis. "Having worked for ABC Sports (after his playing career), I can kinda compare these other coaches. As far as being able to capture the moment and analyze the situation, Barry's better than anybody at being able to motivate a kid to play above his ability.

"He's very honest with his team, honest with this players. When we'd play someone that wasn't very good, he'd say, 'Let's go hang half a hundred on them, and let's go out and have a good time tonight.'

"When we had a tough challenge, he'd trust our intelligence. You could sense it from his personality and the way he and the assistant coaches were."

PUREST RUNNER Washington, whose unpredictable, darting style often left opponents grabbing nothing, was as exciting as he was effective. He finished his brilliant career with 3,995 yards rushing, still an OU record.

"To me, Washington was the purest runner that we've ever had – just hand the ball to him and let him make things happen," said Switzer. "He was probably the best we've ever had. Billy Sims (who played at OU in 1975-79) was bigger, stronger, and faster, more elusive. But none was more exciting than Joe Washington.

"Darrell (Texas coach Darrell Royal) said he was like 'smoke through a keyhole.' That's what he was. He did things that I have never seen any other backs do."

The Monster was thriving.

The Sooners were brought back down to earth in 1976, a season laced with turmoil and injuries. Even so, OU posted a 9-2-1 record, impressive by most standards, shared the Big Eight championship and beat Wyoming in the Fiesta Bowl with quarterback Thomas Lott and corner-back Terry Peters being named the outstanding players.

Thomas Lott was the only Wishbone quarterback in the country who wore a bandana.

INJURIES HIT "We were young at quarterback; Thomas Lott made his emergence then," said Switzer. "We were struggling. The whole offense was young at the time."

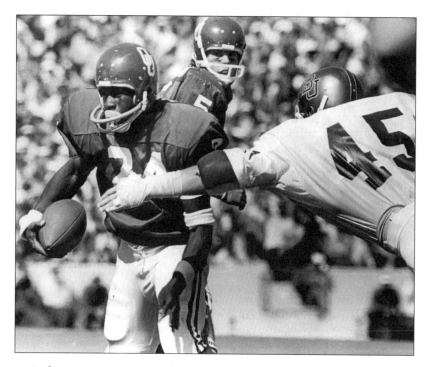

And OU's inexperienced defense lost two of its veterans, safety Scott Hill and cornerback Jerry Anderson, to injuries against Kansas in the fourth game of the year. Their absence cost the Sooners dearly in two crucial contests later.

Still OU and Texas entered their annual meeting with 4-0 records and ranked third and sixth, respectively.

But the circumstances surrounding the classic clash were even more intense than usual. Switzer and Texas Coach Darrell Royal had made public statements that widened the rift between them. President Gerald Ford flipped the coin before the game with Switzer and Royal flanking him. Neither spoke nor looked at the other.

"I wish it hadn't occurred," Switzer said years later.

ROYAL SICK The game also was a standoff, ending in a 6-6 tie. Switzer still had not lost to Texas, and Royal retired after the season, having not defeated OU in his final six tries.

"I never felt as sick as I felt about that one," said Royal. "I wanted that game more than any I competed in or coached."

OU lost back-to-back games for the first time since early in the 1970 season. Oklahoma State claimed its first win over the Sooners since 1966 in a 31-24 triumph, and Colorado scored the final 22 points in a 42-31 jolt

Joe Washington races past Baylor's Don Bockhorn after taking a handoff from Steve Davis.

of the Sooners.

Nebraska also struggled in 1976, entering the clash with OU at Lincoln with an uncharacteristic 7-2-1 record. The Sooners and Cornhuskers were ranked eighth and 10th in the nation at the time, but many observers considered Nebraska the better team.

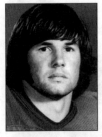

THE PRAYER The game is remembered for several events, including what perhaps is considered the most memorable pregame prayer in OU history. Switzer had asked Hill, a cocaptain who had refused surgery in hopes of continuing to play in his last season, to lead the team in prayer. Hill's prayer, which is credited with relieving some of the pregame pressure, was: "Please, dear Lord, don't let any injury or harm come to any player. And please, please, please, dear Lord, please don't let the best team win."

But it looked as though the better team would win when Nebraska held a 17-13 lead and OU was pinned on its own 15-yard line, facing a 35 m.p.h. wind with only 3 1/2 minutes remaining.

Safety Scott Hill was an OU captain who led the team in a memorable pregame prayer in 1976.

"SANDLOT PLAYS" Switzer substituted a seldom-used halfback, Woodie Shepard, who had carried the ball only nine times all year but could heave the ball a mile. On first down, Shepard passed 47 yards to freshman split end Steve Rhodes at the Nebraska 37-yard line. Six plays later on a third down, quarterback Dean Blevins passed 14 yards to Rhodes, who caught the ball on the Nebraska 20. As the Cornhuskers converged on him, Rhodes flipped a lateral to halfback Elvis Peacock who raced to the two-yard line. Peacock scored the winning touchdown on the next play with only 38 seconds remaining.

Once again Nebraska had been denied its first victory over OU since 1971; this time on what some of its coaches called "sandlot plays."

Sooner Magic.

The Sooners tied Colorado and OSU for the conference title and were ranked fifth in the nation.

Halfback Elvis Peacock scored the winning touchdown against Nebraska in 1976.

SWC VILLAINS In 1977, OU was ranked No. 1 in the preseason AP poll, but two Southwest Conference teams would spoil OU's bid for a sixth national title.

OU's first clash with Ohio State, in the third game of the season, produced one of the Sooners' most exciting triumphs and perhaps the most memorable field goal in school history. OU marched 43 yards on 12 plays with halfback Elvis Peacock scoring on a 1-yard run with 1:29 left in the game. But Peacock's run for a two-point conversion was halted, and it appeared the Buckeyes would win, 28-26.

However, OU's bouncing kickoff was muffed by a Buckeye and recovered by Mike Babb at the 50-yard line. But the Sooners were stalled on the 23 on fourth down.

VON FOOT Uwe von Schamann waited through two time-outs by Ohio State before attempting a 41-yard field goal. The sellout crowd of 87,900 at Columbus, Ohio, began to chant, "Block that kick." Von Schamann, who was known as Von Foot by his teammates, also was Von Cool and responded in two ways: First, he led the crowd in the chant as though he were a band director. Then he kicked the field goal for a 29-28 win with only three seconds left.

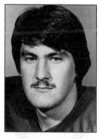

Kicker Uwe von Schamann was known as "Von Foot" among his teammates.

"Football games are 60 minutes, aren't they?" Switzer said afterward, when questioned about the comeback. "This game had more tension, more drama than any game I've ever been associated with. That last field goal was one of the greatest plays I have ever seen in intercollegiate football."

Ohio State's Woody Hayes viewed the events differently, commenting: "I would rather have it dull and win."

OU was ranked second and Texas third going into their 1977 meeting. "We stopped Texas, but we just couldn't stop Earl Campbell," said Switzer of the Longhorns' 1977 Heisman Trophy winner who rushed for 124 yards in Texas' 13-6 win.

OU had not lost to an opponent other than a Big Eight team in Switzer's head coaching career and not lost

Fullback Kenny King and quarterback Thomas Lott show perfect form on the primary Wishbone play where the quarterback keeps the ball or hands to the fullback, depending on the reaction of the defense.

to Texas since 1970, at the dawn of the Sooners' Wishbone era.

However, OU extended its scoring streak to 124 games, bettering the previous NCAA record, also held by the Sooners.

Safety Zac Henderson was a consensus All-American in 1977.

AWESOME ARKANSAS The Sooners went on to win the Big Eight title and gain a berth in the Orange Bowl against Switzer's alma mater, Arkansas. The Razorbacks had suffered their only setback to Texas, 13-9. Arkansas was plagued by disciplinary problems. Three players, including leading rusher Ben Cowins, who had gained 1,192 yards and scored 14 touchdowns, were suspended for the bowl game. Arkansas Coach Lou Holtz played up how strong OU was and how weak his Razorbacks were.

The afternoon before the game, No. 1-ranked Texas had lost to Notre Dame, 38-10, in the Cotton Bowl. Once again the door was open for OU to claim the national title.

Switzer normally preferred for OU to kickoff. But he choose to receive the kickoff against the Razorbacks.

"We did it because we felt like we had to go play for the national championship," Switzer explained. "We thought we had to come out gunning because everybody expected us to beat Arkansas. We had to win big. We're an 18-point favorite going into the game. But we never should have taken the kickoff."

After receiving the opening kickoff, OU lost a fumble on the fourth play, and Arkansas scored two plays later. The game never was close. The Razorbacks won, 31-6, to hand OU its most decisive defeat of the Switzer era and its most decisive loss since bowing to Kansas State, 59-21, in 1969.

"We were lulled to sleep by their problems," Switzer said. "I was disappointed in the way we played. Obviously our coaches and our players were overconfident going into the game. But Arkansas was well-prepared and well-coached."

OU posted a 10-2 record and was ranked seventh in the nation.

FATEFUL FUMBLES   The Sooners went virtually unchallenged in 1978, until their annual test of the Big Reds. (The exception was a 17-16 win over Kansas that wasn't decided until a Jayhawks' conversion pass failed with 15 seconds left.)

This time the game at Lincoln pitted the nation's top scoring teams, each averaging 40 points a game. OU was ranked No. 1, and once-beaten Nebraska was No. 4.

With the Cornhuskers' leading, 17-14, early in the final quarter, it appeared that Sooner Magic was going to take over again. Riding the power running of halfback Billy Sims, OU got to the Nebraska 20-yard line before Sims lost a fumble at the 8:10 mark and got to the Cornhusker 3-yard line before Sims lost another fumble at the 3:27 mark.

OU quite possibly could have won consecutive national championships in 1978 and 1979 had it not been for two losses. No team was all-victorious in 1978, so an all-victorious OU team would have been a popular choice. The issue would have been unclear in 1979 because eventual national champion Alabama was all-victorious. OU and Alabama could not have met in 1979 because their conferences were committed to different bowls.

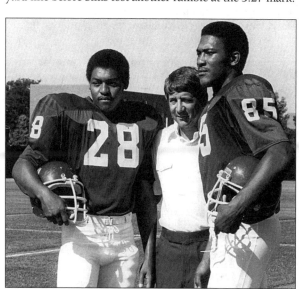

Assistant coach Warren Harper was proud of his All-American linebackers, George Cumby (28) in 1979 and Daryl Hunt in 1978.

Nebraska gained its first win over OU since 1971 and the first victory over the Sooners for head coach Tom Osborne in six tries.

Sims rushed for 153 yards and scored both of OU's touchdowns.

Fumbles or no fumbles, Sims became the sixth junior to win the Heisman Trophy.

"We have had great backs here, but we have never had a back with Sims' combination of speed and power," said Switzer.

Darrol Ray was an all-conference safety in 1978 and 1979.

SECOND CHANCE OU also got a second chance when Nebraska lost to Missouri, 35-31, in its final regular-season game. The Sooners and Cornhuskers tied for the Big Eight title.

"It was an ideal situation for us," said Switzer when the Orange Bowl pitted the Big Eight powers in a rematch. "We really looked forward to it, because we thought we were the better team. There wasn't any question in my mind."

The determined Sims rushed for 134 yards and two touchdowns to win the Most Valuable Player Award in OU's 31-24 triumph in the Orange Bowl.

OU finished the season with an 11-1 record and was ranked third behind Alabama, which was No. 1 in the AP poll, and Southern California, which was No. 1 in the UPI poll.

Thomas Lott, Sammy Jack Claphan, Louis Oubre and Greg Roberts leave the field against OSU after their last home game in 1978.

"We were the best team in the country," said Switzer. "We were a great, great football team.

"(Quarterback) Thomas Lott was a great football player. He was a great competitor. Excellent option quarterback. He had the mechanics and understanding. Daryl Hunt and Reggie Kinlaw were great players, but they were underrated."

RAPID ROBERTS

Greg Roberts faced bitter disappointment in his first month at OU: Coach Barry Switzer had changed him from a linebacker and tossed him into the mass of anonymous offensive linemen. But, as usual, Switzer's judgment of player skills proved correct.

In 1978, Roberts not only was a consensus All-America choice as an offensive guard but won the coveted Outland Trophy as the nation's best interior lineman. OU became the first school to have four winners of the honor, and the 6-3, 283-pound native of Nacogodoches, Texas, become only the third offensive lineman to win the award since the elimination of limited substitution rules.

Roberts was a powerful blocker who also was known for his quickness. In fact, some opposing coaches yelled foul so much, Switzer started warning officials before games that Roberts might

Greg Roberts

look like he was offside.

"We didn't really single out individuals, but we are aware," said Bruce Finlayson, supervisor of Big Eight officials at the time. "I didn't tell the officials to watch No. 65, but it's natural they do. My reports are that he went with the ball 95 percent of the time. I didn't feel you should penalize a boy for being quick. But the guy was uncanny, like his head and the ball were in synchronization."

"He's probably the most talented offensive lineman we've ever had," said Switzer. "He had great quickness coming off the ball. He had great strength and pulling ability. He was a great, great competitor and had a lot of pride."

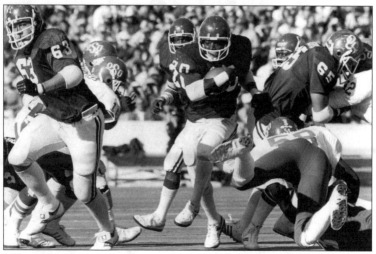

Fulback Kenny King finds a big opening, courtesy of Sammy Jack Claphan (63) and Greg Roberts (65).

SOONER QUIZ

43. Name the Sooner who holds the Big Eight career scoring record.

Linebacker Hunt was a three-year all-conference choice. Nose guard Kinlaw also was named Most Valuable Player in the Orange Bowl. The bowl started selecting two MVPs each year in 1970.

Uwe von Schamann established several records, including NCAA career conversion kicking marks of 125 straight and 140 of 141. Safety Darrol Ray tied the OU season mark with seven interceptions.

TEXAS SPOILER In 1979, The Sooners repeated their 11-1 performance, claimed another conference title and won again in the Orange Bowl.

Once again the season turned on the clash with Texas. Longhorn John Goodson kicked two field goals in the final quarter to seal fourth-ranked Texas' 16-7 triumph over third-ranked OU.

"Texas was a great defensive team," said Switzer. The Longhorns allowed only Arkansas more than two touchdowns all season.

Billy Sims follows tight end Forest Valora.

The Sooners had three consensus All-Americans: halfback Billy Sims in 1978 and 1979, offensive guard Greg Roberts in 1978 and linebacker George Cumby in 1979. Also Sims won the Heisman Trophy and Roberts won the Outland Trophy as the nation's outstanding lineman in 1978.

"In the 1979 season, the things that stand out in my mind are the last two (regular season) games and Billy Sims," said Switzer.

The Sooners survived against Missouri, 24-22, at Columbia. Five-foot-nine Jay Jimerson batted down a pass to 6-4 Missouri end Andy Gibler in the end zone on the Tigers' try for a tying conversion.

SOONER QUIZ

ONE MORE Sims was particularly motivated because his mother, who lived in St. Louis, attended the game. He rushed for 282 yards, a record against Missouri, and scored on a 70-yard run.

"Billy and I were sitting at practice Thursday before the Nebraska game," Switzer recalled. "It's going to be his last home game. I asked him: I said, 'You got one more in you?' He grinned, laughing, and said, 'I got one more, coach. I got one more.' Against Nebraska – a great performance against a team that had only given up 70 yards rushing a game. A very rare moment in sports."

Sims rushed for 247 yards (a 68-yard touchdown run was nullified by a penalty) as OU overcame a 7-3 deficit to defeat the all-victorious and third-ranked Cornhuskers, 17-14.

OU NO. 3 The Sooners faced all-victorious and fourth-ranked Florida State in the Orange Bowl. This time the Sooners overcame a 7-0 deficit to win 24-7. Sims rushed for 164 yards, but quarterback J.C. (Julius Ceasar) Watts

44. Who became the first Sooner to rush for more than 1,000 yards in one season?

J. C. Watts was OU's starting quarterback in 1979 and 1980.

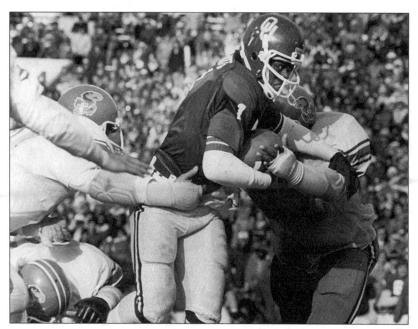

and cornerback Bud Hebert, who intercepted three passes, claimed the MVPs. Watts raced 61 yards for one touchdown and made a picture-perfect option pitchout to Sims on a 34-yard TD run.

OU finished third in the nation behind Alabama and Southern California.

WORLD'S GREATEST Billy Sims was one of the most highly recruited players in Texas in 1974. But it took him four seasons to hit his stride at OU and prompt Barry Switzer to call him "the greatest football player in the world."

Sims' mother sent him from St. Louis to live with his grandmother in Hooks, a northeastern Texas community of 2,000, when he was 13 years old. He not only escaped the evils of the big city but became a high-school legend.

OU Assistant Coach Bill Shimek was still smarting from losing another highly regarded back, Jerry Eckwood, to Arkansas and was determined to get Sims to OU. Between September 1974 and the February 20, 1975, national signing date, Shimek spent 77 nights in Hooks, not counting the Friday nights before OU home games when he and Switzer flew to Hooks to see Sims play.

"The first time I saw Billy, he was carrying two five-gallon cans of cow feed like they were water glasses," said Shimek. "From the waist up, he looked like a Greek god. He only weighed 179, but I thought, 'Lordy, he's strong.' "

Billy Sims dives for a touchdown against Colorado.

"He had it all when he came to OU," Switzer said. "You looked at him and it made you laugh and giggle to know he was coming here. You took great pride in the fact that he came to Oklahoma."

LATE BLOOMER Sims did not reach his full potential until his fourth season at OU. He played sparingly as a freshman, suffered a shoulder injury in his first appearance as a sophomore — receiving another year of eligibility on a conference hardship ruling — and was hampered by an ankle injury the next season.

But Sims made up for lost time in his final two seasons. At 6 feet and 210 pounds, Sims was strong enough to run over defenders and fast enough to outrun most of them.

In 1978, he led the nation in rushing with 1,762 yards, a Big Eight record, and in scoring with 120 points on 20 touchdowns. He rushed for more than 100 yards in every game except one (he left the 66-7 rout of Rice after the first quarter). He rushed for more than 200 yards in three straight games against Iowa State, Kansas State, and Colorado. His 221 yards was the most ever against the Golden Buffaloes.

Sims won the Heisman Trophy in 1978. He received 827 points to 750 for Chuck Fusina, but the Penn State quarterback received more first-place votes, 163 to 151.

ALL THINGS WELL "He's stronger than any running back we've ever had," said Switzer. "He can bench press 350 pounds. That's fullback strength. He's got great strength in his legs, and he's like all of our backs, who run 4.5 or 4.4 in the 40."

Sims was hampered by nagging injuries in 1979 but still topped 100 yards in nine of OU's 12 games. He rushed for 1,506 yards, averaging 6.7 yards a carry, and led the nation in scoring with 132 points on 22 touchdowns. But some of his most impressive performances came late in the season and Southern California tailback Charles White finished ahead of Sims in the balloting for the Heisman Trophy.

"Billy did all the things well," said Switzer. "That's the thing about him. Never a disciplinary problem. Never asked you for anything. He went to class. He got his degree."

BACKING J. C. Mistakes and a couple of opposing quarterbacks nearly wrecked OU's 1980 season. But J.C. Watts and a group of unheralded seniors held things together.

OU lost five of six fumbles and quarterback John Elway bombed the Sooners by completing 20 of 34 passes for 237 yards and three touchdowns to boost Stanford to a 31-14 win in the second game of the season.

The next week OU nearly destroyed Colorado and the record books in an 82-42 triumph in Boulder. However, the Sooners lost four fumbles and yielded four interceptions the next week against Texas. Longhorn quarter-

SOONER QUIZ

45. Name the two Sooners who were No. 1 choices in the NFL draft.

SOONER QUIZ

46. Name the four former Sooners who became OU head coach.

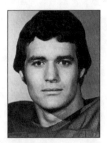

The Tabor twins were all-conference selections: Phil (above) as a defensive tackle in 1978 and Paul (below) as a center in 1979.

back Donnie Little rushed for 110 yards and passed for 99 in the 16-7 win, Texas' third straight in the series.

"Coach Switzer stuck with me 100 percent," said Watts, who was receiving a lot of public criticism. "He came up to me more than once — and this was when things were really going bad and we were 2-2 — and said 'J.C. Watts is my quarterback. I don't care what people say. And that's that.'

"The North Carolina game was the turning point."

The Tar Heels, led by All-America linebacker Lawrence Taylor, had won 10 straight games, including seven in 1980, and were ranked sixth in the nation. With Watts' three touchdowns and 139 yards leading the land rush, OU won, 41-7.

TWO MORE COMEBACKS Once again the Sooners made one of their storied comebacks against Nebraska. Trailing 17-14, OU started on its own 20-yard line with only 3:16 left.

"I had no idea what was going to happen, but I knew something good was going to happen," said Watts. "Louis always helped me out," he said, referring to offensive tackle Louis Oubre, who was a consensus All-American that season. "I'd never say anything to an offensive lineman. But I'd say, 'Louis, get on him for me.' He was the catalyst in the offensive line."

The Sooners capped the grueling drive when freshman halfback George "Buster" Rhymes scored from the 1-yard line with only 56 seconds left. OU 21, Nebraska 17.

Sooner Magic.

OU claimed the conference title and its fourth-straight trip to the Orange Bowl. For the second year in a row, OU faced Florida State, which this time had a 10-1 record and was ranked second in the nation. Trailing, 17-10, fourth-ranked OU got the ball on its own 22-yard line with 3:19 left. The Seminoles had not allowed a point in the fourth quarter all season.

J.C. MVP AGAIN Watts, who had been stunned earlier and did not remember a lot about the drive, completed four passes for 74 yards, including an 11-yard toss to split end Steve Rhodes for a touchdown with 1:27 left. Then he arched another pass to tight end Forest Valora for the crucial conversion and an 18-17 win. Valora had caught only five passes all season.

Watts became the first player to win the Most Valuable Player Award in the Orange Bowl two years in a role.

The Sooners posted a 10-2 record and were ranked third in the nation.

On the main street in Eufaula, a sign read: "Welcome

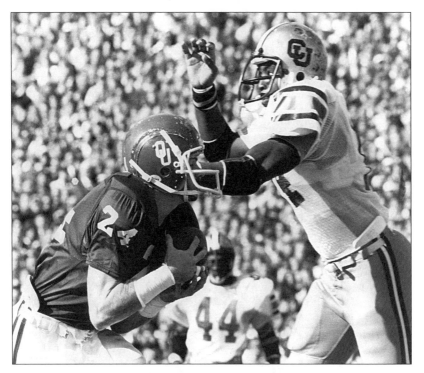

to Eufaula. Home of OU's Finest." The Selmon brothers were listed on it. They added J.C. Watts' name.

DEPRESSION All great programs and successful coaches are susceptible to a depression period. OU and Switzer suffered through one with a 7-4-1 record in 1981 and 8-4 records the next two years. At least, it seemed like a depression by OU standards. The Sooners had suffered only nine losses the previous eight seasons. Ten of OU's 12 losses during 1981-83 came against teams ranked in the nation's Top 20 at the end of the seasons.

In 1981, Nebraska won the first of three straight Big Eight titles, marking the first time since Switzer became head coach that OU hadn't won or shared the title. OU defeated Houston, 40-14, in the Sun Bowl. Quarterback Darrell Shepard was named the Outstanding Player and defensive tackle Rick Bryan was named the Outstanding Lineman. OU was ranked 20th in the nation.

KEY AWARD Offensive guard Don Key had started every game at OU for nearly three seasons before he suffered a kidney injury against Missouri in 1981. The injury ended Key's football career but may have saved his life because doctors discovered cancer during surgery.

The next year Switzer established the Don Key

Split end Steve Rhodes did not catch many passes, but OU went to him in crucial situations.

Guard Don Key had to give up football after suffering a kidney injury and has a special award named for him.

Stanley Wilson started at fullback for portions of four seasons and made all-conference in 1981.

Award, which has been presented each year to the OU senior who best reflects the high standards demonstrated by Key during his career.

SOONER QUIZ

47. Name the OU head coaches who played at Big Ten schools.

DUPREE ARRIVES In 1982, Switzer recruited one of the outstanding prospects in the nation, but even Marcus Dupree wasn't able to stem the Sooners' decline.

Southern California defeated OU, 12-0, in the third game of the season, ending OU's NCAA record scoring streak at 181 games.

The Philadelphia, Miss., running back set an OU freshman record with 905 yards rushing, averaged seven yards a carry, and scored 12 touchdowns although he didn't start playing regularly until the fourth game of the year. The '82 Sooners did upset all-victorious Texas, 28-22, for OU's first win over the Longhorns in four campaigns. Dupree, who rushed for 239 yards, and center Paul Ferrer were named the outstanding players in OU's 32-21 loss to Arizona State in the Fiesta Bowl in Tempe, Ariz.

The 16th-ranked Sooners had an 8-4 record.

Marcus Dupree reacts after scoring a touchdown in OU's 1982 win over Texas.

DUPREE DEPARTS With the 6-3, 230-pound Dupree at tailback, OU expected an improved season in 1983. But a hint of problems came early when Dupree reported late for fall practice and overweight. After a 28-16 loss to Texas dropped OU to 3-2, Dupree left school, ending what could have been one of the most outstanding careers in OU history.

KICKOFF MIX-UP The sagging Sooners escaped with a 21-20 win over Oklahoma State at Stillwater the next week when Tim Lashar of Dallas kicked a 46-yard field goal with 1:14 remaining. After scoring 18 points in the final quarter and trimming its deficit to 20-18, OU planned to kick off deep. But no one told Lashar, who earlier had been instructed to boot an onside kick. That's what Lasher did. The line-drive kick bounced off the helmet of OSU's Chris Rockins and was recovered by Sooner Scott Case, setting up the winning drive.

Sooner Magic.

Rick Bryan, who Switzer described as "the best defensive tackle at OU since Lee Roy Selmon," was a consensus All-American in 1982 and 1983.

Spencer Tillman set a freshman record with 1,047 yards rushing, and Earl Johnson rushed for 945 yards, which bettered the previous freshman mark. Each had been redshirted the previous season.

For the only time in Switzer's head coaching career,

SOONER QUIZ

48. Name the Sooner who played on national championship teams in two sports.

Jackie Shipp (49) and Thomas Benson were OU's starting line-backers in 1981-83.

OU was not ranked in the nation's Top 20.

Asked about what some called OU's down cycle, Switzer said: "I believe in players, not cycles."

The players Switzer sought had been assembled by 1984. A rare combination of depression-hardened seniors and juniors, redshirt sophomores, and regular and redshirt freshmen brought OU back to the brink of glory and foretold of the future.

OU spiced its Wishbone to aid its passing attack, a boost to senior quarterback Danny Bradley. Freshman Lydell Carr provided what every Wishbone attack must have — a threat at fullback. Freshman tight end Keith Jackson became a starter in his first college game. And senior Steve Sewell provided flexibility as a runner and

Quarterback Danny Bradley was named Offensive Player of the Year in the Big Eight Conference in 1984.

receiver at several positions.

The defense centered on junior nose guard Tony Casillas, two steady ends — junior Kevin Murphy and freshman Darrell Reed — and Brian Bosworth, an unheralded linebacker, who saw to it that he was not unheralded for long.

TEXAS CONTROVERSY The Sooners won their first four games before being tied, 15-15, by Texas in a controversial finish. Safety Keith Stanberry caught a Texas pass in the end zone in the closing seconds, but the officials ruled Stanberry was out of bounds before he gained possession. Then Texas kicked the tying field goal. After reviewing the films, the officials announced that Stanberry had made a legal interception, meaning OU should have won, 15-12. But that didn't change the score.

AIKMAN'S DEBUT OU suffered its first loss of the 1984 campaign when its first- and second-team quarterbacks were sidelined in one week. That meant 17-year-old Troy Aikman was forced into the starting assignment. He was being redshirted and had not worked out with the varsity. Kansas benefited, 28-11.

Bradley returned at quarterback, and the Sooners returned to the Big Eight throne room by defeating nationally No. 1-ranked Nebraska, 17-7, in Lincoln. OU scored 10 points in the fourth quarter and stopped the Cornhuskers twice on the OU one-yard line. Bosworth had one of his best games, making 19 tackles.

The second-ranked Sooners returned to the Orange

Safety Keith Stanberry intercepts a pass in the closing seconds against Texas in 1984. Officials ruled Stanberry was out of bounds and Texas kicked a field goal in the 15-15 deadlock. After viewing films, the officials said the catch was legal.

Versatile Steve Sewell played every position in the backfield except quarterback before his OU career ended in 1984.

Bowl for the first time in four years and for the first of four consecutive appearances. Senior-laden Washington, which had lost to Southern California in a 10-1 season, overcame a 17-14 deficit in its 28-17 win.

OU finished sixth in the nation with a 9-2-1 record.

The foundation was set for three remarkable seasons in which the Sooners had a realistic opportunity to win three straight national championships. But Hurricane warnings were stirring in Florida.

BACK TO 'BONE In 1985, OU was forced into a history-making change on offense and relied on an incredible defense that stumbled in only one game.

The Sooners returned to the Wishbone as a basic attack but included some other formations to take advantage of the passing of quarterback Troy Aikman and the receiving of Jackson. The star-studded defense included ends Murphy and Reed; nose guard Casillas; the linebacking duo of Bosworth and Danté Jones, and safety Rickey Dixon.

OU nipped Texas, 14-7, when halfback Patrick Collins raced 45 yards to the winning touchdown in the fourth quarter. The Sooners allowed the Longhorns only four first downs, none in the second half.

STARS FALL But the next week with Casillas sidelined with a knee injury, disaster struck. OU was rallying for a

End Kevin Murphy (39) and nose guard Tony Casillas (92) chase Nebraska quarterback McCathorn Clayton in OU's 1985 win.

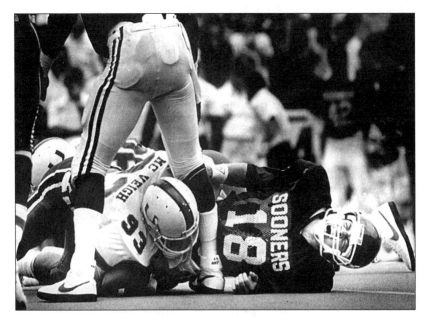

comeback against Miami, when Aikman, who had passed for 131 yards and one touchdown, suffered a broken ankle in the second quarter. OU had lost its second-team quarterback earlier in the season and the duties fell to freshman Jamelle Holieway. Miami won, 27-14, as quarterback Vinny Testaverde passed for 270 yards and two touchdowns. Miami's players chanted "OU Who?" after the conquest. Bosworth made 19 tackles, 13 unassisted.

Quarterback Troy Aikman suffered a broken ankle against Miami in 1985 and missed the rest of the season.

Ironically, Miami was coached by Jimmy Johnson, who played at Arkansas when Switzer was an assistant coach there and was recommended for his first college job at Iowa State by Switzer. But that didn't stop Johnson from dealing Switzer and OU misery for two more years.

ENTER HOLIEWAY "Jamelle is too short (5-9) to drop back and throw the ball," said Switzer of the 1985 contest. "We'll have to change some things offensively with him at quarterback."

What OU changed was its offense. It went back to the Wishbone, which was perfect for Holieway, a natural option quarterback with neck-cracking quickness and surprising strength for a 180-pounder.

Once again Nebraska stood between OU and the Big Eight title. But the Sooners handled the No. 2-ranked Cornhuskers, 27-7. Nebraska's only points came on a 76-yard return of a fumble by tackle Chris Spachman with only 26 seconds remaining.

"They have as good a defense as they ever had and

Safety Sonny Brown was named the Outstanding Back in the 1986 Orange Bowl.

Freshman Jamelle Holieway was the quarterback of OU's last national championship team in 1985.

Holieway became OU's starting quarterback in 1985 after Troy Aikman was injured.

that includes back when the Selmons were playing," said Nebraska coach Tom Osborne.

OU, which seemed destined for disaster in October, finished the regular season ranked No. 3 in the nation and facing all-victorious and No. 1-ranked Penn State in the Orange Bowl. The Nittany Lions claimed a 7-0 lead in the first quarter, but OU rallied after hearing that Tennessee had stunned No. 2-ranked Miami, 35-7, in the Sugar Bowl. OU combined back-breaking touchdown plays of 71 yards on a pass from Holieway to Jackson and a 61-yard run by fullback Lydell Carr and field goals of 26, 31, 21, and 22 yards by Tim Lashar for a convincing 25-10 triumph. C.D. "Sonny" Brown, who intercepted two passes and broke up two others, was named the Outstanding Back and, in a unique choice, Lashar was named the Outstanding Lineman.

NATIONAL CHAMPS Sophomore Bosworth received the first Butkus Award as the nation's best linebacker.

OU finished with an 11-1 record and was named the national champion for the third time in Switzer's career and the sixth time overall. The Sooners allowed eight opponents seven or fewer points each and led the nation in total defense and passing defense and were second in

THE DOMINATOR

Tony Casillas was the heart, both physically and spiritually, of the national champions' outstanding defense in 1985.

The 6-3, 280-pound senior repeated as a consensus All-American, won the Lombardi Award as the nation's outstanding college lineman and was named Lineman of the Year by UPI.

"Tony Casillas was just a dominant factor," said Coach Barry Switzer.

However, it wasn't always that way. Casillas had played behind All-America Rick Bryan at tackle in 1982. But after being moved to nose guard, Casillas became the "dominator."

Tony Casillas

"Being right there in the middle, it seems like there's more happening and everything's happening faster," said Casillas. "It wasn't long before I really began to enjoy it."

Buddy Burris, who played middle guard at OU in late 1940s, called Casillas the best OU football player at any position he had ever seen.

Nose guard Tony Casillas pressures Kansas State quarterback Donnie Campbell. Casillas was a consensus All-American in 1984 and 1985 and won the Lombardi Award in 1985.

rushing defense.

OU's 1986 season was almost a repeat of the 1985 campaign. But the "almost" was a significant one.

Before the season, Switzer had decided to use Jamelle Holieway at quarterback and stay with the Wishbone. He arranged for Troy Aikman, who would have been relegated to a reserve role, to transfer to UCLA without losing any eligibility. Switzer thought it was only right that Aikman play in a program where his passing skills could be utilized.

49. Name the national television anchorman who once was radio broadcaster for OU football games.

MIAMI MISERY No. 1-ranked OU faced Miami in a regular-season return match in the Orange Bowl, but the outcome was nearly the same. Bad blood on and off the field existed. Miami fans wore T-shirts that read: "What is a Boz worth? Not much in Miami." The captains refused to shake hands at the pregame coin toss. The Hurricanes came from behind in the second half to claim a 28-16 win as quarterback Vinny Testaverde had another brilliant performance, completing 21 of 18 passes for 261 yards and four touchdowns. Bosworth was booed on each of his 22 tackles.

For the second straight year, OU and Nebraska entered the Big Eight championship game with the Cornhuskers ranked No. 2 and OU No. 5 nationally. This time, the Cornhuskers, wearing red jerseys and red pants instead of their usual white pants at home, grabbed a 17-7 margin going into the final quarter.

But once again, Sooner Magic and Keith Jackson took over. Jackson caught a 17-yard pass from Holieway for a touchdown and made a one-handed grab of a 41-yard

Keith Jackson, racing to a touchdown against Miami in the 1987 Orange Bowl, may have been OU's most versatile tight end.

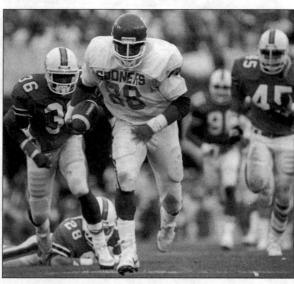

pass to set up the winning field goal by Lashar.

"We've done it so many times, the players just believed they could win the ball game," said Switzer after the 20-17 triumph.

ONE FOR BARRY OU returned to the Orange Bowl and blasted Arkansas, 42-8, in the only game Switzer said he asked one of his teams to win for him. Halfback Spencer Tillman, who rushed for 109 yards, and linebacker Danté Jones, who had nine tackles, were named the Outstanding Back and Lineman, respectively.

The NCAA dealt OU a surprising turn of events when Bosworth was declared ineligible for the bowl game because he failed a test for steroids. Switzer later told Bosworth he would not be welcome for his senior year.

The Sooners finished 11-1 again, were ranked No. 3 in the nation and claimed another conference championship. OU led the nation in all major defensive categories – total defense, passing, rushing and scoring – the first time that had been done since the NCAA started

Halfback Spencer Tillman was named the Outstanding Back in the 1987 Orange Bowl.

Linebacker Brian Bosworth, Butkus Award winner in 1985 and 1986, usually backed up his boasts with outstanding play.

Linebacker Danté Jones was named the Outstanding Lineman in the 1987 Orange Bowl.

compiling such statistics in 1937.

"This is probably the best defensive team we've ever had," Switzer said after the season.

Jackson and Bosworth were consensus All-Americans, and Bosworth won the Butkus Award for the second straight season.

DISASTER LURKS OU returned an explosive offensive unit, including Jackson and Holieway, and a defense rebuilt around three seniors — Reed, Jones, and Dixon. But crippling injuries and the spoiler awaited the Sooners, who were ranked No. 1 from the start of the 1987 season.

Once again, OU dominated Texas, 44-9, as the Sooners picked off seven pass interceptions. Dixon grabbed two as OU claimed its third straight win in the classic series.

After nine convincing victories, disaster struck against intrastate rival Oklahoma State. Running the option, Holieway fell untouched to the turf in pain. His left knee had collapsed and OU lost the player Switzer already had called "the best option quarterback we've ever had." Veteran fullback Lydell Carr also suffered a knee injury against the Cowboys. In one game, OU had lost the two players who formed the primary basis for the Wishbone attack. OU survived, 29-10. But the next week with freshman Charles Thompson at quarterback, the Sooners struggled to a 17-13 win over Missouri and were replaced in the No. 1 spot by Nebraska.

SILENCING HUSKERS In uncharacteristic fashion, some of the Cornhuskers boasted publicly that there would be no Sooner Magic in 1987. The clash between all-victorious Nos. 1 and 2 was played in Lincoln for the second straight year, because of a conference scheduling adjustment.

Safety Rickey Dixon was a consensus All-American and co-winner of the Thorpe Award in 1987.

It appeared that the Cornhuskers might make good on their boast before a record crowd of 76,663 fans as Nebraska led, 7-0, at halftime. But OU allowed the Cornhuskers into Sooner territory only three times in the entire contest for a 17-7 triumph that was not as close as the score. Jones had 12 tackles, 10 unassisted, and set up one score with a pass interception, and Dixon intercepted two passes, setting up a field goal with a 24-yard return.

"We didn't need Sooner Magic today," said Switzer, who had reminded the Sooners before the game that none of the boasting Nebraska players had ever beaten OU. "We dominated from start to finish."

"Of all the losses I've been associated with, this may be the most disappointing," said Nebraska's Tom Osborne.

SAME OLD MIAMI But the biggest test came in the Orange Bowl, which had matched No. 1 OU against No. 2

Lydell Carr started at fullback for most of four years before his OU career ended in 1987.

Miami, each all victorious. Benefiting from Holieway's absence and a sub-par Carr, Miami shut down OU's attack and gained a 20-7 lead in the fourth quarter. OU's score came after Dixon's interception set up a 1-yard TD run by halfback Anthony Stafford. Then the Sooners pulled a desperate trick play: the quarterback put the ball on the ground and guard Mark Hutson picked it up and ran 29 yards for a touchdown with 2:05 left.

Trailing, 20-14, OU's hopes ended when Miami's Bernard Clark recovered a fumble by quarterback Charles Thompson with only 33 seconds remaining.

For the third season in a row, OU posted an 11-1 record and lost to Miami. The Sooners were ranked third in the nation, behind Miami and Florida State, which the Hurricanes had beaten, 26-25.

Jackson, Hutson, Jones, and Dixon were consensus

Consensus All-American guard Mark Hutson (left) scored a touchdown in the 1988 Orange Bowl.

Keith Jackson (middle) was a four-year starter at tight end and consensus All-American in 1986 and 1987.

End Darrell Reed (right) was an all-conference choice for four seasons ending in 1987.

SOONER QUIZ

50. What is OU's
mascot?

*R.D. Lashar (left)
bettered his brother's
school record by
scoring 320 points
by kicking in 1987-
90.*

*Quarterback Charles
Thompson (middle)
led OU to key wins
in 1987 and 1988
when Jamelle
Holieway was
injured.*

*Guard Anthony
Phillips (right) was
a consensus All-
American in 1988.*

All-America choices. Dixon also shared the Jim Thorpe
Trophy as the nation's best defensive back with Miami's
Bennie Blades. Reed, who received one of the Most
Valuable Player awards in the Orange Bowl, became a
four-time all-conference selection.

RECORD CROWD The Sooners faced a rebuilding year in
1988 with only nine of 22 starters returning.

OU got a jolt in the third game when Southern
California won, 23-7. Jamelle Holieway, who carried 11
times for net yardage of zero, had not regained his
quickness after the injury he suffered in 1987. The
setback marked the first loss to a nonconference team
other than Miami since the 1984 season. The game was
played before 86,124 fans at the Los Angeles Coliseum,
the largest crowd ever to see the Sooners play.

RECORD ENDS OU escaped two close calls. R.D. Lashar,
Tim's brother and successor, hit a 22-yard field goal in
the fourth quarter to beat Colorado, 17-14. And OU
nipped Oklahoma State, led by 1988 Heisman Trophy
winner Barry Sanders. The Sooners survived, 31-28,
when Lashar kicked an 18-yard field goal with 2:33 left
and Cowboy Brent Parker dropped a 34-yard pass in the
end zone with 43 seconds remaining.

The Big Eight championship again came down to OU,
ranked ninth, and Nebraska, ranked seventh. The once-
beaten Cornhuskers marched 80 yards to a touchdown
on their first series and made it stand up. OU trimmed
the count to 7-3 but never got past the Nebraska 48 after
that. Nebraska claimed the championship and ended
OU's streak of 31 straight league wins, second only to
OU's 44 straight in the 1950s.

Osborne revealed that since August, Nebraska had
worked on Mondays and open dates on a defense similar
to the one used by Miami to combat OU's Wishbone.

SOUR CITRUS When OU was offered a bid to the Florida
Citrus Bowl in Orlando, Fla., Switzer asked: "Miami
won't be there, will it?" But neither was starting

Brian Boswoth protested being barred from the 1988 Orange Bowl because of steroid use.

quarterback Thompson, who had suffered a fractured ankle in the Nebraska loss. Holieway, who had played only sparingly the last half of the season, was forced back into the starting role. OU's attack sputtered, and the game ended unceremoniously with the Sooners on the Clemson 14-yard line and the Tigers leading, 13-6.

OU posted a 9-3 record and was ranked 14th in the nation.

All-American Anthony Phillips, who Switzer called "the best offensive guard I ever coached," was named all-conference for the fourth straight season.

OU was saddled with a series of devastating events in late 1988 and early 1989.

In September 1988, Brian Bosworth's autobiography, *The Boz: Confessions of a Modern Anti-Hero*, was highly critical of Switzer and the OU program.

"Bosworth's book was like a knife in my back," said Switzer.

STINGING SANCTIONS In December 1988, the NCAA placed OU on three years' probation for violations including illegal recruiting tactics and resale of tickets by players. Sanctions included no bowl games in 1989 and 1990, no games on television in 1989 and crippling restrictions on scholarships and recruiting.

The probation was a particularly difficult blow to Switzer, who had prided himself on the fact that OU had not been charged with infractions while he was head coach.

In January, an OU player received a five-year deferred sentence for shooting a teammate, and three players were charged with rape. Two of them were later convicted. A

SOONER QUIZ

51. Who was OU's first Wishbone fullback?

SOONER QUIZ

52. After what game in 1983 did OU's players award a game ball to the OU band.

few days after being dismissed from the team in February, star quarterback Charles Thompson was charged with selling cocaine to an FBI agent. Thompson pleaded guilty in April and was sent to a federal prison.

SWITZER DEFENDED Some of Switzer's former players pointed out that the OU program should not be judged by the actions of five players.

Even so, the darkest chapter in OU history was taking its toll. Switzer, who also had suffered injuries to both knees in a skiing accident, looked tired and lacked his usual enthusiasm and optimistic outlook during spring practice in 1989.

BUCKET EMPTY In an unexpected move, Switzer resigned as OU head football coach on June 19, 1989.

"My emotional bucket was empty," he said. "I didn't have any enthusiasm for doing the things that must be done for this program. I am tired."

At the time, Switzer and OU officials denied that any pressure was put on Switzer to resign. However, Switzer later revealed he felt threatened by some unsubstantiated charges that might have required him to defend himself in a public forum. No charges ever were brought by OU or law enforcement officials.

Barry Switzer was 51 years old and had the best win-loss record of any active football coach in the nation. His record of 157 wins, 29 losses and 4 ties and .837 percentage placed him fourth in the history of the game.

Within a few years, his batteries charged, he returned to coaching — this time with the Dallas Cowboys of the NFL. He resumed his winning ways, leading the Cowboys to victory in the 1996 Super Bowl. Interestingly, Troy Aikman was his star quarterback.

SOONER QUIZ

53. Name the OU coach who won a Pulitzer Prize in history.

COMPLEX Barry Switzer remains one of the most complex coaches in the game.

From the start, he was outspoken and did not gain favor with some of the nation's most influential coaches, partly because he was so successful and partly because he did not play politics.

Remarkably, he was never named Coach of the Year by the American Football Coaches Association or the Football Writers Association of America.

One of the amazing things about his 16-year career is that if his teams had never done better than his worst record — 7-4-1 in 1981 — he still would have ranked in the top 25 active coaches in the nation by the time he resigned.

The prevailing idea that OU's practices were loosely organized or carefree was not true. "I don't believe they smoke cigars and throw Frisbees in practice," Tom

Barry Switzer wipes his face at the press conference where he announced his resignation in 1989.

Osborne said, after some of the Sooners did just that in a Friday practice at Lincoln before facing the Cornhuskers one year. But Switzer wanted his opponents to think his practices were casual.

Some thought he gave his players too much freedom.

"I don't want a bunch of robots who dress the same and think the same," he once said.

"He works at recruiting harder than 99 out of 100 coaches," said Arkansas' Frank Broyles. Switzer promoted the idea that his teams won because of his players.

SOONER MAGIC "Sooner Magic is composed of three things," he said. "First, it's outstanding players. Then, it's good assistant coaches. And third, you create an atmosphere in which the players want to excel."

Those who knew Switzer also knew he was the biggest soft touch around.

He remains an avid supporter of the Special Olympics and was involved in the program before it was popular with other celebrities. In fact, he often hosted the youngsters at OU practices.

Even at the height of his financial problems during the oil bust in the early 1980s, Switzer remained generous with money, sometimes helping strangers.

54. Six of the last eight OU head coaches had been assistant coaches at OU. Name the two who were not.

Before Bud Wilkinson

John A. Harts got the idea for starting football at OU in 1895.

Yes, there was football at OU before Bud Wilkinson.
In the fall of 1895, 20-year-old John A. Harts came to the new university on the prairie in Oklahoma Territory to study and teach a class in public speaking. If that is all he had done, hardly anyone would have remembered that Harts even attended the University of Oklahoma.

But one day in September at Bud Risinger's barber shop on Main Street in downtown Norman, Harts came up with an idea that assured him a place in OU athletic history. Harts, who had played football at Winfield College in Kansas, suggested forming a football team at OU, which at the time had 148 students — 121 of them doing high-school preparatory work.

THE FIRST GAME   The idea was not a rousing success, but Harts got enough players together for one game. The members of that first team were John P. Evans of Pond Creek, Bert Long of Norman, Horace Simmons of Fort Sill, Ed Barrow of the Chickasha Nation, Fred Bean of Oklahoma City, Bernard Reuter of Fort Reno, Newt Medlock of Noble, Bert Dunn of Lexington, and Will Short, Jasper Clapham and Joe Merkle, whose home towns aren't known. They made their own uniforms and lost their only game, 34-0, to an Oklahoma City town team made up of students from high schools and a Methodist college.

Harts suffered a knee injury in practice and did not play. He recruited Risinger and Fred Perry of Norman, although neither was a student.

May Overstreet, the only woman faculty member, and students Ray Hume and Ruth House selected the school colors: crimson and cream, the official colors today.

Harts left school at the end of the term to prospect for gold in the Arctic, never knowing that what he had started would turn to gold half a century later.

OTHER FIRSTS   Naturally, the next few years were filled with OU football firsts.

Even without an official coach, OU claimed its first win, beating Norman High twice in 1896. In 1897, OU hired Vernon Parrington to head the English Department. Parrington, who had played football at Harvard, also added organization to the football team. OU beat Kingfisher College at Guthrie in its first clash with another college team in 1897. The local sheriff had never seen a football game and stopped the contest, thinking it was a drunken brawl. School officials persuaded him to let

Vernon Parrington brought organization to the English Department and the football team in 1897.

it continue. Even so, the game played second fiddle to the Territorial Intercollegiate Oratorical Contest.

The Monster had yet to be created.

In 1898, OU beat the Arkansas City, Kans., town team in its first game with a team from outside the territory and beat Fort Worth University in its first game against a college team in Norman. OU bowed to Texas in its first clash in that classic series in 1900. And OU lost to the Dallas Athletic Club in 1902 in its first appearance at the Texas State Fair.

ROBERTS RETURNS Fred Roberts, who had played at OU in 1899 and at Washburn College in Topeka, Kans., in 1900, returned to OU as player-coach in 1901. Thus, he became the first OU alumnus to coach at OU.

OU played the first game in what later became known as the Bedlam Series in 1904. OU and Oklahoma A&M clashed at Guthrie, the territorial capital. OU won, 75-0, but the contest is best remembered for the most unusual

SOONER QUIZ

55. *Name the Big Eight teams — in the correct order — that placed 1-2-3 in the national rankings in 1971.*

Bennie Owen was OU coach for a record 22 years and was instrumental in adding to the football facilities.

play in OU football history. On the fourth play of the game, an Aggie punted the ball straight up into a strong wind from his own end zone. The ball ended up in nearby Cottonwood Creek and was retrieved by OU's Ed Cook, who brought it ashore and scored a touchdown.

SOONER STABILITY In 1905, Benjamin Gilbert Owen brought what proved to be three vital factors to OU football in one package. He was experienced as a player in a successful program at Kansas under the famed Fielding H. Yost. He was experienced as a coach at Washburn College in Topeka, as an assistant at Michigan, and as a highly successful head coach at Bethany College in Lindsborg, Kans. And he brought stability. OU had five coaches in the first 10 years of its football history. Owen coached at OU for 22 years, longer than anyone else in the school's history.

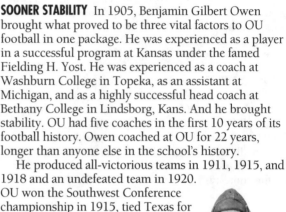

In 1913, Claude Reeds was the first OU player to receive All-American mention.

He produced all-victorious teams in 1911, 1915, and 1918 and an undefeated team in 1920. OU won the Southwest Conference championship in 1915, tied Texas for the title in 1918, and won the Missouri Valley Conference championship in 1920.

Owen provided a great deal of foresight. He helped lay out Boyd Field, where the OU Press is located today, and participated in a campaign to construct Owen Field in 1923.

The school song and nickname also were established during Owen's reign. Arthur M. Allen, a student of history and physiology, in 1905 wrote the lyrics for "Boomer Sooner," using the tune from Yale's "Boola, Boola." Sooners became the official nickname in 1907, replacing Rough Riders and Boomers.

Forest Park Geyer was nicknamed Spot for his passing accuracy in 1915.

The most outstanding players from the Owen era were fullback Claude Reeds, who was named on the All-America honor roll by Outing magazine in 1913, and Forest Park Geyer, who was selected on the 1915 Newspaper

Dewey "Snorter" Luster was OU captain in 1920 and head coach in 1941-45.

Enterprises Association All-America team. He was nicknamed Spot because of his passing accuracy.

The Sooners won 18 straight games during the 1914, 1915, and 1916 seasons, a record streak that stood until 1949.

In 1925, Owen promoted a campaign to build what is now the west side of Memorial Stadium, dedicated to the memory of university students, alumni, and patrons who had died in World War I.

His teams had a record of 122-54-16. The number of victories stood as a school record for 34 years. Bennie Owen was inducted into the Helms Foundation Football Coaches Hall of Fame in 1969, one year after his death.

During the next 19 seasons, 1927 through 1945, OU had five coaches.

Paul Young was the OU center and captain in 1932.

J. W. "Dub" Wheeler (left) was the first Sooner taken in the NFL draft when it was started in 1936. Green Bay selected Wheeler as the 15th player in the second round.

GOING BOWLING The most successful of that group were Tom Stidham and Dewey "Snorter" Luster.

Stidham's teams posted a 27-8-3 record in 1937-40 and claimed OU's first championship in the Big Six Conference in 1938. (In 1928, OU, Iowa State, Kansas, Kansas State, Missouri, and Nebraska left the Missouri Valley Conference to form the new league.) The '38 Sooners posted a 10-0 record while allowing only 12 points before bowing to Tennessee, 17-0, in the Orange Bowl in OU's first bowl appearance. OU also was nationally ranked for the first time, finishing fourth in The Associated Press poll.

End Roland "Waddy" Young, a dominating defender and excellent receiver, became OU's first consensus All-American when he was named to a majority of the teams selected in 1938.

Luster was the fiery captain of the 1920 Sooners and became the second OU alumnus to coach the Sooners. His 1943 and 1944 teams claimed Big Six championships, and his teams had an overall record of 27-18-3. In 1941, Luster divided his team into two groups with the seniors and juniors known as the Big Red. It is thought to be the first time the name was used at OU.

Frank "Pop" Ivy (center) was an OU end in 1937-39 and later was an assistant coach.

Tom Stidham (right) coached the Sooners to their first national ranking and first bowl game in 1938.

Between Bud & Barry

Gomer Jones was OU head coach in 1964 and 1965 after being Bud Wilkinson's No. 1 assistant for 17 years.

Tackle Ralph Neely was a consensus All-American in 1964.

OU did not look long or far for a successor to Bud Wilkinson.

Gomer Jones, Wilkinson's right-hand man for 17 years, was named athletic director and head football coach one week after Wilkinson's resignation in 1964.

"I believed that he deserved the opportunity, if he wanted it," President Cross said. "But I didn't know if he could be successful."

Jones had turned down other opportunities, stating: "Why should I become a head coach? I already have an ulcer."

NO. 2 BECOMES NO. 1 But the popular, 49-year-old Jones was succeeding a legend.

The 1964 Sooners, led by offensive tackle Ralph Neely, fullback Jim Grisham and linebacker Carl McAdams, one of OU's all-time greats, posted a 6-4-1

record after losing three of their first four games. The 17-14 upset of Big Eight champion Nebraska on Thanksgiving Day was the highlight of the campaign. Once again OU robbed the Cornhuskers of their first all-victorious season since 1915.

All-American linebacker Carl McAdams chases Iowa State's Tim Van Galder in 1965.

But the year ended in bitter disappointment in the Gator Bowl. Starters Grisham, Neely, and halfback Lance Rentzel were declared ineligible two days before the game after signing undated professional contracts. Florida State bombed the Sooners, 36-19.

Struggling on offense, OU went 3-7 in 1965 and bowed to Oklahoma State, 17-16 — the Cowboys' first win in the series in 20 years.

Two days later, on December 6, Jones resigned as head coach.

The Monster demanded more.

Jones remained as athletic director until his death. He suffered a fatal heart attack in March 1971 while on a basketball trip in New York City.

WILL IT BE ROYAL? Many of Wilkinson's former players campaigned for OU to hire Darrell Royal away from Texas.

Jim Mackenzie (left) and Chuck Fairbanks don't have the best seats in the house. Mackenzie was OU head coach in 1966. Fairbanks was OU head coach in 1967-72.

SOONER QUIZ

56. Name the OU coaches who had teams in the Orange Bowl in the same decade.

Cross didn't think Royal would leave Texas, but the OU president knew he could not afford to alienate some of OU's most vital supporters. So Cross persuaded the regents to allow him to make a public offer of a six-year contract at $32,000 a year to Royal. Four days later, Royal publicly turned down the offer, leaving Cross free to seek another coach — with the blessing of the ex-players.

YEAR OF MACKENZIE On December 22, OU hired Jim Mackenzie, who had been associated with two of the nation's most successful coaches. The 35-year-old Mackenzie had played for Paul "Bear" Bryant at Kentucky and was an assistant to Frank Broyles at Arkansas.

Mackenzie slept through his airplane's stop in Oklahoma City on his way to interview for the OU job. After returning on a flight from Denver, he told the regents: "I had read about Royal and Dooley, and thought I'd act disinterested, too." (Vince Dooley of Georgia also had turned down the OU job.) The remark gave an indication of the personality that would brighten the OU scene, if only for one year.

Mackenzie knew what it would take to revive the Sooners. Five of his eight-man staff became head coaches – two of them, Chuck Fairbanks and Barry Switzer, at OU. He ordered the Sooners to trim off 1,000 pounds in a Bryant-style off-season program. And he started plans to improve OU's outdated facilities.

WIN OVER TEXAS OU won its first four games in 1966, including an 18-9 triumph over Texas, the Sooners' first victory over the Longhorns in nine seasons.

OU was ranked No. 10 when it faced eventual national champion Notre Dame and suffered its most

Pat James brought fire and brimstone to OU as Jim Mackenzie's defensive line coach in 1966.

SOONER QUIZ

57. If OU had not lost to Miami in 1985, 1986, and 1987, the Sooners would have won 38 straight games. What teams would have beaten OU at the start and the end of that streak?

decisive loss in 21 years. After the 38-0 setback, Mackenzie summed things up with his opening statement in his postgame news conference: "Well, gentlemen, it's not far from the castle to the outhouse."

OU finished 6-4, but not before another upset win over another previously all-victorious Nebraska team, 10-9. Unfortunately the Sooners bowed for a second straight season to OSU, 15-14.

On April 28, 1967, after returning from a recruiting trip, Mackenzie suffered a fatal heart attack during the night at his home.

The OU athletic community was in turmoil, and once again Cross stepped in.

Without regents approval, he appointed his own choice for head coach, 33-year-old Chuck Fairbanks, who had just been elevated from secondary coach to offensive coordinator.

"I wanted to get someone appointed immediately," explained Cross, whose bold move might have been viewed as even bolder if he hadn't already announced his intention to retire in 1968. "The regents were reluctant, but I appointed Fairbanks by executive order, subject to the approval of the board."

The Michigan State graduate became OU's fourth head coach in only five years. The reluctant regents gave him

Chuck Fairbanks became the OU head coach in 1967 and brought the Sooners back to the Top 10.

an abbreviated contract that expired on January 31, 1968.
INDELIBLE MARKS Fairbanks, who lacked Mackenzie's
outgoing personality, remains perhaps the most
underrated and most overlooked coach in recent OU
history.

In a relatively short span — six seasons — Fairbanks'
teams left indelible marks on OU football. In his first
season, the Sooners would finish in the top 10 for the
first time since Wilkinson's reign. OU would suffer only
one loss in each of three seasons, (although one of those
records later was wiped out by forfeits). Tailback Steve
Owens would become OU's second Heisman Trophy
winner. OU would make a daring and perhaps program-
saving shift to the Wishbone attack three games into the
1970 campaign. The Sooners and Nebraska would clash
in the Game of the Century in 1971.

*Bob Warmack was
OU's quarterback in
1966-68.*

Fairbanks also relaxed hair and dress codes during a
rebellious period when many coaches remained
inflexible. And OU opened the door wider for black
players: Fairbanks' first team in 1967 had three black
players on the varsity roster, but when he left after the
1972 season, OU had tripled that number.

SURPRISING SOONERS Even Fairbanks and Cross had to
be surprised by the 1967 Sooners. Unheralded OU was
built around lightning-quick nose guard Granville
Liggins on defense, quarterback Bob Warmack,
sophomore tailback Steve Owens, wingback Eddie
Hinton, and the senior leadership of tackle Bob Kalsu on
offense. OU, which claimed its first conference title since
1962, lost only to Texas, allowed no foe more than two
touchdowns during the regular season and was ranked
third in the nation behind Southern California and
Tennessee.

In the Orange Bowl, the Sooners survived a late rally
by No. 2 Tennessee to win, 26-24, (OU did not move up
in the national rankings. The AP did not adopt its policy
of voting after bowl games until 1968, one year late for
the Sooners.)

Even before the bowl game, the once-reluctant
regents extended Fairbanks' contract.

Liggins was named national Lineman of the Year by
UPI.

*Bob Stephenson
returned an
interception to set up
OU's winning
touchdown against
Tennessee in the
1968 Orange Bowl.*

SOONERS SLIP OU slipped to 7-4 in 1968, despite
returning Warmack, Owens, Hinton, and tight end Steve
Zabel on offense. But with Zabel also playing linebacker
to boost the defense, OU defeated previously unbeaten
Kansas, 27-23, to tie for the Big Eight title and finish
11th in the nation. However, the Jayhawks got the bid to
the Orange Bowl.

Nose guard Granville Liggins, shown with coach Pat James, was the heart of the OU defense in 1967.

RUNNING TO HEISMAN In 1969, OU didn't do as well on the field, finishing 6-4, but the program was buoyed by another prestigious individual honor.

The Sooners returned Owens and Zabel and had a new quarterback, the highly recruited Jack Mildren. But the OU defense allowed 27, 59, 44, and 44 points in losses to Texas, Kansas State, Missouri, and Nebraska, respectively. For the only time in Fairbanks' head coaching career, OU was not nationally ranked.

Steve Owens had come to OU with a football under one arm and left with the Heisman Trophy under the other arm.

The determined, 6-2, 215-pound workhorse took

Eddie Hinton, one of OU's most overlooked stars, still holds school records of 114 receptions and 1,735 yards receiving in his career and 60 receptions in one season (1968).

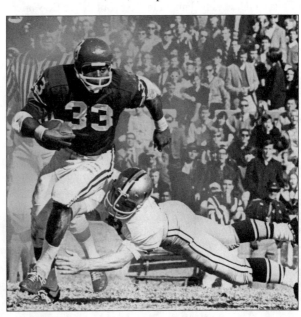

Steve Zabel played end on offense and linebacker on defense in 1968 and 1969.

some of the sting out of the disappointing 1969 campaign by rewriting the NCAA record book and becoming the nation's outstanding college player.

During his career, the native of the northeastern Oklahoma town of Miami established seven NCAA records, five other Big Eight records and three other school records. His national marks included rushing for more than 100 yards in 17 straight regular-season games, 56 touchdowns and 336 points in a three-year career, 905 career rushes, 3,867 career rushing yards, 358 carries in one season (1968), and 55 carries in one game.

On November 25, Owens and his wife, Barbara, were summoned to the office of OU President J. Herbert Hollomon. Word had leaked out, and students left their classrooms and ran across campus with the couple in a scene that was straight out of Hollywood.

When Owens was told on the telephone, "You are the winner," no one had to ask of what.

Owens took fullback Mike Harper, who was in effect his blocking back in the I formation, to New York with him for the Heisman award ceremony. In a tearful acceptance speech, Owens thanked everyone in Oklahoma.

The OU athletic family suffered a severe jolt before the 1970 season.

When informed that his 1967 team captain, Bob Kalsu, had been killed while serving with the 101st Airborne Division in Vietnam on July 21, 1970, coach

Steve Owens became OU's second Heisman Trophy winner when he shattered seven NCAA records in 1969.

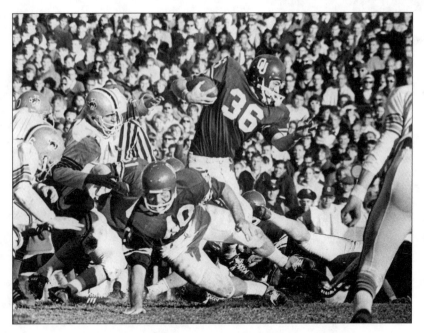

Steve Owens charges through a hole that fullback Mike Harper (40) helped open.

Chuck Fairbanks' left eye twitched and the normally self-contained coach remarked, "What a waste," before turning away.

Kalsu is thought to be the only NFL player killed in Vietnam.

BRING ON WISHBONE A glance at OU's record in 1970 (the Sooners finished 7-4-1) can't begin to reflect the drama that took place in the locker room as the season unfolded.

OU had changed to the Houston Veer attack but struggled in its first three contests. With a week off before the clash with Texas, offensive coordinator Barry Switzer persuaded Fairbanks to take the daring step of changing to the Wishbone. Switzer, who believed OU's personnel were suited to the Wishbone, was just as convinced that at the rate OU was going, the coaches would be fired.

Texas, the best Wishbone team in the nation and ranked No. 3, romped to a 41-9 win.

But OU improved steadily, losing only 28-21 to national champion Nebraska late in the season.

A major factor in the change was the ability of quarterback Jack Mildren to adapt to his third offensive formation in two seasons. Also a substitute sophomore split end was thrust into the lineup as a halfback and led OU to a 29-28 victory over Iowa State, after the Cyclones had jumped to a 21-point lead. Greg Pruitt and the

SOONER QUIZ

58. What team has been OU's opponent most often in bowl games?

Bob Kalsu, OU captain in 1967, was killed in Vietnam in 1970.

Wishbone were made for each other. Pruitt would be named the Outstanding Player in OU's 24-24 tie with Alabama in the Astro-Bluebonnet Bowl.

OU shared 20th in the nation at the end of the season.

UNSTOPPABLE OU and the Big Eight had a landmark year in 1971.

OU had one of its all-time best teams, built around center Tom Brahaney, Mildren, and Pruitt on offense; and linebacker Steve Aycock, tackles Derland Moore and Lucious Selmon, end Raymond "Sugar Bear" Hamilton, and safety John Shelley on defense.

The Sooners' Wishbone was unstoppable. OU scored 30 points or more in every game except one and defeated four teams that finished in the nation's Top 20.

Pruitt put together the three most impressive consecutive performances in OU history. He rushed for 205 yards and three touchdowns against No. 5-ranked Southern California, 216 yards and three touchdowns

59. Name the four players from the same home town who started for OU in 1954.

Quarterback Jack Mildren guided OU in three different offensive systems during his career but became best known as the Sooners' first Wishbone quarterback.

Tom Brahaney was a consensus All-America center in 1971 and 1972.

against Texas, and 190 yards and two touchdowns against all-victorious Colorado.

"You can't compare outstanding teams, but OU has the best team I've seen in my 15 years at Texas," said Darrell Royal.

GAME OF CENTURY But the season came down to one game. Anticipation grew all season as No. 2 OU was considered the only serious challenger to defending national champion Nebraska.

Finally, on Thanksgiving Day, November 25, 1971, what was billed and remains the Game of the Century was played in Norman. Neither team had been seriously challenged all year. They assembled a star-studded cast. Between them, the teams had 12 All-Americans and 14 other players who made all-conference during their careers. Ten assistant coaches, five from each team, later would hold major-college head coaching jobs.

This clash of Nos. 1 and 2 teams lived up to, if not exceeded, expectations.

Boosted by a 72-yard punt return for a touchdown by 1972 Heisman Trophy winner Johnny Rodgers, the Cornhuskers took a 14-3 lead. But the Sooners battled back, 17-14, at halftime. Nebraska claimed a 28-24 lead going into the final quarter. Once again, OU rallied for a 31-28 margin. But Nebraska had the last word when tailback Jeff Kinney scored his fourth touchdown of the game on a 2-yard run with 1:38 left.

Nebraska, which eventually extended its winning streak to 32 games, triumphed, 35-31. Mildren played perhaps his best game, rushing for 130 yards and two touchdowns and passing for 137 yards and two touchdowns with split end and former high-school teammate Jon Harrison his primary receiver. Nebraska allowed its other 12 foes an average of only 5.6 points a game in 1971.

OU LAND RUN OU led the nation by averaging 472.4 yards rushing and 44.9 points a game. The rushing mark still stands as the NCAA record. Pruitt, who often wore a T-shirt with "Hello" on the front and "Goodbye" on the

All-conference linebacker Steve Aycock was an OU captain in 1971.

Greg Pruitt received the Outstanding Player Award from Weldon Humble after OU's 24-24 tie with Alabama in the 1970 Astro-Bluebonnet Bowl in Houston.

Split end Jon Harrison caught two touchdown passes in the 1971 Game of the Century against national champion Nebraska.

Sooner nose guard Lucious Selmon smothers Nebraska quarterback Jerry Tagge in the 1971 Game of the Century.

back, established a Big Eight record with 1,665 yards rushing. Mildren, perhaps OU's most effective Wishbone quarterback, set a school total offense record with 2,018 yards and became the first major-college quarterback to top 1,000 yards rushing with 1,140. Pruitt and Mildren became only the second pair of teammates to top 1,000 yards rushing in the same season.

The '71 Sooners took another step forward when defensive back Glenn King of Jacksboro, Texas, became the first black player to be elected a varsity football captain.

With Nebraska ranked No. 1, OU No. 2, and Colorado No. 3, the Big Eight became the only conference ever to achieve such dominance.

COLORADO COOLER In 1972, OU returned a veteran team with Brahaney and Pruitt leading the offense and Hamilton, Lucious Selmon, and Moore getting a boost on defense from two sophomores, linebacker Rod Shoate and safety Randy Hughes.

But, once again, an obstacle appeared. This time OU bowed on the edge of the Rockies in a 20-14 upset by Colorado. OU's only other close contests that season came in a 17-14 triumph over Nebraska and a 14-0 win

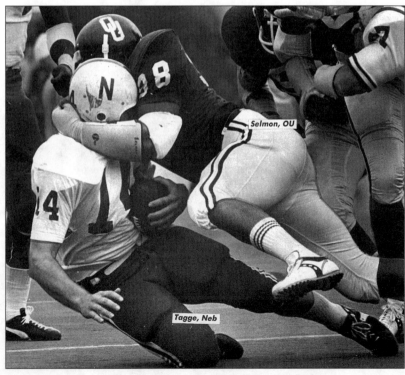

over Penn State in the Sugar Bowl. OU overcame a 14-0 deficit against the Cornhuskers when two freshmen, halfback Joe Washington and split end Tinker Owens (who were forced into action by injuries), and a senior, quarterback Dave Robertson, played key roles.

OU claimed the Big Eight title and finished second in the nation to all-victorious Southern California.

BEST ALL-AROUND Fairbanks called the '72 Sooners his best "all-around" team.

Less than a month after the season, Fairbanks was named head coach and general manager of the New England Patriots of the NFL.

But OU was stunned two months later, when the NCAA ruled that freshman quarterback Kerry Jackson's transcript at Galveston (Texas) Ball High School had been altered to make him eligible for college. OU had to forfeit its conference victories over Kansas, Missouri, and Oklahoma State, games in which Jackson had played. The Sooners' season mark went from 11-1 to 8-4, and Nebraska was awarded the Big Eight title.

Derland Moore was an All-America defensive tackle in 1972.

After Barry Switzer

Gary Gibbs came to OU in 1970 and worked his way up to starting linebacker on the Sooners' 1974 national championship team in his senior year. Twenty-four years after he arrived, Gibbs resigned as OU head coach, citing lack of support for himself and his team, primarily from the public.

Once again, the task of being the immediate successor of a legend, this time Barry Switzer, and pleasing the insatiable Monster proved to be overwhelming.

BRILLIANT CAREER Gibbs' brilliant career as an OU assistant coach paralleled that of his playing days: His football smarts helped him move ahead of better athletes as a player and later allowed him to move ahead of more experienced coaches. When he was only 28 years old,

Cale Gundy rewrote the Sooners' passing records in 1990-93.

Switzer promoted Gibbs to defensive coordinator over more experienced assistants, some of whom were Gibbs' former coaches. The move helped produce some of the most effective defensive teams in the nation in the 1980s and in OU history.

When Switzer resigned in 1989, OU already had the mechanisms in place to restore public confidence in a program that had its image shattered by probation and player arrests. Hiring Gibbs as head coach provided the school with a "Mr. Clean" leader.

But the Sooners, hampered by recruiting restrictions, couldn't win enough and didn't defeat the foes that all OU coaches eventually must conquer.

OU had 9-3 records in 1991 and 1993 and was ranked 16th in the nation in 1991 and 17th in 1990 and 1993.

The Sooners' outstanding players during the Gibbs era were quarterback Cale Gundy, 1991 All-America linebacker Joe Bowden, three-time all-conference defensive tackle Scott Evans, two-time all-conference

Gary Gibbs was a starting linebacker on OU's 1974 national champion-ship team, an OU assistant coach in 1975-88, and head coach in 1989-94.

Scott Evans was a three-time all-conference selection at defensive tackle.

SOONER QUIZ

60. Name the two Sooners who were all-conference in football and basketball.

safety Jason Belser, and running back Mike Gaddis, who rushed for 1,240 yards and 14 touchdowns in 1991. The OU attack was designed to complement Gundy's passing skills, and he responded by setting OU records of 14 touchdowns in 1993, 341 yards passing against Texas Tech in 1992, 2,096 yards passing in 1993, and 35 touchdown passes and 6,142 yards passing in 1990-93. He also passed for 329 yards and two touchdowns and was named Most Valuable Player in OU's 48-14 win over Virginia in the 1991 Gator Bowl.

But Gibbs' teams struggled against the foes the Monster relishes to devour. OU had 1-5 records against Texas and Nebraska and a 4-1-1 record against intrastate rival OSU. Also regular home sellouts dwindled to no sellouts.

BULLET HOLES Rumors of Gibbs' departure became rampant late in the 1994 campaign. One week after he told his staff and players he would not resign, 42-year-old Gary Gibbs announced his resignation at his regular Monday news conference. He had not told his coaches or players what was coming.

"I've taken a bunch of bullet holes in the last 5 and one-half years," he said. "This program is better now than it was in 1989. It was a hell hole then. It isn't now."

Gibbs' persona was the direct opposite of Switzer's. In fact, some of Gibbs' players considered him to be aloof. But during his reign, the Sooners did avoid scandal while improving graduation rates.

Nearly a month later, OU sent veteran observers reeling when it hired 61-year-old Howard Schnellenberger as head coach.

"I would have applied, but I wasn't old enough," remarked former OU assistant coach Larry Lacewell.

Schnellenberger had coached Miami to its first national championship in 1983. He then moved to Louisville, a university better known for its basketball teams. During his 10 years there, his teams were 54-56-2.

Howard Schnellenberger was the head coach at OU in 1995.

SOONER NATION He coined the term Sooner Nation and approached his players with a military — some said dictatorial — air. He did, however, institute one masterstroke: Before home games, OU players would mix briefly with fans and supporters while walking en masse across the campus to the stadium. Even so, Schnellenberger was considered pompous and even arrogant by some observers.

However, he told OU fans what they wanted to hear: The Sooners, who finished 6-6 in 1994 and had not been nationally ranked since 1991, would be back in the chase for the national championship in 1995, he said. It didn't

happen. In fact, OU improved little if at all, posting a 5-5-1 record.

Halfback Jerald Moore rushed for 1,001 yards in 1995.

DISPUTE But Schnellenberger's fate was sealed by something that occurred before the season started. When he withheld water from players during practice in the searing heat of August, two freshmen, Brian Ailey and Aaron Findley, suffered heat exhaustion. Ailey came close to dying, doctors said, before being revived at Norman Regional Hospital. Schnellenberger dismissed the incident.

OU President David Boren did not. In fact, Schnellenberger was ordered to resume the routine procedure of having liquids available for players when they wanted them. Schnellenberger did not fully follow the directions.

Less than a month after the final 1995 game and one year and two days after becoming OU head coach, Schnellenberger resigned in a written statement released December 18. The coach and OU officials denied his action had anything to do with OU's disappointing record.

Before the end of the month, OU hired one of its own, John Blake a member of the Sooner Family, to try to revive the Monster.

SOONER QUIZ

61. Name OU's first mascot.

By the Numbers

The statistics, lists and records that appear in this chapter are taken from the OU football media guide, which is produced by the OU Sports Information Office. The text was updated through the 1995 season.

YEAR-BY-YEAR RECORDS

Year	W-L-T	Pct.	Pts.	Opp.	Coach	Captain(s)
1895	0-1-0	.000	0	34	John A. Harts	John A. Harts
1896	2-0-0	1.000	28	4	None	Ray Hume
1897	2-0-0	1.000	33	8	Vernon Parrington	C. C. Roberts
1898	2-0-0	1.000	29	0	Vernon Parrington	C. C. Roberts
1899	2-1-0	.677	61	28	Vernon Parrington	C. C. Roberts
1900	3-1-1	.700	118	28	Vernon Parrington	C. C. Roberts
1901	3-2-0	.600	93	29	Fred Roberts	Ray Crowe
1902	6-3-0	.667	175	60	Mark McMahan	Clyde Bogle
1903	5-4-3	.542	126	85	Mark McMahan	Clyde Bogle
1904	4-3-1	.563	204	96	Fred Ewing	Byron McCreary
1905	7-2-0	.777	229	55	Bennie Owen	Byron McCreary
1906	5-2-2	.667	124	36	Bennie Owen	James Monnett
1907	4-4-0	.500	181	75	Bennie Owen	Bill Cross
1908	8-1-1	.850	272	35	Bennie Owen	Key Wolf
1909	6-4-0	.600	202	110	Bennie Owen	Charlie Armstrong
1910	4-2-1	.643	163	31	Bennie Owen	Cleve Thompson
1911	8-0-0	1.000	282	15	Bennie Owen	Fred Capshaw
1912	5-4-0	.555	197	80	Bennie Owen	Glenn Clark
1913	6-2-0	.750	323	44	Bennie Owen	Hubert Ambrister
1914	9-1-1	.864	440	96	Bennie Owen	Billy Clark
1915	10-0-0	1.000	370	54	Bennie Owen	Forest Geyer
1916	6-5-0	.545	472	115	Bennie Owen	Homer Montgomery
1917	6-4-1	.591	451	103	Bennie Owen	Frank McCain
1918	6-0-0	1.000	278	7	Bennie Owen	Hugh McDermott
1919	5-2-3	.650	275	63	Bennie Owen	Erl Deacon
1920	6-0-1	.929	176	51	Bennie Owen	Dewey Luster
1921	5-3-0	.625	127	102	Bennie Owen	Lawrence Haskell
1922	2-3-3	.438	64	114	Bennie Owen	Howard Marsh
1923	3-5-0	.375	144	111	Bennie Owen	Peter Hammert
1924	2-5-1	.313	28	80	Bennie Owen	Obie Bristow
1925	4-3-1	.563	93	44	Bennie Owen	Eddie Brockman
1926	5-2-1	.661	137	52	Bennie Owen	Pollack Wallace
1927	3-3-2	.500	122	101	Adrian "Ad" Lindsey	Granville Norris
1928	5-3-0	.625	120	88	Adrian "Ad" Lindsey	Bill Hamilton
1929	3-3-2	.500	81	81	Adrian "Ad" Lindsey	Frank Crider
1930	4-3-1	.563	100	57	Adrian "Ad" Lindsey	Bob Fields
1931	4-7-1	.375	88	108	Adrian "Ad" Lindsey	Guy Warren
1932	4-4-1	.500	90	81	Lewie Hardage	Paul Young
1933	4-4-1	.500	83	70	Lewie Hardage	Bill Pansze
1934	3-4-2	.428	64	43	Lewie Hardage	Art Pansze
1935	6-3-0	.667	99	44	Lawrence "Biff" Jones	Morris McDannald
1936	3-3-3	.500	84	67	Lawrence "Biff" Jones	Connie Ahrens
1937	5-2-2	.667	98	39	Tom Stidham	Al Corrotto
1938	10-1-0	.909	185	29	Tom Stidham	Gene Corrotto, Earl Crowder
1939	6-2-1	.722	186	62	Tom Stidham	Noval Locke
1940	6-3-0	.667	121	105	Tom Stidham	Gus Kitchens
1941	6-3-0	.667	218	95	Dewey "Snorter" Luster	Orville Mathews, Rogers Eason
1942	3-5-2	.400	135	78	Dewey "Snorter" Luster	Bill Campbell, W. G. "Dub" Lamb
1943	7-2-0	.778	187	92	Dewey "Snorter" Luster	W. C. "Dub" Wooten, Bob Brumley
1944	6-3-1	.650	227	149	Dewey "Snorter" Luster	W. C. "Dub" Wooten, Bob Mayfield
1945	5-5-0	.500	169	138	Dewey "Snorter" Luster	Omer Burgert
1946	8-3-0	.727	309	120	Jim Tatum	Jim Tyree
1947	7-2-1	.750	194	161	Bud Wilkinson	Jim Tyree, Wade Walker
1948	10-1-0	.909	350	121	Bud Wilkinson	Wade Walker, Homer Paine
1949	11-0-0	1.000	399	88	Bud Wilkinson	Stanley West, Jim Owens
1950	10-1-0	.909	352	148	Bud Wilkinson	Harry Moore, Norman McNabb
1951	8-2-0	.800	321	97	Bud Wilkinson	Bert Clark, Jim Weatherall
1952	8-1-1	.850	407	141	Bud Wilkinson	Eddie Crowder, Tom Catlin
1953	9-1-1	.864	293	90	Bud Wilkinson	Larry Grigg, Roger Nelson
1954	10-0-0	1.000	304	62	Bud Wilkinson	Gene Mears, Gene Calame, Carl Allison
1955	11-0-0	1.000	385	60	Bud Wilkinson	Bo Bolinger, Cecil Morris, Bob Loughridge
1956	10-0-0	1.000	466	51	Bud Wilkinson	Ed Gray, Jerry Tubbs
1957	10-1-0	.909	333	89	Bud Wilkinson	Don Stiller, Clendon Thomas
1958	10-1-0	.909	300	55	Bud Wilkinson	Joe Rector, Bob Harrison
1959	7-3-0	.700	234	146	Bud Wilkinson	Gilmer Lewis, Bobby Boyd

Year	W-L-T	Pct.	Pts.	Opp.	Coach	Captain(s)
1960	3-6-1	.350	136	158	Bud Wilkinson	Ronnie Hartline, Marshall York
1961	5-5-0	.500	122	141	Bud Wilkinson	Billy White
1962	8-3-0	.727	267	61	Bud Wilkinson	Wayne Lee, Leon Cross
1963	8-2-0	.800	236	137	Bud Wilkinson	John Garrett, Larry Vermillion
1964	6-4-1	.591	207	170	Gomer Jones	Newt Burton, John Garrett
1965	3-7-0	.300	106	150	Gomer Jones	Mike Ringer, Carl McAdams
1966	6-4-0	.600	192	122	Jim Mackenzie	Ed Hall, Jim Riley
1967	10-1-0	.909	290	92	Chuck Fairbanks	Bob Kalsu
1968	7-4-0	.636	343	225	Chuck Fairbanks	Bob Warmack, John Titsworth, Steve Barrett
1969	6-4-0	.600	285	289	Chuck Fairbanks	Steve Zabel, Steve Owens, Jim Files, Ken Mendenhall
1970	7-4-1	.625	305	239	Chuck Fairbanks	Monty Johnson, Steve Casteel
1971	11-1-0	.917	534	217	Chuck Fairbanks	Jack Mildren, Glenn King, Steve Aycock
1972	*8-4-0	.667	385	74	Chuck Fairbanks	Tom Brahaney, Greg Pruitt
1973	10-0-1	.995	400	133	Barry Switzer	Eddie Foster, Gary Baccus, Tim Welch, Lucious Selmon
1974	11-0-0	1.000	473	92	Barry Switzer	Steve Davis, Kyle Davis, Rod Shoate, Randy Hughes
1975	11-1-0	.917	344	154	Barry Switzer	Lee Roy Selmon, Dewey Selmon, Joe Washington, Steve Davis
1976	9-2-1	.792	326	192	Barry Switzer	Mike Vaughan, Scott Hill, Jerry Anderson
1977	10-2-0	.833	411	217	Barry Switzer	Karl Baldischwiler, Zac Henderson
1978	11-1-0	.917	440	151	Barry Switzer	Daryl Hunt, Greg Roberts, Phil Tabor, Thomas Lott
1979	11-1-0	.917	406	145	Barry Switzer	Billy Sims, Darrol Ray, Sherwood Taylor, George Cumby, Paul Tabor
1980	10-2-0	.933	396	209	Barry Switzer	J. C. Watts, Richard Turner, Steve Rhodes, David Overstreet, Louis Oubre
1981	7-4-1	.625	341	193	Barry Switzer	Terry Crouch, Ed Culver, Johnnie Lewis
1982	8-4-0	.667	317	203	Barry Switzer	Game Captains
1983	8-4-0	.667	312	222	Barry Switzer	Rick Bryan, Scott Case, Danny Bradley, Paul Parker
1984	9-2-1	.791	289	136	Barry Switzer	Danny Bradley, Chuck Thomas, Tony Casillas, Kevin Murphy, Keith Stanberry
1985	11-1-0	.917	346	93	Barry Switzer	Tony Casillas, Kevin Murphy, Eric Pope
1986	11-1-0	.917	466	73	Barry Switzer	Brian Bosworth, Steve Bryan, Sonny Brown, Spencer Tillman
1987	11-1-0	.917	479	82	Barry Switzer	Patrick Collins, Mark Hutson, Greg Johnson, Danté Jones, Darrell Reed, David Vickers
1988	9-3-0	.750	326	147	Barry Switzer	Scott Garl, Jamelle Holieway, Anthony Phillips, Anthony Stafford
1989	7-4-0	.636	380	200	Gary Gibbs	Scott Evans, Ken McMichael, Leon Perry, Kevin Thompson, Mark Van Keirsbilck
1990	8-3-0	.727	401	174	Gary Gibbs	Scott Evans, Larry Medice, Mike Sawatsky, Chris Wilson
1991	9-3-0	.750	335	143	Gary Gibbs	Jason Belser, Joe Bowden, Brandon Houston, Mike McKinley, Randy Wilson, Chris Wilson
1992	5-4-2	.545	271	196	Gary Gibbs	Reggie Barnes, Cale Gundy, Kenyon Rasheed, Darnell Walker
1993	9-3-0	.750	406	145	Gary Gibbs	Cale Gundy, Aubrey Beavers, Corey Warren, Mike Coats
1994	6-6-0	.500	225	238	Gary Gibbs	Garrick McGee, Albert Hall, John Anderson, Darrius Johnson
1995	5-5-1	.500	233	277	Howard Schnellenberger	Game Captains

* Season record was 11-1 before forfeiting three games because of an ineligible player.

COACHING RECORDS

Seasons	Coach and School	Year(s)	W-L-T	Pct.	Pts.	Opp.
1895	John A. Harts (Southwest Kansas)	1	0-1-0	.000	0	34
1897-1900	Vernon Parrington (Harvard)	4	9-2-1	.792	241	64
1901	Fred Roberts (Oklahoma)	1	3-2-0	.600	93	29
1902-03	Mark McMahan (Texas)	2	11-7-3	.548	301	145
1904	Fred Ewing (Knox)	1	4-3-1	.563	204	90
1905-26	Bennie Owen (Kansas)	22	122-54-16	.677	5132	1426
1927-31	Adrian "Ad" Lindsey (Kansas)	5	19-19-6	.500	511	435
1932-34	Lewie Hardage (Vanderbilt)	3	11-12-4	.481	237	194
1935-36	Lawrence "Biff" Jones (Army)	2	9-6-3	.583	183	111
1937-40	Tom Stidham (Haskell)	4	27-8-3	.750	590	218
1941-45	Dewey "Snorter" Luster (Oklahoma)	5	27-18-3	.594	936	552
1946	Jim Tatum (North Carolina)	1	8-3-0	.727	309	120
1947-63	Charles "Bud" Wilkinson (Minnesota)	17	145-29-4	.826	5092	1793
1964-65	Gomer Jones (Ohio State)	2	9-11-1	.452	294	284
1966	Jim Mackenzie (Kentucky)	1	6-4-0	.600	192	122
1967-72	Chuck Fairbanks (Michigan State)	6	*49-18-1	.728	2142	1136
1973-88	Barry Switzer (Arkansas)	16	157-29-4	.837	6093	2425
1989-94	Gary Gibbs (Oklahoma)	6	44-23-2	.652	2018	1096
1995	Howard Schnellenberger (Kentucky)	1	5-5-1	.500	233	277

* 52-15-1 before forfeiting three games because of an ineligible player in 1972.

TEAM RECORDS

MOST RUSHES

Game   88 vs. Oklahoma State, 1972
Season   813 in 1974
Per Game   73.9 in 1974

MOST RUSHING YARDS

Game   768 vs. Kansas State, 1988
Season   5196 in 1971

RUSHING YARDS PER ATTEMPT

Game   10.6 (72-768) vs. Kansas State, 1988
Season   7.3 (710-5196) in 1971

MOST PASSING ATTEMPTS

Game   45 vs. Kansas State, 1994
Season   288 in 1994
Per Game   26.2 in 1994

MOST PASSING COMPLETIONS

Game   27 vs. Virginia, 1991 (Gator Bowl)
Season   158 in 1992
Per Game   14.3 in 1992

FEWEST PASSING ATTEMPTS

Season   58, 1976
Per Game   5.3, 1976

FEWEST PASSING COMPLETIONS

Game   0, Several Times (last vs. Arizona, 1989)
Season   21, 1976
Per Game   1.9, 1976

MOST YARDS PASSING

Game   357 vs. Virginia, 1992 (Gator Bowl)
Season   2214 in 1992
Per Game   201.3 in 1992

PASSING COMPLETION PERCENTAGE

Game   1.000, several times
Season   58.4 in 1993

MOST PASSING YARDS PER ATTEMPT

(Minimum 5 attempts)
Game   25.7 vs. Colorado, 1962
Season   13.2 in 1971

MOST PASSING YARDS PER COMPLETION

Game   36.1 vs. Colorado, 1962
Season   27.3 in 1971

MOST PASSES INTERCEPTED

Game   5 vs. Kansas State, 1969
Season   17 in 1992

TOTAL OFFENSE

Game   875 vs. Colorado, 1980
Season   6232 in 1971
Per Game   566.5 in 1971

MOST OFFENSIVE PLAYS

Season   953 in1972
Per Game   86.6 in 1972

OFFENSIVE YARDS PER PLAY

Game   10.9 vs. Colorado, 1980
Season   7.9, 1971

FEWEST TURNOVERS

Game   0, several times (last vs. Oklahoma State, 1994)
Season   16 in 1993
Per Game   1.5 in 1993

SCORING

Game   82 vs. Colorado, 1980
Season   494 in 1971
Per Game   44.9 in 1971

MOST TOUCHDOWNS

Game   12 vs. Colorado, 1980
Season   66 in 1971
Per Game   6.0 in 1971

MOST RUSHING TOUCHDOWNS

Game   12 vs. Colorado, 1980
Season   58 in 1957
Per Game   5.8 in1957

MOST PASSING TOUCHDOWNS

Game   4 vs. Colorado 1951, vs. Kansas, 1950
Season   14 in 1993
Per Game   1.3 in 1993

FIELD GOALS

Game   4 vs. Texas, 1966; vs. Penn State, 1986; vs. Oklahoma State, 1986
Season   16 in 1992
Per Game   1.45 in 1992

FIELD GOAL PERCENTAGE

Game   1.000, several times
Season   88.9 in 1992

MOST EXTRA POINTS

Game   11 vs. Missouri, 1986
Season   60 in 1986

EXTRA POINT PERCENTAGE

Game   1.000, several times (last vs. Kansas, 1994, 2-2)
Season   1.000, several times (last in 1990, 45-45)

MOST PUNTS

Game   18 vs. Santa Clara, 1941
Season   58 in 1994

PUNTING AVERAGE

Game   56.3 vs. Kansas State, 1981
Season   43.0 in 1982

MOST PUNT RETURN YARDS

Game   227 vs. Kansas State, 1948
Season   963 in 1948
Per Game   57.1 in 1971

MOST KICKOFF RETURN YARDS

Game   207 vs. Santa Clara, 1941
Season   629 in 1971
Per Game   57.1 in 1971

FEWEST RUSHING YARDS ALLOWED

Game   -52 vs. Kansas State, 1986
Season   668 in 1986
Per Game   60.7 in 1986

FEWEST RUSHING ATTEMPTS

Season   387, 1984
Per Game   35.1, 1984

FEWEST RUSHING YARDS PER ATTEMPT

Season   1.6, 1986

FEWEST PASSING YARDS ALLOWED

Game   -2 vs. Oklahoma State, 1993
Season   555 in 1956
Per Game   55.5 in 1956

FEWEST PASSING ATTEMPTS

Season   47 in 1960
Per Game   4.7 in 1960

MOST SACKS

Game   7 vs. Texas, 1989
Season   40 in 1989
Per Game   3.6 in 1989

FEWEST POINTS ALLOWED – DEFENSE

Game   0, several times (last vs. Okla. State, 1993)
Season   29 in 1938
Per Game   2.6 in 1938

FEWEST TOUCHDOWNS ALLOWED – DEFENSE

Game   0, several times (last vs. Okla. State, 1993)
Season   29 in 1938
Per Game   2.6 in 1938

FEWEST TOUCHDOWNS ALLOWED – DEFENSE

Game   0, several times (last vs. Okla. State, 1993)
Season   2 in 1938
Per Game   0.5 in 1938

INDIVIDUAL RECORDS

MOST RUSHES

Game   55, Steve Owens vs. Okla. State, 1969
Season   358, Steve Owens, 1969
Career   905, Steve Owens, 1967-69

RUSHING YARDAGE

Game   294, Greg Pruitt vs. Kansas State, 1971
Season   1762, Billy Sims, 1978
Career   3995, Joe Washington, 1972-75

RUSHING YARDS PER ATTEMPT

Game   26.8 (6-161), Eric Mitchel vs. Kansas
State, 1988
Season   9.41, Greg Pruitt, 1971 (NCAA Record)

200-YARD RUSHING GAMES

Season   4, Billy Sims, 1978
Career   6, Billy Sims, 1975-79

RUSHING YARDS BY A FRESHMAN

Game   259, Earl Johnson vs. Colorado, 1983
Season   1047, Spencer Tillman, 1983 (redshirt)
905, Marcus Dupree, 1982 (true)

YARDS RUSHING BY A QUARTERBACK

Game   162, Jamelle Holieway vs. Kansas, 1985
Season   1140, Jack Mildren, 1971
Career   2699, Jamelle Holieway, 1985-88

RUSHING TOUCHDOWNS

Game   5, Steve Owens vs. Nebraska, 1969
5, Jerald Moore vs. Oklahoma State, 1994
Season   23, Steve Owens, 1969
Career   56, Steve Owens, 1967-69

ALL-PURPOSE RUNNING YARDS

Game   374, Greg Pruitt vs. Kansas State, 1971
(294 Rushing, 34 Receiving, 46 Return
Yards)
Season   1940, Greg Prutt, 1971 (1665 Rushing,
103 Receiving, 172 Return Yards)
Career   5784, Joe Washington, 1972-75 (3995
Rushing, 254 Receiving, 1535 Return
Yards)

MOST PASS ATTEMPTS

Game   45, Garrick McGee vs. Kansas State, 1994
Season   284, Garrick McGee, 1994
Career   751, Cale Gundy, 1990-93

PASS COMPLETIONS

Game   25, Cale Gundy vs. Virginia, 1991
Season   149, Garrick McGee, 1994
Career   420, Cale Gundy, 1990-93

PASS COMPLETION PERCENTAGE

Game   1.000 (9-9), Jack Jacobs vs. Kansas, 1941
Season   .708, (17-24), Tommy McDonald, 1955
Career   .559, (420-751), Cale Gundy, 1990-93

PASSES HAD INTERCEPTED

Game   5, Jack Jacobs vs. Kansas State, 1940
Season   15, Cale Gundy, 1992
Career   31, Cale Gundy, 1990-93

LOWEST INTERCEPTION PERCENTAGE

Season   .000, Monte Deere, 1960
Career   .036, Bob Warmack, 1966-68

MOST YARDS PASSING

Game   341, Cale Gundy vs. Texas Tech, 1992
Season   2096, Cale Gundy, 1993
Career   6142, Cale Gundy, 1990-93

300-YARD PASSING GAMES

Season   2, Cale Gundy, 1992 & 1993
Career   5, Cale Gundy, 1990-93

TOUCHDOWN PASSES

Game   4, Claude Arnold vs. Kansas, 1950
4, Eddie Crowder vs. Colorado, 1951
Season   14, Cale Gundy, 1993
Career   35, Cale Gundy, 1990-93

MOST TOTAL OFFENSE YARDS

Game   351, Cale Gundy vs. Iowa State, 1992
(333 Passing, 18 Rushing)
Season   2291, Cale Gundy, 1993 (2096 Passing,
195 Rushing)
Career   6389, Cale Gundy, 1990-93 (6142
Passing, 247 Rushing)

MOST PASSES CAUGHT

Game   10, Gordon Brown vs. Okla. State, 1965
10, Eddie Hinton vs. Okla. State, 1968
Season   60, Eddie Hinton, 1968
Career   114, Eddie Hinton, 1966-68

MOST YARDS GAINED RECEIVING

Game   187, Corey Warren vs. Texas, 1992
Season   967, Eddie Hinton, 1968
Career   1735, Eddie Hinton, 1966-68

YARDS PER RECEPTION

Season   29.1, Jon Harrison, 1971
Career   27.4, Jon Harrison, 1970-71

MOST TOUCHDOWN PASSES CAUGHT

Season   6, Eddie Hinton, 1968
Career   13, Keith Jackson, 1984-87

MOST PUNTS

Game	18, Jack Jacobs vs. Santa Clara, 1941
Season	49, Michael Keeling, 1982
	49, Brad Reddell, 1992
Career	185, Brad Reddell, 1989-92

BEST PUNTING AVERAGE

Game	56.3, Michael Keeling vs. Kansas, 1981
Season	50.2, Joe Washington, 1975
Career	42.3, Jack Jacobs, 1939-41

MOST PUNT RETURNS

Game	8, Jack Jacobs vs. Santa Clara, 1941
Season	34, Darrius Johnson, 1994
Career	88, Joe Washington, 1972-75

MOST PUNT RETURN YARDS

Season	515, Jack Mitchell, 1948
Career	922, Jack Mitchell, 1946-48

BEST PUNT RETURN AVERAGE

Season	45.0, Merrill Green, 1953
Career	23.4, Jack Mitchell, 1946-48

MOST KICKOFF RETURNS

Game	6, Basil Banks vs. Colorado, 1980
Season	18, Everett Marshall, 1969
Career	48, Buster Rhymes, 1980-84

MOST KICKOFF RETURN YARDS

Season	386, Everett Marshall, 1969
Career	1037, Buster Rhymes, 1980-84

BEST KICKOFF RETURN AVERAGE

Season:	35.5, Buster Rhymes, 1980
Career	25.9, Lance Rentzel, 1962-64

MOST POINTS SCORED

Game	30, Steve Owens vs. Nebraska, 1968
	30, Jerald Moore vs. Okla. State, 1994
Season	138, Steve Owens, 1969
Career	336, Steve Owens, 1967-69

MOST TOUCHDOWNS

Game	5, Steve Owens vs. Nebraska, 1968
	5, Jerald Moore, vs. Okla. State, 1994
Season	23, Steve Owens, 1969
Career	56, Steve Owens, 1967-69

MOST EXTRA POINTS MADE

Game	11, Tim Lashar vs. Missouri, 1986
Season	60, Tim Lashar, 1986
Career	194, R.D. Lashar, 1987-90

MOST EXTRA POINTS ATTEMPTED

Game	11, Tim Lashar vs. Missouri, 1986
Season	62, John Carroll, 1971
Career	213, R.D. Lashar, 1987-90

MOST CONSECUTIVE EXTRA POINTS

Season	60, Tim Lashar, 1985
Career	135, Tim Lashar, 1983-86

MOST FIELD GOALS

Game	4, Mike Vachon vs. Texas, 1966
	4, Tim Lashar vs. Penn State, 1985
	Orange Bowl and vs. Okla. State, 1986
Season	16, Scott Blanton, 1992
Career	43, Tim Lashar, 1983-86

MOST POINTS BY A KICKER

Season	96, Tim Lashar, 1986
Career	320, R.D. Lashar, 1987-90

TOTAL TACKLES

Game	22, Brian Bosworth vs. Miami, 1986
Season	182, Jackie Shipp, 1981
Career	506, Daryl Hunt, 1975-78

TACKLES BY A LINEMAN

Game	17, Dewey Selmon vs. Texas, 1974
Season	144, Kevin Murphy, 1983
Career	352, Rick Bryan, 1980-83

TACKLES BY A DEFENSIVE BACK

Game	21, John Anderson vs. Missouri, 1993
Season	97, Monty Johnson, 1970
Career	291, Zac Henderson, 1974-77

TACKLES FOR LOSS

Game	4, Lucious Selmon vs. Kansas, 1973
Season	20, Jimbo Elrod, 1975
Career	44, Jimbo Elrod, 1973-75

INTERCEPTIONS

Season	8, Rickey Dixon, 1987
	8, Scott Case, 1983
Career	17, Darrell Royal, 1946-49

SACKS

Season	14, Cedric Jones, 1994
Career	24, Scott Evans, 1987-90

YEAR BY YEAR LEADERS

RUSHING

Year	Name	Att.	Yds.	TD
1995	Jerald Moore	165	1001	9
1994	Jerald Moore	129	659	10
1993	James Allen	153	788	1
1992	Dewell Brewer	120	561	4
1991	Mike Gaddis	221	1240	14
1990	Dewell Brewer	154	872	8
1989	Mike Gaddis	110	829	10
1988	Charles Thompson	145	829	9
1987	Jamelle Holieway	142	860	10
1986	Jamelle Holieway	139	811	8
1985	Jamelle Holieway	161	861	8
1984	Lydell Carr	138	625	3
1983	Spencer Tillman	188	1047	9
1982	Marcus Dupree	129	905	13
1981	Stanley Wilson	156	1008	4
1980	David Overstreet	96	678	6
1979	Billy Sims	224	1506	22
1978	Billy Sims	231	1762	20
1977	Thomas Lott	139	760	12
1976	Kenny King	141	791	4
1975	Joe Washington	171	871	11
1974	Joe Washington	194	1321	13
1973	Joe Washington	176	1173	10
1972	Greg Pruitt	152	938	13
1971	Greg Pruitt	178	1665	17
1970	Joe Wylie	159	984	12
1969	Steve Owens	358	1523	23

1968	Steve Owens	357	1536	21
1967	Steve Owens	190	808	12
1966	Ron Shotts	149	535	5
1965	Larry Brown	102	344	3
1964	Jim Grisham	146	535	5
1963	Jim Grisham	153	861	8
1962	Joe Don Looney	137	852	9
1961	Mike McClellan	82	508	2
1960	Ronnie Hartline	138	688	0
1959	Prentice Gautt	130	674	4
1958	Prentice Gautt	105	627	2
1957	Clendon Thomas	130	816	9
1956	Tommy McDonald	119	853	12
1955	Tommy McDonald	103	702	14
1954	Bob Herndon	98	588	7
1953	Larry Grigg	130	792	12
1952	Billy Vessels	67	1072	17
1951	Buck McPhail	101	865	3
1950	Billy Vessels	135	870	15
1949	George Thomas	133	859	19
1948	George Thomas	126	835	10
1947	Jack Mitchell	125	573	8
1946	Joe Golding	122	890	13

PASSING

Year	Name	Att.	Cmp.	Int.	Yds.	TD
1995	Eric Moore	200	90	9	1,375	7
1994	Garrick McGee	284	149	13	1,909	8
1993	Cale Gundy	243	144	6	2,096	14
1992	Cale Gundy	227	131	15	1,914	9
1991	Cale Gundy	172	91	7	1,228	8
1990	Cale Gundy	109	54	3	904	4
1989	Steve Collins	49	18	3	442	3
1988	Jamelle Holieway	41	27	2	548	5
1987	Jamelle Holieway	62	21	4	548	7
1986	Jamelle Holieway	63	30	6	541	4
1985	Jamelle Holieway	58	24	2	517	5
1984	Danny Bradley	130	67	6	971	8
1983	Danny Bradley	143	61	8	1,125	7
1982	Kelly Phelps	91	33	9	492	1
1981	Darrell Shepard	56	26	6	371	3
1980	J.C. Watts	78	35	10	905	2
1979	J.C. Watts	81	39	5	785	4
1978	Thomas Lott	55	21	4	440	6
1977	Dean Blevins	29	16	4	347	4
1976	Dean Blevins	44	18	5	370	2
1975	Steve Davis	56	19	7	438	1
1974	Steve Davis	63	26	4	601	11
1973	Steve Davis	92	38	6	934	9
1972	Dave Robertson	110	56	4	1,054	9
1971	Jack Mildren	64	31	2	878	10
1970	Jack Mildren	110	54	1	1,818	7
1969	Jack Mildren	172	79	12	1,319	9
1968	Bob Warmack	186	106	6	1,548	10
1967	Bob Warmack	151	80	6	1,136	8
1966	Bob Warmack	103	57	4	843	4
1965	Gene Cagle	80	34	8	382	0
1964	John Hammond	38	16	1	284	1
1963	Bobby Page	45	13	6	198	2
1962	Monte Deere	65	38	0	789	9
1961	Bobby Page	40	17	6	233	2
1960	Jimmy Carpenter	40	25	3	357	3
1959	Bobby Boyd	54	19	8	256	0
1958	Bobby Boyd	50	24	1	353	5
1957	David Baker	18	12	0	261	3
1956	Jimmy Harris	37	23	1	482	8
1955	Tommy McDonald	24	17	0	265	0
1954	Buddy Leake	26	12	2	249	3
1953	Buddy Leake	21	9	4	138	2
1952	Eddie Crowder	52	30	3	704	6
1951	Eddie Crowder	57	30	1	475	5
1950	Claude Arnold	114	57	1	1,048	13
1949	Darrell Royal	63	34	1	509	4
1948	Darrell Royal	37	18	2	302	5
1947	Jack Mitchell	22	14	2	169	0
1946	Dave Wallace	58	18	7	262	2

PASS RECEIVING

Year	Name	No	Yds	TD
1995	Stephen Alexander	43	580	2
1994	Albert Hall	36	515	0
1993	Rickey Brady	35	536	2
1992	Corey Warren	35	659	3
1991	Corey Warren	26	366	3
1990	Adrian Cooper	13	301	2
1989	Arthur Guess	9	357	5
1988	Eric Bross	14	279	3
1987	Keith Jackson	13	358	4
1986	Keith Jackson	14	403	5
1985	Keith Jackson	20	486	2
1984	Steve Sewell	16	315	2
1983	Buster Rhymes	32	747	3
1982	David Carter	11	218	0
1981	Bobby Grayson	12	249	0
1980	Bobby Grayson	14	389	1
1979	Freddie Nixon	13	257	0
1978	Bobby Kimball	12	198	2
1977	Steve Rhodes	12	226	2
1976	Steve Rhodes	6	160	0
1975	Tinker Owens	9	241	1
1974	Tinker Owens	18	413	5
1973	Tinker Owens	18	472	3
1972	John Carroll	17	343	3
1971	Jon Harrison	17	494	4
1970	Greg Pruitt	19	240	2
1969	Steve Zabel	22	203	1
1968	Eddie Hinton	60	967	6
1967	Eddie Hinton	28	427	3
1966	Ben Hart	33	565	2
1965	Gordon Brown	35	413	1
1964	Lance Rentzel	18	268	2
1963	John Flynn	8	115	1
1962	John Flynn	10	247	1
1961	Jimmy Carpenter	12	143	0
1960	Jerry Payne	6	140	2
1959	Brewster Hobby	10	143	1
1958	Dick Carpenter	11	103	2
1957	Dick Carpenter	8	90	2
1956	Tommy McDonald	12	282	4
1955	Joe Mobra	6	126	1
1954	Max Boydston	11	276	2
1953	Larry Grigg	3	102	1
1952	Max Boydston	13	334	4
1951	John Reddell	13	362	3
1950	Billy Vessels	11	229	2
1949	Jim Owens	15	207	1
1948	Frankie Anderson	9	210	2
1947	Jim Tyree	10	138	1
1946	Jim Owens	19	262	3

SCORING

Year	Name	TD	PAT	2-Pt	FG	Pts
1995	Jeremy Alexander	0	23-24	0	14-17	65
1994	Jerald Moore	11	0	0	0	66
1993	Scott Blanton	0	41-41	0	10-16	71
1992	Scott Blanton	0	27-30	0	16-18	75
1991	Mike Gaddis	14	0	0	0	84
1990	R.D. Lashar	0	50-50	0	15-24	95
1989	R.D. Lashar	0	45-45	0	13-16	84
1988	Charles Thompson	9	0	1	0	56
1987	R.D. Lashar	0	59-63	0	10-15	89
1986	Tim Lashar	0	60-60	0	12-15	96
1985	Tim Lashar	0	43-43	0	15-21	88
1984	Tim Lashar	0	33-34	0	10-13	63

Year	Name					
1983	Spencer Tillman	10	0	0	0	60
1982	Marcus Dupree	13	0	0	0	78
1981	Darrell Shepard	13	0	1	0	80
1980	J.C. Watts	18	0	0	0	108
1979	Billy Sims	22	0	0	0	132
1978	Billy Sims	20	0	0	0	120
1977	Uwe von Schamann	0	47-47	0	14-23	89
1976	Horace Ivy	11	0	0	0	66
1975	Joe Washington	12	0	1	0	74
1974	Joe Washington	14	0	0	0	84
1973	Steve Davis	18	0	0	0	108
1972	Greg Pruitt	14	0	0	0	84
1971	Jack Mildren	17	0	0	0	102
1970	Joe Wylie	13	0	0	0	78
1969	Steve Owens	23	0	0	0	138
1968	Steve Owens	21	0	0	0	126
1967	Steve Owens	12	0	0	0	72
1966	Mike Vachon	0	17-20	0	9-16	44
1965	Gene Cagle	4	0	0	0	24
1964	Lance Rentzel	6	0	0	0	36
1963	Jim Grisham	8	0	0	0	48
1962	Joe Don Looney	10	0	1	0	62
1961	Bobby Page	6	0	1	0	38
1960	Mike McClellan	5	0	0	0	30
1959	Bobby Boyd	10	0	1	0	61
1958	Bobby Boyd	6	0	0	0	36
1957	Clendon Thomas	9	0	0	0	54
1956	Clendon Thomas	18	0	0	0	108
1955	Tommy McDonald	16	0	0	0	96
1954	Buddy Leake	9	25-33	0	0	79
1953	Larry Grigg	13	0	0	0	78
1952	Billy Vessels	18	0	0	0	108
1951	Buddy Leake	13	0	0	0	78
1950	Billy Vessels	15	0	0	0	90
1949	George Thomas	19	3-5	0	0	117
1948	George Thomas	10	0	0	0	60
	Jack Mitchell	10	0	0	0	60
1947	Jack Mitchell	8	0	0	0	48
1946	Joe Golding	13	0	0	0	78

TACKLES

Year	Name	Total
1995	Tyrell Peters, LB	121
1994	Tyrell Peters, LB	101
1993	John Anderson, DB	89
1992	Mike Coats, LB	95
1991	Joe Bowden, LB	127
1990	Joe Bowden, LB	116
1989	Frank Blevins, LB	114
1988	Frank Blevins, LB	92
1987	Danté Jones, LB	118
1986	Brian Bosworth, LB	136
1985	Brian Bosworth, LB	131
1984	Brian Bosworth, LB	128
1983	Kevin Murphy, DE	144
1982	Jackie Shipp, LB	142
1981	Jackie Shipp, LB	142
1980	Mike Coast, LB	111
1979	George Cumby, LB	152
1978	Daryl Hunt, LB	145
1977	Daryl Hunt, LB	152
1976	Daryl Hunt, LB	172
1975	Lee Roy Selmon, DT	132
1974	Rod Shoate, LB	155
1973	Rod Shoate, LB	126
1972	Rod Shoate, LB	132
1971	Steve Aycock, LB	130
1970	Steve Aycock, LB	164

TACKLES FOR LOSS

Year	Name	Total
1995	Baron Tanner, T	7
1994	Tyrell Peters, LB	11
1993	Ricky Wren, NG	4

Year	Name	Total
	John Anderson, DB	4
1992	Ricky Wren, NG	3
	Tremayne Green, LB	3
1991	Reggie Barnes, LB	5
1990	Reggie Barnes, LB	4
1989	Frank Blevins, LB	4
1988	Scott Garl, DB	5
1987	Darrell Reed, DE	5
1986	Brian Bosworth, LB	12
1985	Kevin Murphy, DE	8
1984	Tony Casillas, NG	11
1983	Tony Casillas, NG	6
1982	Kevin Murphy, DE	10
1981	Rick Bryan, DT	9
1980	Scott Dawson, DE	7
1979	Bruce Taton, DE	11
	Johnnie Lewis, NG	11
	Barry Burget, DE	11
1978	Daryl Hunt, LB	10
1977	Phil Tabor, DT	7
	Reggie Kinlaw, DT	7
1976	Reggie Kinlaw, DT	11
1975	Jimbo Elrod, DE	20
1974	Lee Roy Selmon, DT	18
1973	Duane Baccus, DE	14
1972	Raymond Hamilton, DE	14
1971	Lucious Selmon, NG	11
1970	Raymond Hamilton, DE	11

PASSES BROKEN UP

Year	Name	Total
1995	Darrius Johnson, CB	7
1994	Darrius Johnson, CB	10
1993	Darrius Johnson, CB	9
1992	Darnell Walker, CB	8
1991	Darnell Walker, CB	11
1990	Jason Belser, S	9
1989	Terry Ray, S	10
1988	Kevin Thompson, CB	12
1987	Rickey Dixon, S	12
1986	Rickey Dixon, S	6
1985	Tony Rayburn, S	10
1984	Jim Rockford, CB	9
1983	Scott Case, S	8
1982	Keith Stanberry, S	11
1981	Dwight Drane, S	6
1980	Darrell Songy, S	6
1979	Darrol Ray, CB	6
1978	Darrol Ray, CB	9
1977	Zac Henderson, S	4
1976	Jerry Anderson, CB	10
1975	Jerry Anderson, CB	10
1974	Randy Hughes, S	12
1973	Durwood Keaton, S	10
1972	Kenith Pope, CB	12
1971	John Shelley, S	12
1970	Monty Johnson, S	7

INTERCEPTIONS

Year	Name	Total
1995	Larry Bush, CB	4
1994	Darrius Johnson, CB	4
1993	Darrius Johnson, CB	5
1992	Darnell Walker, CB	5
1991	Charles Franks, S	5
	Jason Belser, S	5
1990	Jason Belser, S	4
	Greg DeQuasie, S	4
1989	Jason Belser, S	4
1988	Kevin Thompson, CB	7
1987	Rickey Dixon, S	8
1986	David Vickers, S	3
	Danté Jones, LB	3
	Rickey Dixon, S	3

1985	Sonny Brown, S	5
1984	Jim Rockford	2
	Rickey Dixon, S	2
1983	Scott Case, S	8
1982	Darrell Songy, S	4
	Dwight Drane, S	4
1981	Gary Lowell, S	3
1980	Gary Lowell, S	4
1979	Darrol Ray, CB	4
1978	Darrol Ray, CB	7
1977	Zac Henderson, S	7
1976	Daryl Hunt, LB	4
1975	Jerry Anderson, CB	5
1974	Randy Hughes, S	5
1973	Randy Hughes, S	5
1972	Dan Ruster, S	7
1971	John Shelley, S	5
1970	Monty Johnson, S	5

SACKS

1995	Cedric Jones, DE	11
1994	Cedric Jones, DE	14
1993	Aubrey Beavers, LB	9
1992	Aubrey Beavers, LB	11.5
1991	Reggie Barnes, LB	9
1990	Scott Evans, DT	9
1989	Scott Evans, DT	7
1988	Scott Evans, DT	7
	James Goode, DE	7
1987	Darrell Reed, DE	8
1986	Troy Johnson, DE	7
1985	Kevin Murphy, DE	5
1984	Tony Casillas, DT	10
1983	Kevin Murphy, DE	7

INDIVIDUAL SEASON BESTS

RUSHING YARDAGE

Name	Year	Att	Yards	Avg
1. Billy Sims	1978	231	1,762	7.6
2. Greg Pruitt	1971	178	1,665	9.4
3. Steve Owens	1968	357	1,536	4.3
4. Steve Owens	1969	358	1,523	4.3
5. Billy Sims	1979	224	1,506	6.7
6. Joe Washington	1974	194	1,321	6.8
7. Mike Gaddis	1991	221	1,240	5.6
8. Joe Washington	1973	176	1,173	6.7
9. Jack Mildren	1971	193	1,140	5.9
10. Billy Vessels	1952	167	1,072	6.4
11. Spencer Tillman	1983	188	1,047	5.6
12. Buck McPhail	1952	161	1,018	6.3
13. Stanley Wilson	1981	156	1,008	6.5
14. Jerald Moore	1995	161	1,001	6.1

ALL-PURPOSE YARDS

Name	Year	Total	Rush	Rec	Ret
1. Greg Pruitt	1971	1,946	1,665	108	173
2. Joe Washington	1974	1,904	1,321	71	512
3. Billy Sims	1978	1,797	1,762	35	0
4. Steve Owens	1968	1,752	1,536	94	122
5. Joe Washington	1973	1,744	1,173	89	482
6. Steve Owens	1969	1,558	1,523	32	3
7. Billy Vessels	1952	1,472	1,072	165	285
8. Joe Washington	1975	1,349	871	56	422
9. Mike Gaddis	1991	1,291	1,240	51	0
10. Buster Rhymes	1983	1,199	0	747	452

PASSING ATTEMPTS

Name	Year	Att	Comp	Pct	Yards
1. Garrick McGee	1994	284	149	.542	1,909
2. Cale Gundy	1993	243	144	.592	2,096
3. Cale Gundy	1992	227	131	.577	1,914
4. Bob Warmack	1968	186	106	.563	1,548
5. Cale Gundy	1991	172	91	.529	1,228
	Jack Mildren	1969	172	79	.459	1,319
7. Bob Warmack	1967	151	80	.530	1,136
8. Danny Bradley	1983	143	61	.427	1,125
9. Danny Bradley	1984	130	67	.515	971
10. Claude Arnold	1950	114	57	.500	1,048

PASS COMPLETIONS

Name	Year	Cmp	Att	Pct	Yards
1. Garrick McGee	1994	149	284	.542	1,909
2. Cale Gundy	1993	144	243	.592	2,096
3. Cale Gundy	1992	131	227	.577	1,914
4. Bob Warmack	1968	106	186	.569	1,548
5. Cale Gundy	1991	91	172	.530	1,228
6. Bob Warmack	1967	80	151	.530	1,136
7. Jack Mildren	1969	79	172	.460	1,319
8. Danny Bradley	1984	67	130	.515	971
9. Danny Bradley	1983	61	143	.426	1,125
10. Bob Warmack	1966	57	103	.553	843
	Claude Arnold	1950	57	114	.500	1,048

PASSING YARDAGE

Name	Year	Yards	Pct	Att	Cmp
1. Cale Gundy	1993	2,096	.592	243	144
2. Cale Gundy	1992	1,914	.577	227	131
3. Garrick McGee	1994	1,909	.542	284	149
4. Bob Warmack	1968	1,548	.563	186	106
5. Jack Mildren	1969	1,319	.459	172	79
6. Cale Gundy	1991	1,228	.529	172	91
7. Bob Warmack	1967	1,136	.530	151	80
8. Danny Bradley	1983	1,125	.427	143	61
9. Dave Robertson	1972	1,054	.509	110	56
10. Claude Arnold	1950	1,048	.500	114	57

PASSING EFFICIENCY

Name	Year	Eff	Att-Comp	Yds	TD-Int
1. Jack Mildren	1971	209.9	64-31	878	10-2
2. Monte Deere	1962	206.1	65-38	789	9-0
3. Steve Davis	1974	166.3	63-26	601	11-4
4. Claude Arnold	1950	163.1	114-57	1,048	13-1
5. Dave Robertson	1972	151.1	110-56	1,054	9-4
6. Steve Davis	1973	145.8	92-38	934	9-6
7. Cale Gundy	1993	145.7	243-144	2,096	14-6
8. Darrell Royal	1949	139.6	63-34	509	4-1
9. Bob Warmack	1968	138.2	186-106	1,548	10-6
10. J.C. Watts	1979	134.5	81-39	785	5-4

COMPLETION PERCENTAGE

(Min 20 Attempts)

Name	Year	Pct	Att	Comp	Yds
1. Tommy McDonald	1955	.708	24	17	265
2. Jamelle Holieway	1988	.658	41	27	548
3. Jack Mitchell	1947	.636	22	14	169
4. Jimmy Carpenter	1960	.625	40	25	357
5. Jimmy Harris	1956	.621	37	23	482
6. Cale Gundy	1993	.592	243	144	2,096
7. Claude Arnold	1949	.590	22	13	288
8. Monte Deere	1962	.585	65	38	789
9. Cale Gundy	1992	.577	227	131	1,914
	Eddie Crowder	1952	.577	52	30	704

TOUCHDOWN PASSES

Name	Year	TD	Att	Cmp	Yards
1. Cale Gundy	1993	14	243	144	2,096
2. Claude Arnold	1950	13	114	57	1,048
3. Steve Davis	1974	11	63	26	601
4. Jack Mildren	1971	10	64	31	878
Bob Warmack	1968	10	186	106	1,548
6. Cale Gundy	1992	9	227	131	1,914
Steve Davis	1973	9	92	38	934
Dave Robertson	1972	9	110	56	1,054
Monte Deere	1962	9	65	38	789
10. Cale Gundy	1991	8	172	91	1,228
Danny Bradley	1984	8	130	67	971
Jack Mildren	1970	8	110	54	818
Bob Warmack	1967	8	151	80	1,136

TOTAL OFFENSE

Name	Year	Rush	Pass	Total
1. Cale Gundy	1993	195	2,096	2,291
2. Jack Mildren	1971	1140	878	2,018
3. Garrick McGee	1994	105	1,909	2,014
4. Cale Gundy	1993	-26	1,914	1,888
5. Steve Davis	1973	887	934	1,821
6. Bob Warmack	1968	266	1,548	1,814
7. Jack Mildren	1969	345	1,319	1,664
8. J.C. Watts	1980	663	905	1,568
9. Danny Bradley	1983	426	1,135	1,551
10. Jamelle Holieway	1987	860	548	1,408

PASS RECEPTIONS

Name	Year	Rec	Yards	TD
1. Eddie Hinton	1968	60	967	6
2. Stephen Alexander	1995	43	580	2
3. Albert Hall	1994	36	515	0
4. Rickey Brady	1993	35	536	2
Corey Warren	1992	35	659	3
Gordon Brown	1965	35	413	1
7. Ben Hart	1966	33	565	2
8. Buster Rhymes	1983	32	747	3
9. P.J. Mills	1994	29	432	2
10. Eddie Hinton	1967	28	427	3

RECEPTION YARDS

Name	Year	Yards	Rec	TD
1. Eddie Hinton	1968	967	60	6
2. Buster Rhymes	1983	747	32	3
3. Corey Warren	1992	659	35	3
4. Stephen Alexander	1995	580	43	2
5. Ben Hart	1966	565	33	2
6. Rickey Brady	1993	536	35	2
7. Albert Hall	1994	515	36	0
8. P.J. Mills	1995	507	25	4
9. Jon Harrison	1971	494	17	4
10. Keith Jackson	1985	486	20	2

TOUCHDOWN RECEPTIONS

Name	Year	TD	Rec	Yards
1. Eddie Hinton	1968	6	60	967
2. Corey Warren	1993	5	26	387
Tinker Owens	1974	5	18	413
4. Albert Hall	1992	4	21	234
Keith Jackson	1987	4	13	358
Jon Harrison	1971	4	17	494
Tommy McDonald	1956	4	12	282
Clendon Thomas	1956	4	12	241
P.J. Mills	1995	4	25	507

*Several players tied with 3 TDs

TOUCHDOWNS

Name	Year	Total	Rush	Rec	Ret
1. Steve Owens	1969	23	23	0	0
2. Billy Sims	1979	22	22	0	0
3. Steve Owens	1968	21	21	0	0
4. Billy Sims	1978	20	20	0	0
5. George Thomas	1949	19	19	0	0
6. J.C. Watts	1980	18	18	0	0
Clendon Thomas	1956	18	14	4	0
Billy Vessels	1952	18	17	1	0
Steve Davis	1973	18	18	0	0
10. Jack Mildren	1971	17	17	0	0
Greg Pruitt	1971	17	17	0	0
Tommy McDonald	1956	17	13	4	0

PUNTING AVERAGE

Name	Year	Avg	Att	Yards
1. Joe Washington	1975	50.20	10	502
2. Jack Jacobs	1940	47.80	30	1,434
3. Joe Don Looney	1962	43.41	34	1,476
4. Michael Keeling	1982	43.00	49	2,107
5. Tom Stidham	1966	42.66	48	2,048
6. Michael Keeling	1979	41.87	32	1,340
7. Michael Keeling	1981	41.64	42	1,749
8. Brad Reddell	1989	41.59	37	1,539
9. Brad Reddell	1990	41.57	45	1,871

KICKOFF RETURN YARDAGE

Name	Year	Yards	Att	Avg
1. Everett Marshall	1969	386	18	21.4
2. Otis Taylor	1990	366	15	24.4
3. Eddie Hinton	1966	337	15	22.5
4. Eddie Hinton	1968	317	16	19.5
5. Billy Vessels	1950	309	13	23.8
Buster Rhymes	1983	309	14	22.1
7. Buster Rhymes	1980	283	8	35.5
8. Anthony Stafford	1987	280	11	25.5
9. Joe Washington	1975	275	15	18.3
10. Buster Rhymes	1984	239	10	23.9

KICKOFF RETURN AVERAGE

Name	Year	Avg	Att	Yards
1. Buster Rhymes	1980	35.5	8	283
2. Lance Rentzel	1963	31.3	7	218
3. Stanley Wilson	1979	27.4	7	192
4. Larry Grigg	1953	26.8	8	215
5. Clendon Thomas	1956	26.3	6	158
6. Anthony Stafford	1987	25.5	11	280
7. Ben Hart	1965	24.9	8	199
8. Joe Wylie	1972	24.5	6	147
9. Otis Taylor	1990	24.4	15	366
10. Buster Rhymes	1984	23.9	10	239

PUNT RETURN YARDAGE

Name	Year	Yards	Att	Avg
1. Jack Mitchell	1948	515	22	23.4
2. Joe Washington	1974	332	24	12.7
3. Fred Nixon	1977	266	22	12.9
4. Basil Banks	1979	260	17	15.3
Joe Washington	1973	260	23	10.4
6. Paul Lea	1962	254	17	14.9
7. Darrius Johnson	1994	254	1	7.9
8. Jakie Sandefer	1957	249	17	14.6
9. Freddie Nixon	1978	243	24	10.1
10. Derrick Shepard	1985	241	29	8.3

PUNT RETURN AVERAGE

Name	Year	Avg	Att	Yards
1. Merrill Green	1953	45.0	5	225
2. Eddie Hinton	1966	29.7	8	233
3. Clendon Thomas	1957	25.4	7	178
4. Virgil Boll	1963	23.6	5	118
5. Jack Mithcell	1948	23.4	22	515
6. Bobby Boyd	1958	22.0	6	132
7. Clendon Thomas	1955	19.9	10	199
8. Marcus Dupree	1982	19.2	6	115
9. Tommy McDonald	1954	19.1	7	134
10. Tommy McDonald	1955	18.8	11	207

FIELD GOALS ATTEMPTED

Name	Year	Att	Made	Pct
1. R.D. Lashar	1990	24	15	.625
2. Uwe von Schamann	1977	23	14	.609
3. Tim Lashar	1985	21	15	.714
4. Tony DiRienzo	1975	19	13	.684
5. Scott Blanton	1992	18	16	.889
6. R.D. Lashar	1989	16	13	.813
Mike Vachon	1966	16	9	.563
Scott Blanton	1994	16	11	.690
Scott Blanton	1993	16	10	.625
9. Tim Lashar	1986	15	12	.800
R.D. Lashar	1987	15	10	.666
Rick Fulcher	1972	15	9	.600
Tim Lashar	1983	15	6	.400

FIELD GOALS MADE

Name	Year	Made	Pct	Att
1. Scott Blanton	1992	16	.889	18
2. Tim Lashar	1985	15	.714	21
R.D. Lashar	1990	15	.625	24
4. Uwe von Schamann	1977	14	.609	23
5. R.D. Lashar	1989	13	.813	16
Tony DiRienzo	1975	13	.684	19
7. Tim Lashar	1986	12	.800	15
8. Scott Blanton	1994	11	.690	16
9. Tim Lashar	1984	10	.769	13
R.D. Lashar	1987	10	.666	15
Scott Blanton	1993	10	.625	16

KICK SCORING

Name	Year	Pts	FG-FGA	PAT-A
1. Tim Lashar	1986	96	12-15	60-60
2. R.D. Lashar	1990	95	15-24	50-50
3. R.D. Lashar	1987	89	12-15	59-63
Uwe von Schamann	1977	89	14-23	47-47
5. Tim Lashar	1985	88	15-21	43-43
6. R.D. Lashar	1989	84	13-16	45-45
7. Uwe von Schamann	1978	80	7-11	59-59
John Carroll	1971	80	9-12	53-62
9. Scott Blanton	1992	75	16-18	27-30
10. Scott Blanton	1993	71	10-16	41-41

SCORING

Name	Year	Pts	TD	FG	PAT
1. Steve Owens	1969	138	23	0-0	0-0
2. Billy Sims	1979	132	22	0-0	0-0
3. Steve Owens	1968	126	21	0-0	0-0
4. Billy Sims	1978	120	20	0-0	0-0
5. George Thomas	1949	117	19	3-5	0-0
6. Steve Davis	1973	108	18	0-0	0-0
J.C. Watts	1980	108	18	0-0	0-0
Clendon Thomas	1956	108	18	0-0	0-0
Billy Vessels	1952	108	18	0-0	0-0

TACKLES

Name	Year	No
1. Jackie Shipp	1981	182
2. Daryl Hunt	1976	172
3. Steve Aycock	1970	164
4. Rod Shoate	1974	155
5. Daryl Hunt	1977	152
6. George Cumby	1979	151
7. Daryl Hunt	1978	145
8. Kevin Murphy	1983	144
9. Jackie Shipp	1982	142
10. George Cumby	1977	140

TACKLES FOR LOSS

Name	Year	No
1. Jimbo Elrod	1975	20
2. Lee Roy Selmon	1974	18
3. Jimbo Elrod	1974	15
4. Gary Baccus	1973	14
Raymond Hamilton	1972	14
6. Brian Bosworth	1986	12
Mike Phelps	1975	12
Vic Kearney	1972	12
9. Several tied with 11		

SACKS

Name	Year	No
1. Cedric Jones	1994	14
2. Aubrey Beavers	1992	11.5
3. Tony Casillas	1984	10
4. Reggie Barnes	1991	9
Scott Evans	1990	9
Aubrey Beavers	1993	9
7. Darrell Reed	1987	8
8. Several tied with 7		

*Sack statistics were not recorded until 1983

INTERCEPTIONS

Name	Year	No	Yards
1. Rickey Dixon	1987	8	214
Scott Case	1983	8	110
3. Darrol Ray	1978	7	99
Zac Henderson	1977	7	89
Huel Hamm	1942	7	68
Darrell Royal	1947	7	38
Steve Barrett	1967	7	32
8. Tommy McDonald	1956	6	136
Larry Shields	1963	6	66
Ed Lisak	1948	6	63
Otis Rogers	1938	6	47
Kevin Thompson	1988	6	42

PASSES BROKEN UP

Name	Year	No.
1. Kevin Thompson	1988	12
Rickey Dixon	1987	12
Randy Hughes	1974	12
Kenith Pope	1972	12
John Shelley	1971	12
6. Darnell Walker	1991	11
Keith Stanberry	1982	11
8. Terry Ray	1991	10
Jerry Parks	1988	10
Tony Rayburn	1985	10
Jerry Anderson	1976	10
Jerry Anderson	1975	10
Durwood Keaton	1973	10
Darrius Johnson	1994	10

INDIVIDUAL HONORS

OU ALL-AMERICANS

* Consensus All-American

1991 Joe Bowden*, Linebacker, Mesquite, Texas

1988 Anthony Phillips*, Guard, Tulsa, Oklahoma

1987 Mark Hutson*, Guard, Fort Smith, Arkansas; Keith Jackson*, Tight End, Little Rock, Arkansas; Rickey Dixon*, Defensive Back, Dallas, Texas; Danté Jones*, Linebacker, Dallas, Texas; Darrell Reed, Defensive End, Cypress, Texas

1986 Brian Bosworth*, Linebacker, Irving, Texas; Keith Jackson*, Tight End, Little Rock, Arkansas; Anthony Phillips, Guard, Tulsa, Oklahoma

1985 Brian Bosworth*, Linebacker, Irving, Texas; Tony Casillas*, Noseguard, Tulsa, Oklahoma; Kevin Murphy, Defensive End, Richardson, Texas

1984 Tony Casillas*, Noseguard, Tulsa, Oklahoma

1983 Rick Bryan*, Defensive Tackle, ; Coweta, Oklahoma

1982 Rick Bryan*; Defensive Tackle, , Coweta, Oklahoma

1981 Terry Crouch*, Guard, Dallas, Texas

1980 Terry Crouch, Guard, Dallas, Texas

1979 George Cumby*, Linebacker, Tyler, Texas; Billy Sims*, Halfback, Hooks, Texas

1978 Billy Sims*, Halfback, Hooks, Texas; Reggie Kinlaw, Noseguard, Miami, Florida; Daryl Hunt, Linebacker, Odessa, Texas; Greg Roberts*, Guard, Nacogdoches, Texas

1977 Zac Henderson*, Defensive Back, Burkburnett, Texas; Daryl Hunt, Linebacker, Odessa, Texas; George Cumby, Linebacker, Tyler, Texas; Greg Roberts, Guard, Nacogdoches, Texas; Reggie Kinlaw, Noseguard, Miami, Florida

1976 Mike Vaughan*, Tackle, Ada, Oklahoma; Zac Henderson, Defensive Back, ; Burkburnett, Texas

1975 Lee Roy Selmon*, Defensive Tackle, ; Eufaula, Oklahoma; Dewey Selmon*, Noseguard, Eufaula, Oklahoma; Terry Webb, Guard, Muskogee, Oklahoma; Mike Vaughan, Tackle, Ada, Oklahoma; Billy Brooks, Split End, Austin, Oklahoma; Jimbo Elrod*, Defensive End, Tulsa, Oklahoma; Tinker Owens, Split End, Miami, Oklahoma; Joe Washington, Halfback, Port Arthur, Texas

1974 Joe Washington*, Halfback, Port Arthur, Texas; Rod Shoate*, Linebacker, Spiro, Oklahoma; Lee Roy Selmon, Defensive Tackle, Eufaula, Oklahoma; Dewey Selmon, Noseguard, Eufaula, Oklahoma; Tinker Owens, Split End, Miami, Oklahoma; John Roush*, Guard, Arvada, Colorado; Randy Hughes, Defensive Back, Tulsa, Oklahoma; Kyle Davis, Center, Altus, Oklahoma

1973 Rod Shoate, Linebacker, Spiro, Oklahoma; Eddie Foster, Tackle, Monahans, Texas; Lucious Selmon, Noseguard, Eufaula, Oklahoma

1972 Tom Brahaney*, Center, Midland, Texas; Rod Shoate, Linebacker, Spiro, Oklahoma; Greg Pruitt*, Halfback, Houston, Texas; Derland Moore, Tackle, Poplar Bluff, Missouri

1971 Jack Mildren, Quarterback, Abilene, Texas; Tom Brahaney*, Center, Midland, Texas; Greg Pruitt*, Halfback, Houston, Texas

1969 Steve Zabel, Tight End, Thornton, Colorado; Steve Owens*, Halfback, Miami, Oklahoma; Ken Mendenhall, Center, Enid, Oklahoma

1968 Steve Owens*, Halfback, Miami, Oklahoma

1967 Granville Liggins*, Noseguard, Tulsa, Oklahoma; Bob Kalsu, Tackle, Del City, Oklahoma

1966 Granville Liggins, Noseguard, Tulsa, Oklahoma

1965 Carl McAdams*, Linebacker, White Deer, Texas

1964 Carl McAdams, Linebacker, White Deer, Texas; Ralph Neely*, Tackle, Farmington, New Mexico

1963 Jim Grisham*, Fullback, Olney, Texas; Ralph Neely, Tackle, Farmington, New Mexico

1962 Leon Cross, Guard, Hobbs, New Mexico; Wayne Lee, Center, Ada, Oklahoma; Joe Don Looney, Halfback, Fort Worth, Texas

1959 Jerry Thompson, Tackle, Ada, Oklahoma

1958 Bob Harrison*, Center, Stamford, Texas

1957 Clendon Thomas*, Halfback, ; Oklahoma City, Oklahoma; Bill Krisher*, Guard, Midwest City, Oklahoma

1956 Jerry Tubbs*, Center, Breckenridge, Texas; Bill Krisher, Guard, Midwest City, Oklahoma; Tommy McDonald, Halfback, ; Albuquerque, New Mexico; Ed Gray, Tackle, Odessa, Texas

1955 Bo Bolinger*, Guard, Muskogee, Oklahoma; Tommy McDonald, Halfback, ; Albuquerque, New Mexico

1954 Kurt Burris*, Center, Muskogee, Oklahoma; Max Boydston*, End, Muskogee, Oklahoma

1953 J.D. Roberts*, Guard, Dallas, Texas

1952 Tom Catlin, Center, Ponca City, Oklahoma; Eddie Crowder, Quarterback, Muskogee, Oklahoma; Billy Vessels*, Halfback, Cleveland, Oklahoma; Buck McPhail, Fullback, Oklahoma City, Oklahoma

1951 Jim Weatherall*, Tackle, White Deer, Texas; Tom Catlin, Center, Ponca City, Oklahoma

1950 Leon Heath*, Fullback, Hollis, Oklahoma; Jim Weatherall*, Tackle, White Deer, Texas; Buddy Jones, Safety, Holdenville, Oklahoma; Frankie Anderson, End, Oklahoma City, Oklahoma

1949 Wade Walker, Tackle, Gastonia, North Carolina; Stanley West, Guard, Enid, Oklahoma; Darrell Royal, Quarterback, Hollis, Oklahoma; Jimmy Owens, End, Oklahoma City, Oklahoma; George Thomas, Halfback, Fairland, Oklahoma

1948 Buddy Burris*, Guard, Muskogee, Oklahoma; Jack Mitchell, Quarterback, Arkansas City, Kansas

1947 Buddy Burris, Guard, Muskogee, Oklahoma

1946 Buddy Burris, Guard, Muskogee, Oklahoma; Plato Andros, Guard, Oklahoma City, Oklahoma; John Rapacz, Center, Kalamazoo, Michigan

1939 Frank "Pop" Ivy, End, Skiatook, Oklahoma; Gilford Duggan, Tackle, Davis, Oklahoma

1938 Walter Young*, End, Ponca City, Oklahoma

1937 Pete Smith, End, Muskogee, Oklahoma

1935 J.W. "Dub" Wheeler, Tackle, Davis, Oklahoma

1934 Cash Gentry, Tackle, Lawton, Oklahoma

1927 Granville Norris, Tackle, Laverne, Oklahoma

1920 Phil White, Halfback, ; Oklahoma City, Oklahoma; Roy "Soupy" Smoot, Tackle, Lawton, Oklahoma

1915 Forest "Spot" Geyer, Fullback, Norman, Oklahoma

1913   Claude Reeds, Fullback, Norman, Oklahoma

THREE-TIME ALL-AMERICANS

| 1946-48 | Buddy Burris |
| 1972-74 | Rod Shoate |

TWO-TIME ALL-AMERICANS

1950-51	Jim Weatherall
1951-52	Tom Catlin
1955-56	Tommy McDonald
1956-57	Bill Krisher
1963-64	Ralph Neely
1964-65	Carl McAdams
1966-67	Granville Liggins
1968-69	Steve Owens
1971-72	Greg Pruitt
1971-72	Tom Brahaney
1974-75	Tinker Owens
1974-75	Dewey Selmon
1974-75	Lee Roy Selmon
1974-75	Joe Washington
1975-76	Mike Vaughan
1976-77	Zac Henderson
1977-78	Reggie Kinlaw
1977-78	Greg Roberts
1977-1979	George Cumby
1977-78	Daryl Hunt
1978-79	Billy Sims
1980-81	Terry Crouch
1982-83	Rick Bryan
1984-85	Tony Casillas
1985-86	Brian Bosworth
1986-87	Keith Jackson
1986-1988	Anthony Phillips

MISSOURI VALLEY CONFERENCE SELECTION

1907   Owen Acton, Back

SOUTHWEST CONFERENCE SELECTIONS

1915   Homer Montgomery, End; Oliver Hott, Tackle; Willis Hott, Guard; Hap Johnson, Back; Elmer Capshaw, Back; Forest Geyer, Back
1916   Willis Hott, Guard
1917   W.E. Durant, End; Walt Abbott, Back
1919   Paul Johnston, Tackle; Claude Tyler, Guard; Sol Swatek, Back; Hugh McDermott, Back

MISSOURI VALLEY CONFERENCE SELECTIONS

1920   Howard Marsh, End; Roy Smoot, Tackle; Bill McKinley, Guard; Harry Hill, Back; Sol Swatek, Back
1921   Howard Marsh, End
1922   Howard Marsh, End
1923   King Price, End
1924   Obie Briston, Back
1926   Roy LeCrone, End; Pollack Wallace, Center; Frank Potts, Back
1927   Roy LeCrone, End

BIG SIX CONFERENCE SELECTIONS

1928   Tom Churchill, End
1929   Frank Crider, Back
1930   Hilary Lee, Guard; Buster Mills, Back
1931   Charles Teel, Guard
1932   Ellis Bashara, Guard; Bob Dunlap, Back
1933   Cassius Gentry, Tackle; Ellis Bashara, Guard; James Stacy, Guard; Robert Dunlap, Back
1934   Dub Wheeler, Tackle; Cassius Gentry, Tackle; James Stacy, Guard; Ben Poyner, Back
1935   Dub Wheeler, Tackle; Ralph Brown, Tackle; Nick Robertson, Back; Bill Breedon, Back
1936   Ralph Brown, Tackle; Red Conkwright, Center
1937   Pete Smith, End; Waddy Young, End; Mickey

Parks, Center; Jack Baer, Back
1938   Waddy Young, End; Gilford Duggan, Tackle; Hugh McCullough, Back; Earl Crowder, Back
1939   Frank Ivy, End; Gilford Duggan, Tackle; Justin Bowers, Tackle; Beryl Clark, Back; Robert Seymour, Back
1940   Bill Jennings, End; Roger Eason, Tackle; Harold Lahar, Guard; John Martin, Back
1941   Roger Eason, Tackle; Jack Jacobs, Back
1942   W.G. Lamb, End; Homer Simmons, Tackle; Clare Morford, Guard; Jack Marsee, Center; William Campbell, Back; Huel Hamm, Back
1943   W.G. Lamb, End; Lee Kennon, Tackle; Gale Fulgham, Guard; Bob Mayfield, Center; Bob Brumley, Back; Derald Lebow, Back
1944   W.G. Wooten, End; John Harley, Tackle; Bob Mayfield, Center; Merle Dinkins, End
1945   Omer Burgert, End; Thomas Tallchief, Tackle; Lester Jensen, Guard; John West, Back; Jack Venable, Back
1946   Warren Geise, End; Homer Paine, Tackle; Wade Walker, Tackle; Buddy Burris, Guard; Plato Andros, Guard; John Rapacz, Center; Joe Golding, Back
1947   Jim Tyree, End; Wade Walker, Tackle; Buddy Burris, Guard; John Rapacz, Center; Jack Mitchell, Back

BIG SEVEN CONFERENCE SELECTIONS

1948   Jim Owens, End; Wade Walker, Tackle; Homer Paine, Tackle; Buddy Burris, Guard; Jack Mitchell, Back; George Thomas, Back
1949   Jim Owens, End; Wade Walker, Tackle; Stan West, Guard; Darrell Royal, Back; George Thomas, Back
1950   Frankie Anderson, End; Jim Weatherall, Tackle; Norman McNabb, Guard; Harry Moore, Center; Tom Catlin, Center; Claude Arnold, Back; Billy Vessels, Back; Leon Heath, Back
1951   Art Janes, Tackle; Jim Weatherall, Tackle; Roger Nelson, Guard; Bert Clark, Guard; Fred Smith, Guard; Tom Catlin, Center; Eddie Crowder, Back; Larry Grigg, Back; Buck McPhail, Back
1952   Max Boydston, End; Ed Rowland, Tackle; Jim Davis, Tackle; J.D. Roberts, Guard; Tom Catlin, Center; Eddie Crowder, Back; Billy Vessels, Back; Buck McPhail, Back
1953   Max Boydston, End; Roger Nelson, Tackle; J.D. Roberts, Guard; Kurt Burris, Center; Gene Calame, Back; Larry Grigg, Back
1954   Max Boydston, End; Carl Allison, End; Bo Bolinger, Guard; Kurt Burris, Center; Buddy Leake, Back; Gene Calame, Back
1955   Ed Gray, Tackle; Cal Woodworth, Tackle; Bo Bolinger, Guard; Cecil Morris, Guard; Jerry Tubbs, Center; Jimmy Harris, Back; Tommy McDonald, Back; Bob Burris, Back
1956   John Bell, End; Ed Gray, Tackle; Tom Emerson, Tackle; Bill Krisher, Guard; Jerry Tubbs, Center; Tommy McDonald, Back; Clendon Thomas, Back
1957   Don Stiller, End; Ross Coyle, End; Bill Krisher, Guard; Clendon Thomas, Back

BIG EIGHT CONFERENCE SELECTIONS

1958   Ross Coyle, End; Steve Jennings, Tackle; Gilmer Lewis, Tackle; Dick Corbitt, Guard; Bob Harrison, Center; Prentice Gautt, Back
1959   Jerry Thompson, Guard; Bobby Boyd, Back; Prentice Gautt, Back

1960 Billy White, Tackle
1961 Billy White, Tackle
1962 Dennis Ward, Tackle; Wayne Lee, Center; Jim Grisham, Back; Joe Don Looney, Back
1963 John Flynn, End; Ralph Neely, Tackle; Newt Burton, Guard; Jim Grisham, Back
1964 Ralph Neely, Tackle; Newt Burton, Guard; Jim Grisham, Back; Carl McAdams, Linebacker
1965 Carl McAdams, Linebacker
1966 Ben Hart, Split End; Ed Hall, Offensive Tackle; Eugene Ross, Linebacker
1967 Bob Kalsu, Offensive Tackle; Steve Owens, Running Back; Bob Warmack, Quarterback; John Koller, Defensive End; Granville Liggins, Noseguard
1968 Steve Zabel, Tight End; Ken Mendenhall, Offensive Guard; Eddie Hinton, Wingback; Steve Barrett, Defensive Back
1969 Steve Zabel, Tight End; Ken Mendenhall, Offensive Guard; Bill Elfstrom, Offensive Guard; Steve Owens, Running Back
1970 Joe Wylie, Running Back; Steve Aycock, Linebacker; Monty Johnson, Defensive Back
1971 Albert Chandler, Tight End; Ken Jones, Offensive Guard; Tom Brahaney, Center; Jack Mildren, Quarterback; Greg Pruitt, Running Back; Raymond Hamilton, Defensive End; Derland Moore, Defensive Tackle; Steve Aycock, Linebacker; John Shelley, Defensive Back
1972 Dean Unruh, Offensive Tackle; Tom Brahaney, Center; Greg Pruitt, Running Back; Leon Crosswhite, Fullback; Derland Moore, Defensive Tackle; Lucious Selmon, Defensive Tackle; Raymond Hamilton, Defensive Tackle; Rod Shoate, Linebacker
1973 John Roush, Offensive Guard; Joe Washington, Running Back; Gary Baccus, Defensive End; Lucious Selmon, Defensive Tackle; Rod Shoate, Linebacker; Randy Hughes, Defensive Back
1974 Wayne Hoffman, Tight End; Tinker Owens, Split End; Jerry Arnold, Offensive Tackle; John Roush, Offensive Guard; Terry Webb, Offensive Guard; Joe Washington, Running Back; Jimbo Elrod, Defensive End; Dewey Selmon, Defensive Tackle; Lee Roy Selmon, Defensive Tackle; Rod Shoate, Linebacker; Randy Hughes, Defensive Back
1975 Mike Vaughan, Offensive Tackle; Terry Webb, Offensive Guard; Joe Washington, Running Back; Tony DiRienzo, Kicker; Jimbo Elrod, Defensive End; Dewey Selmon, Middle Guard; Zac Henderson, Defensive Back
1976 Mike Vaughan, Offensive Tackle; Daryl Hunt, Linebacker; Zac Henderson, Defensive Back; Scott Hill, Defensive Back
1977 Karl Baldischwiler, Offensive Tackle; Greg Roberts, Offensive Guard; Thomas Lott, Quarterback; Reggie Kinlaw, Noseguard; George Cumby, Linebacker; Daryl Hunt, Linebacker; Zac Henderson, Defensive Back
1978 Greg Roberts, Offensive Guard; Thomas Lott, Quarterback; Billy Sims, Running Back; Uwe von Schamann, Kicker; Reggie Mathis, Defensive End; Phil Tabor, Defensive Tackle; Reggie Kinlaw, Noseguard; Daryl Hunt, Linebacker; George Cumby, Linebacker; Darrol Ray, Defensive Back
1979 Louis Oubre, Offensive Tackle; Paul Tabor, Center; Billy Sims, Running Back; John

Goodman, Defensive Tackle; George Cumby, Linebacker; Darrol Ray, Defensive Back
1980 Forrest Valora, Tight End; Louis Oubre, Offensive Tackle; Terry Crouch, Offensive Guard; Richard Turner, Defensive Tackle
1981 Lyndle Byford, Offensive Tackle; Terry Crouch, Offensive Guard; Don Key, Offensive Guard; Stanley Wilson, Running Back; Rick Bryan, Defensive Tackle
1982 Steve Williams, Offensive Guard; Paul Parker, Offensive Guard; Marcus Dupree, Running Back; Kevin Murphy, Defensive End; Rick Bryan, Defensive Tackle; Jackie Shipp, Linebacker
1983 Chuck Thomas, Center; Kevin Murphy, Defensive End; Rick Bryan, Defensive Tackle; Jackie Shipp, Linebacker; Scott Case, Defensive Back
1984 Danny Bradley, Quarterback; Darrell Reed, Defensive End; Tony Casillas, Noseguard; Brian Bosworth, Linebacker
1985 Jamelle Holieway, Quarterback; Anthony Phillips, Offensive Tackle; Mark Hutson, Offensive Guard; Keith Jackson, Tight End; Darrell Reed, Defensive End; Kevin Murphy, Defensive End; Tony Casillas, Noseguard; Brian Bosworth, Linebacker
1986 Jamelle Holieway, Quarterback; Anthony Phillips, Offensive Tackle; Mark Hutson, Offensive Guard; Keith Jackson, Tight End; Tim Lashar, Kicker; Brian Bosworth, Linebacker; Darrell Reed, Defensive End; David Vickers, Defensive Back; Steve Bryan, Defensive Tackle; Rickey Dixon, Defensive Back
1987 Mark Hutson, Offensive Guard; Keith Jackson, Tight End; Greg Johnson, Offensive Tackle; Bob Latham, Center; Anthony Phillips, Offensive Guard; Rickey Dixon, Defensive Back; Danté Jones, Linebacker; Darrell Reed, Defensive End; David Vickers, Defensive Back
1988 Anthony Phillips, Offensive Guard; Charles Thompson, Quarterback; Scott Evans, Defensive Tackle; Scott Garl, Defensive Back; Curtice Williams, Defensive Tackle; Tony Woods, Noseguard
1989 Frank Blevins, Linebacker; Scott Evans, Defensive Tackle; Dante Williams, Noseguard
1990 Adrian Cooper, Tight End; Mike Sawatzky, Offensive Guard; Scott Evans, Defensive Tackle; Joe Bowden, Linebacker; Jason Belser, Defensive Back
1991 Reggie Barnes, Defensive End; Jason Belser, Defensive Back; Joe Bowden, Linebacker; Brian Brauninger, Offensive Tackle; Mike Gaddis, Running Back
1992 Darnell Walker, Defensive Back
1993 Aubrey Beavers, Linebacker; Rickey Brady, Tight End; Mario Freeman, Linebacker; Cale Gundy, Quarterback
1994 Cedric Jones, Defensive End; Darrius Johnson, Defensive Back; Scott Blanton, Kicker
1995 Stephen Alexander, Tight End; Tyrell Peters, Linebacker; Jeremy Alexander, Kicker

HEISMAN MEMORIAL TROPHY

(Player of the Year)
1952 Billy Vessels, Halfback, Cleveland, Okla.
1969 Steve Owens, Tailback, Miami, Okla.
1978 Billy Sims, Halfback, Hooks, Texas

MAXWELL MEMORIAL AWARD

(Player of the Year)
1956 Tommy McDonald, Halfback, Albuquerque, N.M.

WALTER CAMP TROPHY

(Player of the Year)
1956 Jerry Tubbs, Center, Breckenridge, Texas
1969 Steve Owens, Tailback, Miami, Okla.
1978 Billy Sims, Halfback, Hooks, Texas

OUTLAND TROPHY

(Outstanding Lineman)
1951 Jim Weatherall, Tackle, White Deer, Texas
1953 J.D. Roberts, Guard, Dallas, Texas
1975 Lee Roy Selmon, Tackle, Eufaula, Okla.
1978 Greg Roberts, Offensive Guard, Nacogdoches, Texas

DICK BUTKUS AWARD

(Outstanding Linebacker)
1985 Brian Bosworth, Linebacker, Irving, Texas
1986 Brian Bosworth, Linebacker, Irving, Texas

VINCE LOMBARDI AWARD

(Outstanding Lineman)
1975 Lee Roy Selmon, Tackle, Eufaula, Okla.
1985 Tony Casillas, Noseguard, Tulsa, Okla.

HELMS AND CITIZENS SAVINGS ATHLETIC FOUNDATION

(Player of the Year)
1954 Kurt Burris, Center, Muskogee, Okla.
1969 Steve Owens. Tailback, Miami, Okla.
1978 Billy Sims, Halfback, Hooks, Texas

THE SPORTING NEWS AWARD

(Player of the Year)
1956 Tommy McDonald, Halfback, Albuquerque, N.M.

FOOTBALL NEWS

(Freshman of the Year)
1982 Marcus Dupree, Tailback, Philadelphia, Miss.

JIM THORPE AWARD

(Outstanding Defensive Back)
1987 Rickey Dixon, Safety, Dallas, Texas

WASHINGTON, D.C., TOUCHDOWN CLUB

(Player of the Year)
1972 Greg Pruitt, Halfback, Houston, Texas
1974 Joe Washington, Halfback, Port Arthur, Texas

CHEVROLET ABC

(Offensive Player of the Year)
1971 Jack Mildren, Quarterback, Abilene, Texas

CHEVROLET ABC

(Defensive Player of the Year)
1973 Lucious Selmon, Noseguard, Eufaula, Okla.

LINEMAN OF THE YEAR

1953 J.D. Roberts, Guard, Dallas, Texas (AP, UPI, Fox Movietime News)
1954 Kurt Burris, Center, Muskogee, Okla. Philadelphia Sports Writers)
1954 Max Boydston, End, Muskogee, Okla. (Washington Touchdown Club)
1956 Jerry Tubbs, Center, Breckenridge, Texas (UPI)
1958 Bob Harrison, Center, Samford, Texas (UPI)
1967 Granville Liggins, Noseguard, Tulsa, Okla. (UPI)
1985 Tony Casillas. Noseguard, Tulsa, Okla. (UPI)

NATIONAL FOOTBALL HALL OF FAME

1961 Claude Reeds, Fullback, Norman, Okla.
1973 Forrest "Spot" Geyer, Fullback, Norman, Okla.
1974 Billy Vessels, Halfback, Cleveland, Okla.
1982 Jim Owens, End, Oklahoma City, Okla.

1985 Tommy McDonald, Halfback, Albuquerque, N.M.
1986 Walter Young, End, Ponca City, Okla.
1988 Lee Roy Selmon, Defensive Tackle, Eufaula, Okla.
1991 Steve Owens, Halfback, Miami, Okla.
1992 Jim Weatherall, Tackle, White Deer, Texas
1993 J.D. Roberts, Guard, Dallas, Texas

NATIONAL FOOTBALL COACHES HALL OF FAME

1951 Bennie Owen, 1905-26
1969 Bud Wilkinson, 1947-63

HELMS AND CITIZENS SAVINGS ATHLETIC FOUNDATION

1969 Buddy Burris, Guard, 1946-48
1975 Jim Weatherall, Tackle, 1949-51
1975 Greg Pruitt, Halfback, 1970-72

HELMS AND CITIZENS SAVINGS ATHLETIC COACHES HALL

1969 Bennie Owen, 1905-26
1969 Bud Wilkinson, 1947-63

NCAA FOOTBALL PLAYER OF THE YEAR

(Selected by Washington, D.C., Pigskin Club)
1972 Greg Pruitt, Halfback, Houston, Texas
1974 Joe Washington, Halfback, Port Arthur, Texas

NEW YORK ATHLETIC CLUB DEFENSIVE BACK OF THE

1977 Zac Henderson, Free Safety, Burkburnett, Texas

DAVEY O'BRIEN AWARD

(Outstanding back from Texas)
1978 Billy Sims, Halfback, Hooks, Texas

NCAA TOP SIX AWARD

1987 Keith Jackson, Tight End, Little Rock, Ark.
1988 Anthony Phillips, Offensive Guard, Tulsa, Okla.

LETTERMEN LIST

According to intercollegiate athletic records, the following men lettered at Oklahoma in the years indicated (through 1995)

* Date unavailable; (M) indicates manager; (T) trainer

A Abbott, George C. 1916; Abbott, Wallace 1917; Acker, Mark (T)*; Acker, Neal W. 1972; Acree, Jim 1949,52,53; Acton, Owen E. 1905,06,07; Adkins, David 1975(M); Adkins, Kevin 1983,84,85; Ahrens, Conrad 1934,35,36; Aikman, Troy 1984,85; Alexander, Stephen 1994,95; Alfieri, Jerry 1963,64,65,66; Alfred, Joey 1994; Aljoe, Mike 1983,84,85; Allen, Fred 1907; Allen, James 1993,94,95; Allen, Keith 1995(M); Allen, Robert L., II 1992,94,95; Allen, Russell 1990,91,92,94; Allen, Sam 1951,52; Allford, V. Larry 1963,64,65; Allison, Carl 1951,52,53,54; Allsup, John V. 1946,47; Allton, Joe 1940,41; Ambrister, Hubert 1910,11,12,13; Andarakes, Drake 1973,74; Anderegg, Dan 1947; Anderson, Bruce 1972(T); Anderson, Frank G. 1947; Anderson, George 1914,15; Anderson, Jerry O. 1975,76; Anderson, John 1991,92,93,94; Anderson, Rotnei 1985,86,87,88; Anderson, Vickey Ray 1977,78; Andros, Dee G. 1949; Andros, Plato 1946; Angel, Keith F. 1980; Antone, Tony 1977,78; Arbuckle, Dale 1923,24,25,26; Armstrong, Charles 1907,08,09; Armstrong, Tyrone 1973; Arnold, Claude 1948,49,50; Arnold, Gerald K. 1972,73,74; Arnold, Lee 1900; Aston, Roscoe 1901; Atkins, Arthur 1994,95; Atyia, Darren 1983; Austman, George 1967; Austin, John 1944; Avent, Bob 1945; Aycock, Steve 1969,70,71.

B Babb, Mike 1976,77,78,79; Baccus, Duane 1974,75,76; Baccus, Gary 1970,72,73; Backes, Tom 1987,88,89,90; Baer, Jack 1935,36,37; Bagby, Boots 1966; Bagwell, Paul W. 1966; Bailey, Calvin 1988; Bailey, Manley 1912; Bailey, Warren 1921; Baily, Gary 1974; Baker, Boone 1942,43; Baker, Charles 1967; Baker, David 1957,58; Baker, Frank 1916; Balcer, Frank 1916; Baldischwiler, Karl 1975,76,77; Baldridge, Richard D. 1967,68,69; Baldwin, James 1989,92; Ball, Fred S., Jr. 1935,36,37; Ballard, Hugh C. 1951,55,56; Banks, Basil M. 1977,78,79,80; Barkett, Woody 1945; Barnes, Reggie 1989,90,91,92; Barnoskie, Gary 1974; Barr, Johnny 1968,69; Barresi, John 1973,74; Barrett, J. Rodney 1986(T); Barrett, Steve J. 1966,67,68; Barrow, Edwin 1896,97; Base, Michael 1963,64,65,66; Basham, Jim 1945; Bashara, Ellis 1931,32,33; Bass, Maurice 1918; Baublit, Randy 1994(M); Bayles, Marion 1963; Beattie, Richard L. 1961; Beavers, Aubrey 1992,93,94; Bechtold, Earl 1917,19; Bechtold, William B. 1979,80,81; Beck, Wesley W. 1933,35; Becker, Max 1902; Beckman, William 1950; Belcher, Page 1918; Bell, Curry 1913,14,15; Bell, Glenn 1988; Bell, John H. 1954,55,56; Bell, Roy Lemount 1969,70,71; Belser, Jason 1988,89,90,91; Bene, Fred 1895; Benien Jr., Paul F. 1959,60,61; Benien, John David 1961; Bennett, W. Gary, Jr. 1985,86,87; Benson, Thomas 1980,81,82,83; Bentley, David P. 1975; Berg, Robert P. 1973,74; Bergman, Deroy 1945; Berry, Curtis 1928,29,30,31; Berry, Harry L. 1926,27,28; Berry, John 1901; Berry, Mike 1978; Berry, Roger E. 1910,11,12; Berryhill, Darin 1981,83,84,85; Bibb, Boyd 1946,47; Bigby, Byron 1966,67,68; Birge, Laddie V. 1940,41; Birks, Mike 1974,75,76; Bishop, Bobby 1979,81; Bishop, Gary 1975; Blake, John 1979,80,81,82; Blanton, Scott 1991,92,93,94; Blevins, Dean 1974,75,76,77; Blevins, Frank 1987,88,89,90; Blodgett, Mark 1988,89,91; Blubaugh, Tom 1984(M); Boatright, Lloyd 1922; Bobo, Robert, 1987(M); Bodenhamer, Bob 1945,47,48,49; Bodin, Jeffrey R. 1974,75; Bodine, Hugh 1904; Bogle, Clyde 1899,1900,01,02,03; Bohannon, Craig 1994; Bolinger, Bo 1953,54,55; Boll, Virgil Lloyd 1961,62,63; Bolton, Jerry 1937,38,39; Bookout, Billy 1951; Borah, Oren 1930,31; Bosworth, Brian K. 1984,85; Boudreau, George 1941; Boudreau, Raphael 1936,37,38; Boudreaux, Richard 1963; Bourland, Joe 1991(T); Bowden, Joe 1989,90,91; Bowen, Jim 1957(M); Bowers, Justin 1938,39; Bowles, R.C. 1921,22,23; Bowman, Charles "Chuck" 1957; Bowman, Dick 1951,52,53; Boyd, Bobby 1957,58,59; Boyd, James 1989; Boydston, Max 1951,52,53,54; Boyle, Dorsey 1917,19; Braden, Kent 1951,52(M); Bradford, Kent 1977,78; Bradley, Danny L. 1981,82,83,84; Bradley, John 1988,91; Bradley, Lester E. 1959; Brady, Barry 1974; Brady, Rickey 1990,91,92,93; Brahaney, Tom 1970,71,72; Brauninger, Brian 1990,91; Breathett, Sherdeill H. 1980,81; Brecht, Martin B. 1974; Breeden, Charles 1943; Breeden Joe, Jr. 1943; Breeden, J.W. 1935,36; Brewer, Dewell 1989,90,91,92; Brewer, George W.,

Jr. 1946,47,48,49; Brewer, Otto 1916; Brewington, Carl 1941; Bridges, John 1935; Bridges, Richard 1984; Briggs, Larry 1975; Brindley, Bob 1945; Brinkman, Wade 1988(M); Briscoe, Albert 1916,19; Bristow, J. Gordon "Obie" 1922,23,24; Britt, Jodie Dean 1985; Brockman, Ed 1923,24,25; Brooks, Bill 1973,74,75; Bross, Eric B. 1986,87,88,89; Bross, Larry A. 1968; Brown, Sidney, Jr. 1974,75,76; Brown, C.D. "Sonny" 1983,84,85,86; Brown, Don K. 1952,53,54; Brown, Gordon 1963,64,65; Brown, Jim 1905; Brown, Joe A. 1917; Brown, Joe 1994,95; Brown, Larry 1963,64,65; Brown, Mart 1925,26,27; Brown, Melvin 1950,52,53; Brown, Ralph 1934,35,36; Brown, Terence 1993,94,95; Brown, Victor Larue 1975,76; Brown, William H. 1955,56; Browne, Howard 1907; Broyles, J. Henry, Jr. 1955,56; Brumley, Bob 1943; Bryan, Mitch W. 1982,83; Bryan, Rick D. 1980,81,82,83; Bryan, Steven R. 1983,84,85; Bryant, Anthony 1973,74,75,76; Bryce, C.F. 1942; Buchanan, Dennis 1972,73,75; Buchanan, James N. 1909; Bullard, David 1994,95; Bumgardner, Allen W. 1962,63,64; Bunge, Paul, 1972; Burch, Wyatt 1901,02,03,06; Burgar, Jim 1966,67; Burgert, Eran Omer, Jr. 1943,44,45; Burgess, Rickey T. 1966; Burget, Barry 1976,77,78,79; Burget, Grant 1972,73,74; Burkett, Vernon D. 1964,65,66; Burkhart, Jon 1992(T); Burks, Brent 1982,83,84; Burns, Artis 1993,94; Burns, Greg 1964; Burns, Mike 1965; Burris, Kurt 1951,52,53,54; Burris, Lynn 1956; Burris, Paul "Buddy" 1946,47,48; Burris, Robert R. 1953,54,55; Burson, H.T. 1896; Burton, Newton 1962,63,64; Burton, Sam 1910,12; Bush, Larry 1992,93,94,95; Butts, Wes 1965,66,67; Buxton, C.C. 1930; Byerly, Jim 1959; Byford, Lyndle 1979,80,81; Bynum, Chester L. 1951,52.

C Cabbiness, Carl 1985,86,87,88; Cabbiness, Chris 1988,89,90; Cagle, Gene 1965,66,67; Calame, Gene 1951,52,53,54; Calonkey, Steve 1973; Campbell, Bill 1940,41,42; Campbell, Chris 1993,94,95; Campbell, David 1992,93,94; Campbell, Ralph 1907,08; Campbell, Roy 1908; Cantrell, Marshall 1973; Capshaw, Elmer 1912,13,14,15; Capshaw, Fred 1908,09,10,11; Carey, Orville J. 1931,32,33; Cargill, Brett 1976,77; Carlyle, Bill 1964,65; Carman, Jack P. 1927; Carnahan, Sam D. 1950; Carner, James 1978,79,80; Carollo, Joe 1993,95; Carpenter, Dick 1957,58,59; Carpenter, E.J. 1958,60,61; Carr, Lydell 1984,85,86,87; Carroll, Hugh 1904; Carroll, John 1971,72,74; Carroll, Tom M. 1953,54; Carter, Bobby 1984; Carter, David, 1981,82; Carter, Gary 1972; Carter, Melvin 1989,90,92; Cartwright, Roy 1954; Case, Scott 1982,83; Casey, Clay 1936; Casillas, Tony 1982,83,84,85; Cason, Owen T. 1933; Cassett, Steve 1968,69,70; Catlin, Tom A. 1950,51,52; Cavil, Ben 1991,92,93,94; Cawthon, Pete W., Jr. 1941,42; Chambers, Evans E. 1931; Chandler, Albert M. 1970,71,72; Chandler, Dwayne 1992,93,94; Chase, Martin 1994,95; Cherry, Fred 1930,31; Chiles, Clay 1933; Chilless, Bill 1947,48,49; Choate, Phillip 1988(T); Chrisman, Gary 1968,69,70; Christian, Brian 1995(M); Christian, Moe 1992(M); Christmon, Drew 1990,91,92; Churchill, Tom, Sr. 1927,28,29; Clammer, Sam 1927; Clapham, Jasper 1895,96,97,98,99; Clapham, Sam 1976,77,78; Clark, Bert 1949,50,51; Clark, Beryl 1938,39; Clark, Carl 1919; Clark, Glenn C. 1909,10,11,12; Clark, Waymon 1973; Clark, William 1912,13,14; Clark, William, N. 1905; Clay, Nigel 1988; Clearman, David 1970(M); Clements, Alex 1902,03; Clewis, Paul 1981,82,83; Clopton, Mike 1983; Coast, Mike 1978,79,80; Coats, Michael 1990,91,92,93; Cobbs, John 1978; Cockrell, Gene 1954; Coffman, Randy 1972; Cohane, Tim 1967; Coker, Jeff 1933,34; Cole, J.W. 1949,50; Coleman, Royce 1979; Collier, Perry 1993,94; Collier, Terry 1992,93,94; Collins, Egean 1983; Collins, Herve T. 1914; Collins, Patrick 1984,85,86,87; Collins, Steve 1989,90,91,92; Collins, Tink 1989,90,91,92; Comeaux, Glenn 1973,74,75; Comer, Jason 1992,93,94,95; Condren, Glen P. 1962,63,64; Conkright, William 1934,35,36; Conrad, J. R. 1992,93,94,95; Conrad, Rich 1988; Coody, Reed 1972; Cook, Edward 1904; Cook, James Duane 1960,61,62; Cook, Paul 1987; Cookman, Jeff 1986(T); Cooper, Adrian 1987,88,89,90; Coots, Earl 1910; Copher, Brian 1985(M); Coppage, Alton 1937,38,39; Corbitt, Dick 1957,58; Corbitt, Tom R. 1964(M); Corey, Orville J. 1931,32,33; Cornelius, George R. 1950,51,52; Cornell, Bob 1958,59,60; Correia, Joe 1992,94; Corrotto, Albert 1935,36,37; Corrotto, Eugene F. 1936,37,38; Coshow,

154   *Sooners Handbook*

Larry 1980; Couch, Jeffrey A. 1979; Counter, Ron 1987; Courtright, Raymond 1911,12,13,14; Covin, Bill 1951; Cowan, Jackie R. 1961,63; Cowling, L.A. 1941; Cox, R.A. 1934; Cox, Thomas S. 1959,60,61; Coyle, Ross 1956,57,58; Crafts, Jerry 1988; Craig, Kevin 1976; Craig, Robert Edward 1965,66,67; Crider, Frank 1927,28,29; Crook, Justin 1988(M); Cross, D. Leon 1960,61,62; Cross, Jerry L. 1953; Cross, Rick D. 1980; Cross, W.J. 1904,05,06,07; Crosswhite, Kenneth 1975; Crosswhite, Leon M. 1970,71,72; Crosswhite, Rodney 1964,65,66; Crouch, Terry 1979,80,81; Crowder, Earl F. 1936,37,38; Crowder, Eddie 1950,51,52; Crowder, Stan 1965; Crudup, Derrick 1985,86,87; Crutchmer, Larry 1965,66,67; Culbreath, James C., Jr. 1975,76; Cullen, Ronald J. 1920,21,22; Culley, Blair 1992; Culver, David 1982; Culver, Ed 1978,79,80,81; Culver, Max 1944; Cumby, George 1976,77,78,79; Cummings, Jim 1979(M); Cummings, Millard 1944; Cunningham, Glenn 1959; Cunningham, Joe 1950; Curnett, E. Lee 1931; Curtis, Joe 1976,77; Cutchall, Dean B. 1935.

D Dalke, Bill 1975,76; Dambro, Guntar 1972(M); Darnell, Bobby J. 1952,53,54,55; Daughtry, Tim 1994,95; Davis, Arlo 1917,19,20; Davis, Danny 1979(M); Davis, Don W. 1966; Davis, Ernest 1945; Davis, George 1975; Davis, Heath 1995(T); Davis, James W. 1957,58,59; Davis, Jim 1951,52; Davis, Kyle 1972,73,74; Davis, Sam A. 1961; Davis, Skivey A.R. 1917,19,20; Davis, Steve 1973,74,75; Davis, Thomas "Eddy" 1941,42,46,47; Davis, Wendell 1994,95; Dawson, Chris 1993,94,95; Dawson, Russell Scott 1977,79,80,81; Day, Ernest B. 1955,56; Day, Lionell 1968,69,70,71; Dayton, Max 1971; Deacon, Erl E. 1917,18,19,20; Deere, Monte M. 1960,61,62; DeLoney, Bruce Edward 1969,70,71; Delozier, Brown 1980,82; Dempsey, Jackie L. "Bud" 1962; Denton, Sammy L. "Bo" 1967,68; Denton, Tim 1994,95; Depue, L. Dale 1956,57; DeQuasie, Brent 1992,93,94,95; DeQuasie, Greg 1988,89,90,91; Derr, Bruce J. 1968,69,70; Derrick, Robert 1954,55,56; Desmond, Jim 1943; Dewberry, Glenn 1969,71; Dickey, Donald F. 1960; Dickson, Wayne 1987,88,89; Dillard, Stacy 1988,89,90,91; Dillingham, David 1983,84; Dillingham, W. David 1969; Dillon, Richard 1984,86,87,88; Dinkins, Merle L. 1943,44,46,47; DiRienzo, Tony 1973,74,75; Dittman, Barry Robert 1975,77,78,79; Dixon, Greg 1987,89; Dixon, Rickey 1984,85,86,87; Dobbs, James Mark 1982(M); Dodd, Carl 1955,56,57; Dodd, Gary Steve 1971,72,73; Dodd, Sidney 1982,83; Dodds, James Lawrence 1974,75,76; Dodson, Ted E. 1963; Dollarhide, Louis 1944; Donaghey, Jerry 1953; Douglas, Alfred G. 1917,18; Douglas, Willard 1906,09; Dowell, Charles 1947,48,49; Downing, Dewayne 1979,82; Downs, Albert 1942; Drake, Bruce 1927,28; Drane, Dwight 1980,81,82,83; Driscoll, Mark W. 1970,71; Dubler, Rick 1984; Duggan, Gilford 1937,38,39; Duke, Richard Lawrence 1975; Duncan, Terry 1990; Dunkleberger, Scott 1994(T); Dunlap, Robert L. 1931,32,33; Dunn, Bert 1895; Dunn, Lewis 1943; Dunng, Holly 1994(T); Dupree, Marcus 1982; Durant, W.E. 1916,17; Durham, Jere 1957,58; Dutton, Richard L. 1974; Dutton, Todd 1975; Dye, Alan 1973; Dykes, Billy 1988,91.

E Earnest, Rick 1988(M); Earthman, Bill 1982,83,84; Eason, Roger 1939,40,41; Eck, Robert 1988; Ederer, John 1955,56,57; Edgeman, Harold C. 1938; Edmonson, A.V. 1920,21,22; Edmonson, Charles Van 1920,21,22; Elam, Willis 1954; Elfstrom, W.W. "Bill" 1967,68,69; Ellington, Sidney 1983(M); Ellis, Harry H. 1933,34,35; Ellis, Richard F. 1951,52; Ellstrom, Marvin 1931; Ellsworth, Ferd 1933,35,36; Elrod, James W. 1973,74,75; Emel, Thomas Jeffrey 1974; Emerson, Thomas E. 1954,55,56; Emerson, John F. 1969,70,71; English, Porter 1908,09; Ervin, Greg 1990,91; Erwin, Bill 1945; Estep, Robert 1943,44; Estes, H.O. 1960; Evans, Chez 1973,74,75,76; Evans, J.C. 1895; Evans, Richard 1958; Evans, Richard W. 1974; Evans, Scott 1987,88,89,90; Evans, Tommy 1994(M); Ewbank, James B. 1948,52; Ewing, Darrell L. 1929,30.

F Farley, Gerald 1992; Farthing, Jody 1976,77,78; Fauble, Don 1942; Favor, Richard E. 1938,39; Feagan, Jimmy 1958; Ferguson, Glenn 1981; Ferguson, Milton 1899; Ferrer, Paul G. 1981,82,84,85; Fields, Jess 1914,16; Fields, Mike 1991,92; Fields, Robert D. 1928,29,30; Fields, Troy 1984; Files, Jim 1967,68,69; Finch, Lonnie 1985,86,87; Fischer, Max 1941,46,47; Fisher, Rod 1988,89,91; Fitch, Ken 1943; Flanagan, Orlando 1980,81; Flanagan, Robert 1965; Fleetwood, Harold E. 1932,33; Fleming, L.B. 1923; Flemons, Tommy 1980,82,83; Fletcher, Ron 1964; Flint, Earl 1928,29; Flood, Alger W. 1969; Flynn, John 1962,63; Fogle, Anthony 1993,94,95; Foley, Mark J. 1980; Fontenette, Johnny

1980,82,83; Ford, Harry 1896,97,98; Forrest, Dugan 1987; Foster, Ed 1971,72,73; Foster, Jerry 1975; Foster, Raybourne 1915; Fox, Dave 1908; Francis, William Raleigh 1933,34,35; Franklin, Willie 1970,71; Franks, Charles 1988,89,90,91; Frazer, David P. 1968; Frazier, Jeff 1994,95; Freeman, Mario 1992,93,94; Friday, Elmer 1945; Friedrichs, L.G. 1939; Fulcher, Rick 1972,73; Fulghum, Gale 1943; Fultz, Eric 1988,90,91; Funk, John H. 1941; Fuqua, Karey A. 1933,34,35.

G Gaddis, Mike 1988,89,91; Gaines, Ryan 1994(T); Gambill, Jess 1898; Gambrell, Bob 1944; Gambrell, Rick E. 1971,72,73,74; Gammil, Floyd 1916; Garl, Michael Scott 1985,86,87,88; Garrett, John C. 1962,63,64; Gary, Keith 1979,80; Gassoway, Jim 1943; Gatewood, Evan 1983,84,85; Gaut, Robert N. 1951,52; Gautt, Prentice 1957,58,59; Gaynor, Joe 1951; Geerts, Greg 1985(M); Gentry, Cash 1933,34; Gentry, Malcomb 1914; Gentry, Weldon C. 1928,29; Geren, David R. 1971; Geyer, Forest 1913,14,15; Gibbons, George 1941,42; Gibbs, Gary L. 1972,73,74; Giese, Warren 1946; Giles, Barry 1994,95; Giller, Tre 1987,88; Gilstrap, Jimmy R. 1961,62,63; Ging, Jack 1951,52,53; Glenn, Ledell 1985; Goad, Robert W. 1946,47,48,49; Goff, Duane 1953,54,55; Golding, Joe 1941,46; Goldsby, Jerry 1963,64; Goodall, Buddy 1942; Goode, James 1988,89,90; Goodlow, Daryl 1980,82,83; Goodman, John 1976,77,78,79; Goodwin, Rick 1965,66,67; Gordon, Murray 1927; Gordon, Tracy 1988,89,90; Gorka, Bryan 1991,92,94; Graalman, Gordon 1931; Grace, George 1936,37; Graham, Bobbye 1994(M); Graham, Elbert 1979,80,81; Graham, Hershel A. 1918,19,22; Graham, Thomas 1916,17; Gravitt, Bert W. 1962; Gray, Edmund 1954,55,56; Gray, Tom 1948,49,50; Grayson, Bobby 1979,80,81; Grayson, Joseph P. 1967; Greathouse, Myrle 1942,46,47,48; Green, Fred 1901,03; Green, John 1987; Green, Karl 1973; Green, Merrill 1950,52,53; Green, Stanley 1942; Green, Tremayne 1992,94; Greenberg, Alan 1945; Greene, Emmitt "Mickey" 1986; Greenlee, C. Wayne 1954,55; Griffin, Bennett 1916; Griffis, Russell D. 1977,78; Grigg, Larry 1951,52,53; Grimmett, Tom 1931; Grisham, Jim C. 1962,63,64; Guess, Arthur 1987,88,89,90; Guffey, Roy 1923,24,25; Gundy, Cale 1990,91,92,93; Gwinn, Richard L. 1956,57,58; Gwinn, Robert, 1989(M).

H Haag, Heinie W. 1931; Haberlein, Jack 1940,41; Haddad, David 1979; Hake, Jeff 1983,84,85; Hale, David 1984; Hale, Earl P. 1946,47,48; Hale, Joe Cliff 1974; Halfman, Peter F. 1970,72; Hall, Albert 1991,92,93,94; Hall, Bernard 1987; Hall, Brian 1980,82,83,84; Hall, Charles E. "Ed" 1964,65,66; Hall, Larry 1963(T); Haller, W.C. 1925,26,27; Hallett, Bill D. 1944,45; Hallum, Ken 1955; Hamilton, Raymond L. 1970,71,72; Hamilton, William 1926,27,28; Hamm, Huel 1940,41,42; Hamm, W. Dow 1918,19,21; Hammert, Pete, Jr. 1922,23; Hammond, John 1963,64,65; Hamon, Claude L. 1960,61; Han, Tony 1990; Hancock, Roy 1916; Harbuck, Jennifer 1992(T); Hardin, Lawrence 1981; Hardin, Robert W. 1979; Hardy, Russell 1918,19; Harley, John, Jr. 1943,44; Harley, John, Sr. 1910; Harman, Jason 1994; Harmon, Ronald E. 1962,63; Harold, James 1921; Harp, Laddie J. 1947; Harper, Gary 1966,67,68; Harper, Mike 1967,68,69; Harper, Scotty 1992; Harrell, Joe 1945; Harris, Bill 1956; Harris, Calvin Roy 1974; Harris, Jack 1933,34,35; Harris, Jerome 1976; Harris, Jim 1954,55,56; Harris, Ralph 1939,40,41; Harrison, Bob 1956,57,58; Harrison, Jon 1970,71; Hart, Ben 1964,65,66; Hartford, Glen 1922,23,24; Hartline, Ronnie 1958,59,60; Harts, John A. 1895; Harvel, Everett 1945; Haskell, Lawrence 1918,19,20,21; Haskins, A. Lynwood 1926,28; Hatcher, Mickey 1976; Haught, Richard 1960; Hawkins, Howard 1945; Haworth, Steve 1979,80,81,82; Hawpe, Mike 1969,72; Haycraft, Hugh 1896; Hayden, Jerry 1963; Hayes, Jim 1983(M); Haynes, Ray 1964,65,66; Heape, Gene G. 1946,49; Heard, Charles 1943,44; Hearon, Darlon N. "Doc" 1951,52,53; Heath, Leon 1948,49,50; Heatly, Dick 1949,50,51; Hebert, Bud 1976,77,79; Hefley, John 1896,97,98,99; Helms, Randy 1985(T); Henderson, Joseph S. 1965; Henderson, R. Alan 1964,65,66; Henderson, Rod 1993,94,95; Henderson, Zac R. 1974,75,76,77; Hendricks, Earl 1920,21,23,24; Hendricks, Viene 1921,23,24; Herndon, Bob D. 1953,54; Hetherington, Jerry 1969; Hetherington, Rickey 1966,68,69; Hettmannsperger, Harry 1966; Hewes, Elmo "Bo" 1934,35,36; Hicks, Victor 1975,76,77; Higginbotham, John 1977; Hill, Harry F. 1918,19,20,21; Hill, Houston "Bus" 1925; Hill, Howard W. "Bill" 1962,63,64; Hill, James 1945; Hill, Kyle 1991,93; Hill, Scott 1973,74,75,76; Hillis, James H. 1982(T); Hines, Percy 1983,84; Hinton, Eddie 1966,67,68; Hobby, Brewster,

1959,60; Hoffman, Wayne 1972,73,74; Hogan, Patrick 1963; Hoge, John 1979; Holieway, Jamelle 1985,86,87,88; Holland, J.D. 1912; Holland, Lonnie 1956; Holland, Weaver 1910; Holloway, Don 1983(M); Holman, Jay 1975; Holt, Jack D. 1958,59; Hood, Fred, 1955; Horkey, Joe R. 1948,49,50; Hotchkiss, Lewis 1938; Hott, Oliver 1913,14,15,16; Hott, Sabert 1910,11,12,13; Hott, Willis 1913,14,15,16; Houston, Brandon 1989,90,91; Houtman, Jay 1992; Hover, Lee 1975,76,77; Howard, James 1979; Hubbard, Edward 1934; Hubble, Rocky 1981,82; Huddleston, Woody 1935,36,37; Hudgens, David 1976,77; Huffman, Bill 1945; Huffman, Eric 1990(M); Hughes, Harry 1904,05,06; Hughes, Randy 1972,73,74; Hull, Ronn 1994; Hunt, Daryl 1975,76,77,78; Husack, John E. 1946,47,48; Hussey, Pat 1972,73,74; Hutson, Mark 1984,85,86,87.

I Ingram, Austin 1952; Ingram, Jerry 1950,51,52; Inman, Richard Walton 1961; Irmscher, Chris 1987(M); Irvin, Darrell 1978,79; Irvin, Kyle 1984; Irvin, Oliver 1906; Ivory, Horace 1975,76; Ivy, Frank 1937,38,39.

J Jackson, Alvin 1921,22; Jackson, Elvin E. 1943,44; Jackson, Grady 1931; Jackson, James Ray 1966; Jackson, Keith 1984,85,86,87; Jackson, Kerry 1972,74; Jackson, Mickey 1957,59; Jacobs, Jack 1939,40,41; Jacobs, Jay 1982; Jamar, Gary 1968; James, Harold L. 1921; Janes, Charles Art 1949,50; Jarman, George W. 1961,63; Jenkins, Delbert 1899; Jenkins, William 1899; Jenkinson, Steve 1974; Jennings, Bill 1938,39,40; Jennings, Doyle D. 1955,56,57; Jennings, Steve 1956,57,58; Jensen, Chris 1991; Jensen, Lester 1945; Jensen, Robert M. 1971,72; Jimerson, Jay 1977,78,79,80; Johnson, Andre 1984; Johnson, Corey 1990,91; Johnson, Darrius 1992,93,94,95; Johnson, E.B. 1921,22,23,24; Johnson, Earl 1983,84,86; Johnson, Graham B. 1916,17; Johnson, Greg 1984,85,86,87; Johnson, Keith 1978(M); Johnson, Mark D. 1980(M); Johnson, Mickey R. 1955,56,57,58; Johnson, Montford 1914,15,16; Johnson, Montford T. III 1969,70; Johnson, Neil R. 1913,14; Johnson, Oscar 1900,01; Johnson, Troy 1984,85,86,87; Johnson, Wallace 1961; Johnson, Wally 1982; Johnston, Paul X. 1918,19,20; Johnston, Ross 1916,17,18; Johnston, W.R. 1916,17,19; Jones, Cedric 1992,93,94,95; Jones, Danté 1984,85,86,87; Jones, Harold 1989; Jones, Jim 1979,80,81; Jones, Ken 1970,71,72; Jones, Russell 1991,92; Jones, W.D. "Buddy" 1947,48,49,50; Jordan, Phil 1969,70,71; Joyce, Micheal R. 1980; Joyner, Barry 1978,79,80; Judkins, John F. 1986.

K Kaighan, Mike 1994; Kalsu, Bob 1965; Kaltanbaher, Jim 1984; Kaspar, Kert 1984,87,88; Keadle, Robert D. 1960; Kearney, Vic 1970,71,72; Keeling, Mike 1979,80,81,82; Keeton, Durwood 1972,73; Keith, Jason 1990,91,92; Keith, Olen 1939,40; Keller, Troy Kay 1950,52,53; Kennedy, Jon R. 1964,65,66; Kennon, Doug, 1986(T); Kennon, Lee V. 1943; Key, Don 1979,80,81,82; Kidd, Summie 1926,27; Killingsworth, Joe 1967,68,69; Killingsworth, T.K. 1974(M); Killion, Kirk 1973,74; Kilpatrick, Darren 1984,85,86,87; Kimball, Robert L. 1977,78; Kindley, Don L., Jr. 1965,66; King, Aubrey 1985,86; King, David W. 1967; King, Glenn 1969,70,71; King, Kenny 1976,77,78; Kinlaw, Reggie 1975,76,77,78; Kirby, Darrell 1990; Kirby, Monty 1976; Kircher, Omer* (M); Kirk, Clyde 1928,29,30; Kitchell, Charles Abe 1928; Kitchens, Gus 1938,39; Klitzman, Robert 1969; Knapp, Jim 1961; Knight, Alford Eugene 1965; Koller, John 1965,66,67; Koontz, Brent 1990,91,92,94; Kosmos, Mark 1965,66; Kramer, Forrest 1916; Kramer, Kyle 1994; Kreik, Edward 1946,47; Krisher, Bill 1955,56,57; Krivanek, Louis 1994(M); Kulbeth, Ralph L. 1975; Kunkle, Steve 1975; Kusiak, Joe 1968,69.

L LaCrosse, Clane 1993; La Rosa, Vince 1969,70; Ladd, Benton 1955,56,57; Lahar, Harold W. 1938,39,40; Lamb, Roy 1923,24; Lamb, W.G. 1940,41,42; Lambert, Chris P., Sr. 1942; Lancaster, Eddie 1967,68; Land, Proctor 1989,90,91; Lane, Lester 1952; Lang, Noland W., Jr. 1949; Lang, Vernon 1958,59,60; Langston, Chuck 1992,93,94,95; Larghe, Steve 1976; Larue, William 1938,39; Lashar, R.D. 1987,88,89,90; Lashar, Tim 1983,84,85,86; Latham, Bob, Jr. 1985,86,87,88; Laurita, Al 1984,85,86,87; Lawrence, J. Adair 1918; Lawrence, Jim 1956,57,58; Lea, Paul 1961,62; Leake, John E. "Buddy", Jr. 1951,52,53,54; Lear, Alvin 1962; Leavell, Ron 1959,60(T); Lebow, Derald 1943,44; Lecrone, Leroy 1925,26,27; Lecrone, Ray 1925,26,27; Ledbetter, Jerome 1980,83,84; Ledbetter, Weldon 1979,80,82; Lee, Frank 1930; Lee, Hillory 1929,30; Lee, John 1928,29; Lee, Steve 1988; Lee, William Wayne 1960,61,62; Legg, Jerry A. 1980; Leggett, Scott 1983; Lemon, William 1907; Lester, Chuck

1977(M); Levonitis, Bill 1959; Levy, Tony 1990,91; Lewis, Fred 1994,95; Lewis, Ike 1989,90; Lewis, Johnnie 1978,79,80,81; Liggins, Granville 1965,66,67; Light, Earl 1917; Link, Donald 1943; Link, Emery A. 1953; Linn, Jim 1968; Linzy, Marceline Chavez 1974; Lisak, Edward J. 1948,49,50; Little, Kenneth 1933,34,35; Littlejohn, Wray 1951,52,53,54; Littrell, Jim 1973,74,75; Lively, William Prentice 1915; Locke, Norval 1936,38,39; Lockett, David M. 1949,50,51; Lohmann, Phil Jay 1959,60,61; Loman, Brad 1980(M); Long, Beede 1933,34; Long, Bert 1895; Long, Charles 1899; Long, Delbert 1954,55,56; Long, Frank 1904,05,06,07,08; Long, Ted 1988,89,90,91; Looney, Joe Don 1962; Lott, Thomas 1976,77,78; Loughridge, Robert E. 1953,54,55; Lovall, Gerald 1945; Lowe, Marcus 1987; Lowell, Gary 1978,80,81,82; Luckey, Stirling 1994; Lucky, Mark 1977,78,79,80; Ludwig, Stephen Lee 1974; Lund, Craig M. 1975; Luster, Dewey 1917,18,19,20.

M Mabry, Jeffrey C. 1974; MacDuff, Larry 1968,69; Mackey, Paul 1896,97,98; Malone, Fred R. 1966,68; Maloney, Don J. 1985; Maloney, Pete 1931; Manley, Leon 1947,48,49; Manly, J.R. 1937,38,39; Manning, Terran 1987,88,89,90; Mantle, Mike 1983,84,85; Manuel, Rod 1993,94,95; Marcum, Delton 1949; Marks, Richard W. 1985,86,87; Marsee, Jack 1939,41,42; Marsh, James H. 1918,19,20,21,22; Marsh, Victor 1927,28,29; Marshall, Everett 1969,70,71; Martin, Bob 1956; Martin, Howard C. 1925,26; Martin, Fred 1918; Martin, Jason 1995(M); Martin, John 1938,40; Martin, Leo 1974,75,76; Martin, Randy 1984; Martin, Robert 1911; Martin, William A. 1938,39,40,41; Mason, Rick 1969,70; Massad, Ernest L. 1929,30,31; Mathes, Donald E. 1922; Mathews, Orville 1939,40,41; Mathis, Reggie 1976,77,78; Mattox, William 1940,41,42; Maxfield, Ralph*; Mayes, Clair S. 1948,49,50; Mayfield, Corey 1989,90,91; Mayfield, R.C. "Bob" 1943,44; Mayhew, J.A. "Al" 1927,28,29; Mayhue, Charles D. 1962,63,64; Mays, Ed B. 1946,47,48,49; McAdams, Carl 1963,64,65; McBride, Brad 1984,85,86,87; McCain, Frank 1915,16,17; McCall, Aubrey 1945; McCampbell, Richard 1976; McCartney, John 1900; McCarty, Howard W. 1937,38; McCasland, T. Howard 1914,15; McClellan, Mike 1959,60,61; McCloud, Marc Dwight 1974; McClure, Bruce 1994,95; McClure, Daniel Edwin II 1974; McCoy, James P. 1961; McCreary, Byrom 1902,03,04,05; McCullough, Hugh 1937,38; McCurdy, Rick 1962,63,64; McCutcheon, Bill 1896,97; McDade, Billy 1991; McDade, Laddie Burl 1949; McDaniel, Edward "Wahoo" 1957,58,59; McDaniel, Mike 1994,95; McDannald, Morris Robert 1933,34,35; McDermott, Hugh V. 1916,17,19; McDonald, Chris 1991(T); McDonald, Don 1942; McDonald, Jeff 1981; McDonald, Tommy 1954,55,56; McDonough, Kevin 1979; McFadden, Alfred 1922,23; McFerron, George 1916; McGee, Garrick 1994,95; McGee, Reece 1948; McGehee, Perry E. 1969; McGlothlin, Claude 1916,17; McGraw, Joseph 1898; McKim, Jay D. 1978,79,80; McKinley, Mike 1987,89,90,91; McKinley, William 1920,21; McLaughlin, John 1971,72; McLaughlin, Mike 1971,72; McMichel, Ken 1986,87,88,89; McNabb, Norman 1946,48,49,50; McPhail, Coleman "Buck" 1950,51,52; McPhail, Gerald 1954,55; McQuarters, Ed L. 1962,63,64; McReynolds, Edwin C. 1910; McReynolds, Joe 1973,75; Meacham, Bill 1960; Meacham, Edgar 1911,12,13; Meacham, Randy 1966,67,68; Mears, Gene 1952,53,54; Medice, Larry 1988,89,90; Medlock, Newt 1895; Meinhert, Lloyd 1943; Melendez, Jaime H. 1973,75,76,77; Melson, Chris 1988,89,90,91; Mendenhall, Ken 1967,68,69; Merkle, Fred 1896,97,98,99; Merkle, Joe 1897,98,99; Merrell, Webber 1936,37; Metcalf, L.A. "Butch" 1962,63,64; Meyer, Clifford 1915; Mickey, Joey 1989,90,91,92; Migliazzo, Paul 1983,84,85,86; Milburn, Glyn 1988; Mildren, Jack 1969,70,71; Mildren, Richard 1973; Miles, Mitch 1990(M); Miller, Jeff 1989,90; Miller, T.B. 1933,34; Mills, Bus 1928,29,30; Mills, P.J. 1992,93,94,95; Mills, Ron 1981; Milstead, Jon 1970,71,72; Milstead, Karl 1959,60,61; Ming, Leslie I. 1948; Miskovsky, John 1933,34,35; Mitchel, Eric 1985,86,87,88; Mitchell, Jack 1946,47,48; Mobra, Joe 1953,54,55; Monnett, Jim 1902,03,04,05,06; Montgomery, Homer 1914,15,16; Montgomery, Sam 1916; Mooney, Prentiss 1926,27; Moore, Billy Jack 1957,58,59; Moore, Derland 1971,72; Moore, Dewayne 1987(M); Moore, Frank 1979; Moore, Grant 1994(T); Moore, Harry 1948,49,50; Moore, Jerald 1993,94,95; Moore, John 1925,26; Moore, Kirk 1988; Moore, Obie 1973,75,76,77; Moreno, Dennis 1986(M); Morford, Clare E. 1941,42; Morford, Robert B. 1957,58,59; Morford, R. Brent 1960; Moriarty, Paul 1991,92; Morris, Lee A., Jr. 1985; Morris, Bill 1941,42,46,47; Morris, Cecil

1953,54,55; Morris, Dennit E. 1955,56,57; Morris, Max 1958,60; Morrison, C.E., "Ram" 1920,21,22,24; Morter, Ray A. 1909,10; Morton, Don 1975; Moseley, Donald G. 1976,77,78(T); Moss, William B. 1911; Muldrow, Alvin 1928; Muldrow, Hal 1925,26,27; Mullen, John Daniel 1970,71,72; Mullen, Michael L. 1969; Mullen, Ray R. 1941,42; Munn, Jeff 1986(T); Munsey, J.S. 1939,40,41; Murphy, Kevin 1981,82,83,85; Murray, Richard 1974,75,76,77.

N Nairn, James 1908,09,10,11; Needs, Al 1945,48,50; Neely, Ralph E. 1962,63,64; Neher, Lee Roy 1941,42,46,47; Nelson, Don 1957; Nelson, F. Wayne 1967; Nelson, George N. 1954; Nelson, John 1994; Nelson, Roger D. 1951,52,53; Nelson, Roy 1929; Nemecek, Vivian 1934,35; Newland, Scott 1982,83,84; Newton, Charles E. 1968; Nicholson, John 1970; Nixon, Fred 1976,77,78,79; Noles, Dan M. 1969; Nolte, David 1982(M); Nordgren, Geoffrey E. 1969,70,71; Norris, Granville T. 1925,26,27; Northcutt, Ken 1954,55,57; Norvell, J.C. 1992(M); Norwood, Pete 1992.

O O'Gara, Bill 1977,78; O'Grady, Kevin 1969,70; O'Neal, Preston, Jr. 1953,54; O'Neal, Benton 1958; O'Neal, Jay 1954,55,56; O'Neal, Pat 1951,52,53,54; O'Neal, Roberto 1992; O'Shaughnessy, Stephen M. 1969,70,71; Oatts, Paul 1993; Ogilive, Frank A. 1920; Orendorff, Bill 1972; Orr, Charles 1912; Orr, Ellis 1928,29; Oubre, Louis 1978,79,80; Oujesky, Joseph B. 1954,55,56,57; Overstreet, David 1977,78,79; Overton, Milton 1992,93,94,95; Owens, Jim 1946,47,48,49; Owens, Roger Ray 1976; Owens, Roy 1983; Owens, Steve 1967,68,69; Owens, Tinker 1972,73,74,75.

P Paaso, Dick 1966,67,68; Pace, Bobby W. 1962,63,64; Pace, Harrison W. 1950; Page, Bobby 1962,63,64; Page, G. Robert 1957,58,59,61; Page, Harland 1934; Paine, Charles W. 1949; Paine, Homer 1946,47,48; Pair, Gayle 1945; Pangburn, Sam L. 1926; Pannell, Larry 1962; Pannell, Tommy 1963,64,65; Pannell, William 1962; Pansze, Art 1932,33,34; Pansze, William N. 1931,32,33; Parham, Duncan 1986,87; Parker, James 1960,62; Parker, Kenneth W. 1947,48,49; Parker, Paul 1981,82,83; Parks, Edward Mickey 1934,37; Parks, Jerry 1988; Parrish, George 1933,34; Parsons, Hillard, Jr. 1943; Pasque, Dan 1985(M); Patterson, Mark 1990(M); Patterson, William A. 1922,24; Paul, Byron 1978,79,80; Paul, Harold 1971; Payne, James H. 1959,62,63; Payne, Jerry 1957,58,59; Payne, Ron 1959,61; Peacock, Elvis 1974,75,76,77; Pearce, Joe 1967,68,69; Pearson, Douglas B. 1974; Pearson, Lindell 1948,49; Pearson, Tom 1954; Peddycoat, Dick 1944; Pegues, Rod 1978,80,81,82; Pelfrey, Carl 1992(M); Pellow, Johnny 1956,57,58; Pemberton, Jerry 1982(T); Pena, Tony III 1992; Pennick, James 1922,23,24; Penny, JaJuan 1992,93,94,95; Perini, Dale 1960,61; Perry, Ed*; Perry, Fred 1895; Perry, Leon 1985,86,88,89; Perryman, A.G. 1970; Peters, Tony L. 1973,74; Peters, Karl 1979; Peters, Terry 1975,76,77; Peters, Tyrell 1993,94,95; Peters, Zarek 1989; Pettibone, Jerry 1961; Pfrimmer, Don 1967,68; Phebus, Wright 1938; Phelps, Kelly 1978,79,81,82; Philips, Leon C. 1915; Philips, Marland 1928; Philips, Martin 1927; Phillips, Anthony 1985,86,87,88; Phillips, Forb L. 1968,69,70; Phillips, Jon 1984,85,86,87; Phillips, Michael F. 1974,75,76; Phillips, T. Ray 1932; Phipps, Mike 1994,95; Pickard, Claude 1904,05,08; Pickett, Jeff 1983,84,85; Pierce, Clovis 1941; Pitchlynn, Thurman J. 1966; Porkorny, Charles D. 1922; Pomeroy, Gary 1982,83; Pope, Eric 1982,83,84,85; Pope, Kenith 1971,72,73; Porter, Jack D. 1966,67,68,69; Porterfield, John L. 1962,63; Poslick, Joe 1965,66,67; Potter, Byron 1939; Potters, Gary 1975; Potts, Frank 1925,26; Powell, Raymond R. 1949,51,52,53; Powell, Roland 1956; Powers, Clyde J. 1971,72,73; Poynor, Ben 1933,34,35; Preston, Gene 1945; Price, Harry 1906,07,10; Price, King 1923; Price, Lance 1985,86,87; Price, William 1945,46,47,48; Pricer, Billy C. 1954,55,56; Prickett, John 1895; Prince, Blair 1985(M); Prince, Tony 1987; Pruitt, Greg 1970,71,72.

Q Qualls, Albert 1969,70,71; Quinn, Daniel 1965,66,67,68(T).

R Radcliffe, Earle 1907,08,10; Raley, John 1979; Randolph, John 1976; Randolph, Tim 1981,83,84; Rapacz, John J. 1946,47; Rasheed, Kenyon 1989,90,91,92; Ray, Darrol 1976,77,78,79; Ray, John 1898; Ray, Terry 1988,89,90,91; Rayburn, Tony 1983,84,85,86; Rector, Joe D. 1956,57,58; Reddell, Brad 1989,90,91,92; Reddell, John C. 1950,51,52; Reed, Chester 1904,05; Reed, Darrell 1984,85,86,87; Reed, Richard 1984,85; Reeds, Artie 1909; Reeds, Clarence 1904; Reeds, Claude E. 1910,11,12,13; Reese, Jerry 1974,75,76;

Reilly, Mike 1977,79,80; Remy, William E. 1949; Rentie, Caesar 1984,85,86,87; Rentzel, Lance 1962,63,64; Resler, Jeff 1991,92,93,94; Rhodes, Roy 1945; Rhodes, Steve 1976,77,78,80; Rhymes, George 1980,81,83,84; Rhynes, Gary 1972; Richardson, Joe A. 1945; Richey, Joey 1993(T); Riley, James 1964,65,66; Ringer, Mike 1963,64,65; Ripley, J.M. "Mickey" 1967,68,69,70; Risinger, R.L. 1895; Roach, Larry 1970,71,72; Roberson, Broderick 1991,92,93,94; Roberts, Donald H. 1968; Roberts, C.C. 1896,97,98,1900; Roberts, Fred 1901; Roberts, Greg 1975,76,77; Roberts, Harold 1929,30; Roberts, Hugh 1908; Roberts, J.D. 1951,52,53; Robertson, Dave 1971,72; Robertson, Melbourne 1933,34,35; Robinson, Bobbie 1965,66; Robinson, Eric 1984; Robison, Leroy 1933,34; Rockford, Jim 1980,81,83,84; Rogers, Tyrone 1988; Rogers, Charles E. 1911,12,13; Rogers, J.W. "Jim" 1907,10; Rogers, Jimmy 1974,76,77,78; Rogers, Otis R. 1936,37,38; Roland, Phil 1977; Rolle, David 1956,57,58; Rollins, Zerrick 1994; Rose, Michael 1994,95; Rosenberg, Collin 1993,94,95; Ross, Alvin 1981,83; Ross, Dwight M. 1920; Ross, Eugene 1964,65,66; Ross, H. Grady 1909; Ross, Ronald K. 1978; Rousey, Tom 1940; Roush, John 1972,73,74; Rowe, William J. 1959; Rowland, Ed 1950,51,52; Royal, Darrell 1946,47,48,49; Royter, (Unknown) 1895; Runbeck, Leonard 1905; Russell, Clyde 1973,74 ; Russell, Kleyn 1972; Ruster, Dan 1970,71,72.

S Salmon, Don E. 1960; Sandefer, J.D. "Jakie" III 1956,57,58; Sanders, Jerry 1978,80,81,82; Sandersfield, Melvin 1959,60,61,62; Santee, Jack H. 1951,52; Santee, Robert P. 1954; Sarratt, Charles 1946,47; Saunders, Thomas W. 1970,71,72; Sawatzky, Mike 1988,89,90; Sawyer, Steve 1944; Schaefer, Herbert 1922,23,24; Schmitt, Pete 1989,90,91,92; Scholl, Robert 1958,59; Schreiner, Carl S. III 1963,64; Schreiner, Carl S., Jr. 1945; Schreiner, Henry F. 1945,49; Scott, Bob 1956,57; Searcy, Byron 1955,56,57; Sellmyer, Greg 1976,78,79; Selmon, Dewey 1972,73,74,75; Selmon, Lee Roy 1972,73,74,75; Selmon, Lucious 1971,72,73; Severin, Robert 1904,05,06; Sewell, Steve 1981,82,83,84; Seymour, Bob 1937,38,39; Shadid, Mitch 1940,41,42; Shane, Dan S. 1967; Shankle, William 1991,92,94; Shanks, Patrick 1941,42; Sharp, Basil 1944,45; Sharp, Mike 1973(M); Sharpe, Louis 1939,40,41; Shaw, Clinton 1917; Shearer, Clifton 1928; Shelley, John A. 1969,70,71; Shepard, Darrell 1980,81; Shepard, Derrick 1983,84,85,86; Shepard, Woodie 1976; Sherrod, Dale 1955,56,57; Shields, Bennie 1961,63; Shields, Larry 1963,64; Shilling, Jack C. 1957,58; Shipp, Jackie 1980,81,82,83; Shirk, John 1937,38,39; Shoate, Myron 1974,76; Shoate, Rod 1972,73,74; Shoemaker, David 1987,88; Shores, Phillip 1982; Short, Dan 1900,01,02,03; Short, Gacicuis, 1927; Short, Harvey 1898,99; Short, Tom M. 1936,37; Shotts, Ron 1965,66,67; Shotts, Steve 1970; Silva, Frank R. 1948,49,50,51,52; Simcik, Douglas W. 1976,77; Simmons, Homer 1940,41,42; Simmons, Milton E. 1953,54; Simms, Dick E. 1930,31; Simon, E.N. 1973,74; Simpson, Broderick 1993,94; Simpson, Travis 1983,84,85; Sims, Billy 1975,77,78,79; Sims, Fred 1981,82; Sims, Jerry L. 1968,69,70; Sims, Richard 1930,31; Singletary, Hinston L. 1928; Sitton, Ken 1979,80; Skidgel, Wesley A. 1962,63; Slater, Bob 1981,82,83; Slough, Elmer 1923,24; Smalley, Harley 1944; Smith, C. Lyle 1939,40,41; Smith, C. Michael 1970; Smith, David 1972,73; Smith, Dean C. 1948,49,50; Smith, Fred 1949,50,51; Smith, Fred C. 1927; Smith, John L. 1899; Smith, Leon L. 1927; Smith, Michael G. "Mike" 1973; Smith, Norman W. 1962,63,64; Smith, Pete 1935,36,37; Smith, Ray 1897; Smith, Robert E. 1968(M); Smith, Todd 1983,84,85; Smith, Travian 1994; Smitherman, Don 1986,88,89; Smoot, Roy 1918,19,20,21; Snell, Ernest B. 1930,31; Snodgrass, M.H. 1925; Songy, Darrell 1979,80,82; Soult, Timothy A. 1984(T); Sparkman, Homer 1943,44; Sparks, Keith 1993,94,95; Spears, Roy A. 1911,12,13; Speegle, Cliff 1938,39,40; Spencer, Micheal L. 1975; Spottswood, Ed 1938; Stacy, James 1932,33,34; Stacy, Ronnie Lee 1970,71; Stafford, Anthony 1985,86,87,88; Stahl, William 1921; Stamps, Harry, Jr. 1992,93,94,95; Stanberry, Keith 1981,82,83,84; Stanley, Raymond 1929,30; Steele, David A. 1969; Steele, Jack 1940,41,42; Steinberger, Clinton C. 1922,23; Steinbock, Delmar 1934,35; Steines, William 1992; Stell, Damon 1984,85,87,88; Stensrud, Bruce 1967,68,69; Stephens, Sam, 1941,42; Stephenson, Robert L. "Bob" 1965,66,67; Stevenson, Ralph 1937,38,39; Steward, J.N. 1945; Stidham, J. Thomas 1966; Stiller, Don 1955,56,57; Stogner, C.H. 1930,31; Stoia, Sam 1984; Stokes, George 1961,62,63; Stokes, Ricky 1971,73; Stone, Clifford O., Jr. 1945; Stout, Mark 1987(T); Stover, Albert 1944,45; Stover, Robert L. 1944; Strouvelle, C.E. 1922; Struck, Mike 1971,72,73; Sturm, Bill 1955; Sullivan, David 1974; Sullivan,

Glenn 1986,87; Sumpter, R.O. "Bob" 1926; Suntrup, Tom 1977; Sutton, Anthony P. 1974; Swank, Floyd 1905; Swanson, Garry F. 1969; Swanson, Lance 1988,89,90, Swanson, T.M. 1922; Swartz, P.W. 1909; Swatek, Charles 1915; Swatek, Roy E. 1918,19,20,21; Swofford, Joe 1931.

T Tabor, Dion 1983(T); Tabor, Paul 1977,78,79; Tabor, Phil 1975,76,77,78; Talbott, George V. 1957; Tallchief, Tom 1945; Tanner, Barron 1994,95; Tarlton, Stephen F. 1968,69,70; Tate, Larry Wayne 1974; Taton, Bruce 1977,78,79; Tatum, John E. 1960,61,62; Taylor, Ben 1925,26,27; Taylor, Fenton 1928,29; Taylor, Jim 1972,73,74; Taylor, L. Geary 1961; Taylor, Otis 1989,90,91,92; Taylor, Ron 1971(M); Taylor, Sherwood A. 1977,78,79; Teel, Charles 1930,31; Teeter, George Howard 1938,40,41; Tennyson, Dewey 1932,34,35; Terrell, David 1967; Thomas, James A., Jr. 1973,74,75; Thomas, Chuck 1981,82,83,84; Thomas, Clendon 1955,56,57; Thomas, George C. 1946,47,48,49; Thomas, Jamie 1973,74,75; Thomas, Jim 1936,37,38; Thomas, Keith 1973,74,75,76; Thomas, W.S. 1964; Thompson, Bobby 1968; Thompson, Charles 1987,88; Thompson, James 1921,22,23,24; Thompson, Jerry 1957,58,59; Thompson, Kevin 1986,87,88,89; Thompson, Michael 1992; Thompson, Scott 1989; Thompson, Scott 1985; Thompson, Travis 1990; Thomsen, Todd 1985,86,87,88; Tigart, Thurman 1943,44,45; Tillery, Jerry 1958,59,60; Tillman, A.M. "Pete" 1946,47,48; Tillman, Donald 1943,45; Tillman, Spencer 1983,84,85,86; Timberlake, R.W. 1954,55,56; Tippens, Trey 1989,90,91,92; Tipps, Ken 1947,48,49; Tipton, Greg 1994(M); Titsworth, John 1966,67,68; Todd, Nelson Page 1969,71; Tolbert, James R. 1916; Tribby, Floyd 1912; Trotter, Jess 1946,47,48; Trousdale, J.R. 1987(T); Truesdell, George 1905,06; Truitt, John 1981,83; Tubbs, Jerry 1954,55,56; Tupper, Jeff 1982,83,84,85; Turner, Richard 1977,78,79,80; Tyler, Claude 1919; Tyler, George 1918,19,20,21; Tyree, James E. 1941,42,46,47.

U Uhles, Ric 1981,82,85; Unruh, Dean 1970,71,72.

V Vachon, Mike 1966,67; Vallance, Chad Y. 1941; Valora, Forrest 1977,78,79,80; Van Burkleo, Bill 1961; Van Camp, Eric 1973,74,75; Van Goethen, Melanie 1992(T); Van Horn, Bruce 1957,58,59,60(M); VanKeirsbilck, Mark 1986,87,88,89; Van Osdol, Scott 1979; Van Pool, Jack 1951,53; Vardeman, Robert 1963,65; Vaughan, Mike 1974,75; Venable, Jack 1945; Venable, Jim 1944,45; Vermillion, Larry 1962,63; Vessels, Billy 1950,51,52; Vickers, David 1984,85,86,87; Vickers, Mike 1989,90(T); Vitito, Tim 1991; Vogel, Al 1944,45; Vogle, Daniel O. 1922; Voiles, John David 1962,63,64; von Schamann, Uwe 1976,77,78; Von Tungelin, Rudolph 1916.

W Wade, Greg 1989(M); Waggoner, Roy 1904,05,06; Waggoner, F.E. "Gene" 1929; Walker, Ab D. 1930,31; Walker, Barrion 1980,81; Walker, Barth P. 1935,36,37;

Walker, Darnell 1990,91,92; Walker, Wade 1946,47,48,49; Wallace, Dave 1946,47; Wallace, Polly 1924,25,26; Wallace, Randy 1988,89,90,91; Walling, Vernon 1906,07,08; Walrond Jr., George A. 1976,77; Wantland, C.W. 1907,08; Ward, Allan 1982; Ward, Bob 1957,58; Ward, Dennis 1961,62; Ward, Jeffery C. 1977,78; Ward, Paul 1926,27,28; Ward, Stanley 1958; Warmack, Bob 1965,66,67,68; Warner, Bobby 1994; Warren, Corey 1990,91,92,93; Warren, Guy 1929,30; Washington, Joe 1972,73,74,75; Waters, Ron L. 1972,73,74; Watkins, Chris 1991; Watkins, Smith 1931; Watkins, Steve 1981(M); Watson, Johnny A. 1968,69,70; Watts, Bennett 1957,59,60; Watts, Bill 1959; Watts, Brad 1973; White, C. 1978,79,80; Weatherford, Jennifer 1994(T); Weatherall, James 1948,49,50,51; Webb, Terry D. 1973,74,75; Weddington, Darrell 1984; Weddington, Mike 1979,80,81,82; Weedn, Henry 1911,12; Welch, Tim 1971,72,73; Wells, Ben D. 1958; Wenzl, Troy 1989,90(T); Wesley, Maylon 1992,93,94,95; West, John 1944,45; West, Mark 1994(T); West, Stanley B. 1946,47,48,49; Wetherbee, Phillip L. 1965; Whaley, Steve 1979,80,81; Wheeler, Gordon 1967; Wheeler, J.W. 1933,34,35; Wheeler, Jeff 1995(T); Whisenant, John B. 1916; White, Billy 1959,60,61; White, Brad 1973; White, C. Lazelle, 1922,23,24; White, Derrick 1984,85,86,87; White, Phil E. 1918,19,20; Whited, Marvin 1939,40,41; Whittington, Claude L. 1931,32,33; Wickersham, Taylor 1994,95; Wilcox, John 1923; Wilhelm, George 1937,38,39; Wilhite, Otto 1909; Wilkins, Greg 1991; Williams, Chad 1987(M); Williams, Charles A. 1966; Williams, Curtice 1985,86,87,88; Williams, Dante 1986,87,88,89; Williams, Dewey 1979; Williams, Earnest 1990,91,92; Williams, Edward 1976; Williams, Gregory 1987,89; Williams, Jeff 1977,81; Williams, Robert 1983,84; Williams, Steve 1979,80,81,82; Williams, Troy 1981; Wilmoth, Evert G. 1916,17; Wilson, Bryon 1989(M); Wilson, Charles Hugh 1930,31; Wilson, Chris 1988,89,90,91; Wilson, Corey 1991,92; Wilson, Danny 1980,81,82,83; Wilson, Keith 1977; Wilson, Matt 1991,94; Wilson, Remardo 1989; Wilson, Stanley 1979,80,81,82; Winblood, Bill 1960; Winchester, Mike 1984,85,86; Winfrey, Ronald M. 1965,66; Wingate, Robert 1899,1900; Winters, Chet 1979,80,81,82; Wise, Mike 1987,88,89; Wolf, Key 1905,06,07,08; Wolfe, Zetta 1925; Wolverton, M.E. "Woody" 1953,54; Wood, Eddie*; Wood, Steven Norvel 1938,39,40; Woods, Billy Joe 1958,59,61,62,; 63(M); Woods, C.A. "Tony" 1985,86,87,88; Woods, Mort 1909,10; Woodson, Paul 1939; Woodsworth, Calvin 1953,54,55; Wooten, W.G. 1942,43,44; Wren, Ricky 1991,92,93; Wright, Curtis Truman 1947,48; Wright, John W. "Bill" 1944; Wright, Lonnie Gene 1975; Wright, Sonny Thelton 1942,43; Wright, Willie 1978; Wyatt, Bobby J. 1961; Wylie, Gary 1960,61,62; Wylie, Joe 1970,71,72.

Y York, Marshall R. 1958,59,60; Young, Dalton 1990; Young, Gary L. 1973,74; Young, Herbert 1979,80; Young, Paul 1930,31; Young, Waddy 1936,37,38.

Z Zabel, Steve 1967,68,69.

TRIVIA ANSWERS

1. Crimson and cream, same as they are now.

2. The Sooners played in the Sugar Bowl twice in 1972 (January 1 and December 31), in the Orange Bowl and Fiesta Bowl in 1976, and in the Orange Bowl and Sun Bowl in 1981.

3. Jim Weatherall in 1951, J. D. Roberts in 1953, Lee Roy Selmon in 1975, and Greg Roberts in 1978.

4. OU did not list a captain for 1982 or 1995.

5. The year was 1967 when tackle Bob Kalsu was captain.

6. Jay Wilkinson played at Duke, and Greg Switzer played at Arkansas.

7. Lucious, Dewey, and Lee Roy Selmon started in 1973.

8. Fullback Leon Crosswhite scored a touchdown in OU's first game in the Wishbone, a 41-9 loss to Texas in 1970.

9. Mickey Hatcher played for the Los Angeles Dodgers.

10. The stadium is named Memorial Stadium and playing field is named Owen Field.

11. Texas' Darrell Royal had the most victories with 13, and OU's Bud Wilkinson had the most losses with 8.

12. 1946. The attendance of 50,000 set a record for watching the game, but it was not a sellout. The game has been a sellout every year since then.

13. OU became a member of the Missouri Valley Conference, which had a rule prohibiting members from playing at a non-campus site. The league later

rescinded the rule.

14. Mike Gaddis in 1991.

15. Wade Walker in 1946-49, Darrell Reed in 1984-87, and Anthony Phillips in 1985-88.

16. Back Sol Swatek was all-conference in the Southwest Conference in 1919 and in the Missouri Valley Conference in 1920.

17. Bennett Watts in 1960 and J. C. Watts in 1979-80.

18. Howard Waugh of Tulsa led the nation in rushing in 1952.

19. Jack Ging.

20. Stanford.

21. Loren and Charles.

22. Orange, Sugar, Gator, Bluebonnet, Fiesta, Sun (John Hancock), and Copper.

23. 14-6 against North Carolina in the 1949 Sugar Bowl for Wilkinson, and 14-6 against Michigan in the 1976 Orange Bowl for Switzer.

24. d) north of Holmberg Hall.

25. Tom Carroll was an OU halfback in the 1950s. Bill Carroll was OU's track-and-field coach. John Carroll was a split end and placekicker at OU in the 1970s.

26. Dick and Chuck Bowman, Pat and Jay O'Neal, and Jerry and Ronny Payne.

27. Phil and Paul Tabor, Steve and Jeff Williams, and Grant and Barry Burget.

28. Bob Warmack — who held records in passing yardage, completions, and attempts — set in 1968.

29. Dewell Brewer, who had 38 rushes against Kansas State in 1968. (Owens' school record is 55 against OSU in 1969.)

30. Monte Deere with 246 yards against Colorado in 1962. (Gundy's school record is 341 yards against Texas Tech in 1992.)

31. The 1956 Sooners averaged 46.6 points a game.

32. Steve Owens in 1967-69, Joe Washington in 1973-75, and Jamelle Holieway in 1985-87.

33. Jamelle Holieway in 1985-88 and Cale Gundy in 1990-93.

34. Tinker Owens in 1973-75 and Keith Jackson in 1985-87.

35. Center Kurt Burris finished second to Wisconsin's Alan Ameche in 1954.

36. Gary and Mike Harper; Bill, Larry and Tommy Pannell; Bill and Bert Gravitt; and Alan and Stan Henderson.

37. Thurman Pitchlynn.

38. Bob Cornell, Brewster Hobby, Joe Rector, and Jerry Thompson.

39. Harry Hettsmannsperger, who lettered in 1966.

40. Against Wyoming in the 1976 Fiesta Bowl.

41. Lance Rentzel, because he brought his trophies from high school to OU with him.

42. Quarterback Danny Bradley.

43. Steve Owens with 336 points in 1967-69.

44. Billy Vessels and Buck McPhail each topped 1,000 yards in 1952. But technically, Vessels, who topped the 1,000 mark two series before McPhail in the final season game, was first.

45. Lee Roy Selmon by Tampa Bay in 1976 and Billy Sims by Detroit in 1980.

46. Fred Roberts in 1901, Dewey "Snorter" Luster in 1941-45, Gary Gibbs in 1989-94, and John Blake, starting in 1996.

47. Bud Wilkinson at Minnesota, Gomer Jones at Ohio State, and Chuck Fairbanks at Michigan State.

48. John Reddell was an end on the 1950 football team and a catcher on the 1951 baseball team.

49. Walter Cronkite.

50. The Sooner Schooner, a covered wagon pulled by ponies, Boomer and Sooner.

51. A. G. Perryman started at fullback in OU's first game in the Wishbone in 1970.

52. OU's 21-20 win over OSU in Stillwater. In fact, the Sooners went to the end zone where the band was seated and gave its members a standing ovation after the contest because of their loyal support.

53. Vernon Parrington, who coached in 1897-1900, and wrote Main Currents of American Thought in 1928.

54. Jim Mackenzie in 1966 and Howard Schnellenberger in 1995. The other six were Bud Wilkinson, Gomer Jones, Chuck Fairbanks, Barry Switzer, Gary Gibbs, and John Blake.

55. 1, Nebraska; 2, Oklahoma; 3, Colorado.

56. Bud Wilkinson in 1963 and Chuck Fairbanks in 1968.

57. Washington in the 1985 Orange Bowl and Southern California in the third game of the 1988 season.

58. Florida State three times.

59. End Max Boydston, guard Bo Bolinger, center Kurt Burris, and halfback Bob Burris from Muskogee.

60. Roy LeCrone in 1927 and Tom Churchill in 1928 and 1929.

61. Mex, a bulldog, was mascot in 1919-1928.

COLLEGE SPORTS HANDBOOKS
Stories, Stats & Stuff About America's Favorite Teams

U. of Arizona	Basketball	Arizona Wildcats Handbook
U. of Arkansas	Basketball	Razorbacks Handbook
Baylor	Football	Bears Handbook
Clemson	Football	Clemson Handbook
U. of Colorado	Football	Buffaloes Handbook
U. of Florida	Football	Gator Tales
Georgia Tech	Basketball	Yellow Jackets Handbook
Indiana U.	Basketball	Hoosier Handbook
Iowa State	Sports	Cyclones Handbook
U. of Kansas	Basketball	Crimson & Blue Handbook
Kansas State	Sports	Kansas St Wildcat Handbook
LSU	Football	Fighting Tigers Handbook
U. of Louisville	Basketball	Cardinals Handbook
U. of Miami	Football	Hurricane Handbook
U. of Michigan	Football	Wolverines Handbook
U. of Missouri	Basketball	Tiger Handbook
U. of Nebraska	Football	Husker Handbook
U. of N. Carolina	Basketball	Tar Heels Handbook
N.C. State	Basketball	Wolfpack Handbook
Penn State	Football	Nittany Lions Handbook
U. of S. Carolina	Football	Gamecocks Handbook
Stanford	Football	Stanford Handbook
Syracuse	Sports	Orange Handbook
U. of Tennessee	Football	Volunteers Handbook
U. of Texas	Football	Longhorns Handbook
Texas A&M	Football	Aggies Handbook
Texas Tech	Sports	Red Raiders Handbook
Virginia Tech	Football	Hokies Handbook
Wichita State	Sports	Shockers Handbook
U. of Wisconsin	Football	Badgers Handbook

Also:

Big 12 Handbook: Stories, Stats and Stuff About The Nation's Best
Football Conference

The Top Fuel Handbook: Stories, Stats and Stuff About Drag Racing's
Most Powerful Class

For ordering information call Midwest Sports Publications at:

1·800·492·4043